an a-z history of huddersfield town football club

the light at the end
of the tunnel

by tony matthews

an official terriers publication

We would like to thank our sponsors:
Graham J Airs, Mrs Stephanie Airs, Edward A Ashton, Stephen Barker, Mrs M Battye,
Alan M Beevers, Simon Blakey, Mrs J Booth, Ashley Booth, Nigel Brook, George Brook,
Andrew Bullock, Ian Michael Carter, Christopher Chambers, John David Clegg,
Lesley Copley, Eddie Cran, Burn Croft, John Dyson, Clark Eastwood, Trevor & Coleen Ellis,
Russell & Thomas Firth, Marcus Garside, Robert Scott Gray, Warren Green, Pamela Haigh,
Claire Hebblethwaite, Ian Hebblethwaite, John Hebblethwaite, Andrew Hepworth, Darren R Herbert,
David Hirst, Ian G Hogbin, David Horsfall, Rob Jepson, Sally Kerry, Andrew Macorison,
Trevor Marsden, Natalie Mason, John Mason, Richard Mason, Micheal Edward Miller, Paul Miller,
Peter North, Mrs Barbara Nutton, Geoffrey David O'Hehir, Geoffrey Oldfield, Hope Prendergast,
M Proctor, George Ramsey, Adam Rothera, David Saville, Hermon Shaw, Roger Stopford,
Rebecca & William Swithenbank, Russell Thomas, Ben J Thornes,
Oliver Thornes - in memory of Dad Stephen, Janet Walker, Keith J Walker, Tim Ward,
The Revd David Wilding, Shaun Withers, GM Wood, JG Wood, Elizabeth Wrigley.

MINUTES
the total football solution

the light at the end of the tunnel -
an a-z history of huddersfield town football club
by tony matthews
published by 90 minutes publications, darwen
Text copyright © tony matthews 2004
printed in the uk by mercer print, accrington
graphic design by darren brown
Photographs courtesy of tony matthews and huddersfield town fc
with thanks to john russell and maureen reed

ISBN 0-9546251-4-5

FOREWORD

Whether you are young or old, this book will fill a vital place on your bookshelf.

It should provide answers to most if not all your questions and queries about Huddersfield Town, its major players and managers over the past 96 years.

There is plenty in this book to keep you occupied, enough information to enable you to get your friends and colleagues talking continuously about the Terriers, whether it is down the pub or club, at the ground, on a street corner, a train or plane, anywhere, in fact, where the subject of conversation is football.

I found it fascinating reading and made me appreciate just how much tradition there is at Huddersfield Town. A tradition that all players, managers and staff past and present, including myself, are justly proud of.

This book not only reflects the pride and tradition of the Club but is also full of fascinating facts and stories.

It is a must for all Terriers fans anywhere.

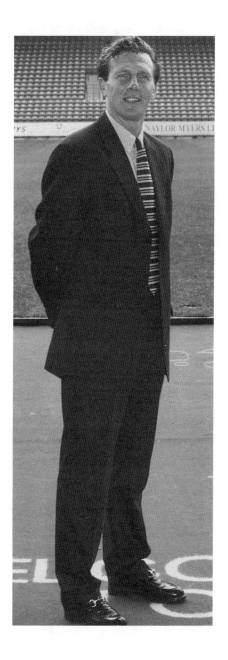

Peter Jackson
Huddersfield Town A.F.C. Manager

Huddersfield Town

A.F.C. LTD.
LEEDS ROAD, HUDDERSFIELD

SECOND DIVISION

WALSALL

SATURDAY, SEPTEMBER 23rd

Official Programme 4d.

the light at the end of the tunnel

A

ABANDONED MATCHES: Details of abandoned games involving Huddersfield:

29.04.1909	v. Hebburn Argyle (a) Eastern League	Heavy storm
11.01.1913	v. Sheffield United (h) FA Cup	Snow
09.02.1918	v. Notts County (h) Midland SPC	Waterlogged pitch
29.05.1940	v. York City (a) Regional League (NE)	Heavy storm
06.12.1941	v. Bradford Park Avenue (a) FL N Reg.	Waterlogged pitch
15.01.1944	v. Bradford Park Avenue (a) FL War Cup	Fog
07.01.1956	v. Bolton Wanderers (a) FA Cup	Bad weather

AFC BOURNEMOUTH: Huddersfield's record against the Cherries:

Football League

Venue	P	W	D	L	F	A
Home	15	5	7	3	16	12
Away	15	6	3	6	17	16
Totals	30	11	10	9	33	28

FA Cup

Away	1	0	0	1	0	1

Huddersfield first met Bournemouth in a League game in September 1973 at Leeds Road. The Third Division clash ended 1-1.

The Cup-tie was a 1st round clash at Dean Court in 1997.

AGE:

- The youngest player ever to appear for Huddersfield in a senior match is Denis Law who was 16 years, 303 days old when he made his League debut against Notts County on 24 December 1956 (Division Two).
- When Law made his debut, his wing partner was Kevin McHale, aged 17 years, 84 days.
- The oldest player to appear in a competitive game for Huddersfield is Billy Smith who was 38 years 263 days old when he made his final bow in a League game against Sheffield United on 10 February 1934, scoring twice in a 4-2 win.
- Stanley Matthews was almost 47 years of age when he played for Stoke against Huddersfield in December 1962 (Division 2), making him the oldest footballer ever to appear against the Terriers in a competitive match.
- The average age of Huddersfield's 1968-69 League side on several occasions was 22.

AGGREGATE SCORES: Over the years several Terriers' Cup-ties have been decided with an aggregate scoreline. Here are some of the interesting two-legged contests:

- Huddersfield beat Mansfield 7-2 on aggregate in a two-legged 1st round League Cup-tie in August/September 1983. They won 2-1 away and 5-1 at home.
- The Terriers defeated Rochdale 7-3 over two legs in a League Cup-tie in September 1981.
- Six years later they lost 7-5 on aggregate to Rotherham in the 1st round of the same competition (August 1987).
- Huddersfield's only two-legged FA Cup-tie was against Sheffield United in January 1946. After drawing the first game 1-1 at Leeds Road, the return leg at Bramall Lane went in favour of the Blades by 2-0 for an aggregate 3-1 scoreline.
- Huddersfield lost 6-4 to West Ham in a two-legged Football League Wartime Cup fixture in May 1940.
- A year later, in February/March 1941, the Terriers were again beaten 6-4 on aggregate by Middlesbrough in a two-legged Football League Wartime Cup-tie.
- Huddersfield lost 7-6 on aggregate to Sunderland in the final of the Combined Counties Cup in May 1943. The Terriers won 4-1 at home after losing 6-2 away,

ALDERSHOT: Huddersfield's record against the Shots:
Football League

Venue	P	W	D	L	F	A
Home	7	4	3	0	10	4
Away	7	2	1	4	6	7
Totals	14	6	4	4	16	11

FA Cup

Venue	P	W	D	L	F	A
Home	1	0	1	0	1	1
Away	1	0	0	1	1	3
Totals	2	0	1	1	2	3

Alan Gowling scored the winning goal (1-0) when Huddersfield met Aldershot for the first time in a League game (15 September 1973).
The FA Cup games were played in 1969-70.

ALLARDYCE, Samuel: Defender: 42 apps. Born: Dudley, 19 October 1954
A solid, hard tackling defender, signed from Coventry, Allardyce served the Terriers in the 1984-85 season. He played for Bolton, Sunderland, Millwall and Tampa Bay Rowdies before Coventry, returning to Bolton from Leeds Road. Later assisted PNE (two spells) and WBA, retiring in 1993 with over 440 League appearances behind him. He has been manager of Bolton since October 1999, having previously been in charge at Preston (as caretaker-boss), Notts County and Blackpool.

ALLISON, Wayne Anthony: Striker: 84 apps. 19 goals
Born: Huddersfield, 16 October 1968

Nicknamed 'The Chief ', 6ft 1" striker Wayne Allison started his career with Halifax before joining Watford for £250,000 in July 1989. A year later he signed for Bristol City for £300,000 and moved to Swindon for £475,000 in July 1995. After helping the Robins win the Second Division title in 1996, his £800,000 switch to Leeds Road followed in November 1997 by which time he had scored 123 goals in competitive football. He did well with the Terriers before transferring to Tranmere for £300,000 in September 1999. From Prenton Park he joined Sheffield United on a 'free' in July 2002, helping the Blades reach two domestic Cup semi-finals and the First Division play-off final in 2003. In June 2004 he signed for Chesterfield.

ANGLO-ITALIAN TOURNAMENT: Huddersfield's record in this competition is:

Venue	P	W	D	L	F	A
Home	2	1	0	1	4	3
Away	2	1	0	1	3	3
Totals	4	2	0	2	7	6

Huddersfield played in this competition in May and June 1971. They beat Sampdoria (h) 2-0 but lost the return in Italy 3-2 and after losing 1-0 away to Bologna, triumphed in the return fixture 3-2. However, they failed to make progress from the 'English' group, Blackpool going on to beat Bologna 2-1 in the final

APPEARANCES: Huddersfield's top appearance-makers
All Major Competitions (League, FA Cup, League Cup, others)

575	Billy Smith
501	Tom Wilson
459	Vic Metcalfe
440	Roy Goodall
403	Malcolm Brown*
394	Hugh Turner
393	David Cowling **
388	Steve Smith ***
381	Bill McGarry
375	Kevin McHale

* Total includes four substitute apps.
** Total includes 10 substitute apps.
*** Total includes 13 substitute apps.

Appearance Facts
* Frank Worthington lies in 16th position in the Football League list of all-time appearance-makers. He played in 737 games between 1966 and 1988.

ARMOUR, Andrew D: Winger: 98 apps. 8 goals Born: Irvine, Scotland, 24 July 1883. Died: 1955.
Andrew Armour was essentially an outside-right who could also play at inside or centre-forward. He served with Irvine Meadow and Queen's Park (1905) before representing the Scottish League in 1909 as a Kilmarnock player. He returned to Queen's Park in 1910, had a second spell with Kilmarnock and joined Huddersfield in December 1911. Rejoining 'Killie' for a third time in September 1914, he assisted Clydebank on loan before retiring.

ARMSTRONG, Steven Craig: Midfield: 119 apps. 5 goals Born: South Shields, 23 May 1975.
A steady, hard working left-sided midfielder, Craig Armstrong played for Nottingham Forest, Burnley, Bristol Rovers (two spells), Gillingham and Watford (two spells) before joining Huddersfield for £750,000 in February 1999. On leaving the Terriers in February 2002, he signed for Sheffield Wednesday for £100,000 and had a loan spell with Grimsby (February-May 2004)

ARSENAL: Huddersfield's record against the Gunners is:
Football League

Venue	P	W	D	L	F	A
Home	32	8	14	10	47	39
Away	32	8	9	15	37	47
Totals	64	16	23	25	84	86

FA Cup

Home	1	0	0	1	0	1
Neutral	1	0	0	1	0	2
Totals	2	0	0	2	0	3

League Cup

Home	3	0	1	2	2	9
Away	4	0	1	3	3	7
Totals	7	0	2	5	5	16

The first time the clubs met in the Football League was on 11 October 1913 when a crowd of 8,000 saw the Gunners win a Second Division game 2-1 at Leeds Road. Huddersfield won the return fixture in mid-February 1-0, Frank Mann the scorer.
Arsenal won 4-0 at Leeds Road in November 1920 before Charlie Wilson scored a hat-trick in each of the two League games against Arsenal in December 1923, the Terriers winning 3-1 away and 6-1 at home. Wilson also netted a treble in a 5-0 win at Highbury in February 1925.
The Terriers lost 6-2 at Arsenal in September 1950 - 10 days after crashing 6-0 at Newcastle.
A crowd of 43,000 saw Huddersfield beat the Gunners 5-3 in London in November 1954.
Arsenal scored in 41 of their 42 League games in 1930-31, the exception being a 0-0 draw with Huddersfield at Highbury.

Huddersfield lost 2-0 to the Gunners in the 1930 FA Cup final, Jack Lambert and Alex James scoring in front of 92,488 spectators.

When the Gunners won a 6th round tie at Leeds Road by 1-0 in February 1932, it ended a run of 25 unbeaten home FA Cup games for Huddersfield, stretching back to January 1914. The Gunners beat Huddersfield over two legs in the semi-final of the 1967-68 League Cup. They won 3-1 at Leeds Road and 3-2 at Highbury for a 6-3 overall victory. Huddersfield suffered their heaviest home defeat in the League Cup when losing 5-0 to Arsenal in a 2nd round, 1st leg encounter in September 1993. They lost the tie 6-1 on aggregate.

Herbert Chapman managed both clubs to League championship and FA Cup triumphs.

ASTON VILLA: Huddersfield's record against the Villa is:

Football League

Venue	P	W	D	L	F	A
Home	32	15	10	7	51	32
Away	32	3	9	20	31	74
Totals	64	18	19	27	82	106
FA Cup						
Away	4	2	0	2	4	5
Neutral	1	0	0	1	0	1
Totals	5	2	0	3	4	6
League Cup						
Away	1	0	0	1	1	4

Huddersfield met Villa for the first time in League combat on 12 March 1921 (Division One). A crowd of 25,000 witnessed the 0-0 draw at Villa Park. A week later a similar crowd saw Frank Mann's goal give Huddersfield a 1-0 win in the return fixture.

Huddersfield lost 1-0 to Villa after extra-time in the 1920 FA Cup final at Stamford Bridge and the following season were knocked out 2-0 in a third round tie at Villa Park. Villa won 4-3 at Leeds Road in March 1923 and in February 1925 George Brown (later to join Villa) scored a hat-trick in a 4-1 home win for the Terriers.

In March 1926, Huddersfield beat Villa 5-1 at home and four years later triumphed 5-3 away but then lost 6-1 both at home and away in 1930-31.

The Terriers ended 1931-32 with a 3-2 win at Villa Park, Dave Mangnall scoring a hat-trick. On Christmas Day 1935, Huddersfield lost 4-1 at Villa Park yet 24 hours later won by the same score in the return fixture.

On their way to the 1930 FA Cup final, Huddersfield beat Villa 2-1 away.

Huddersfield's first League Cup-tie saw them lose 4-1 at Villa Park in October 1960.

ATKINS, Denis: Full-back: 214 apps. Born: Bradford, 8 November 1938

Atkins conceded a penalty when making his league debut for Huddersfield against Sunderland in February 1960. He went on to serve the club for 15 years, receiving two benefits while making over 200 appearances. He signed professional forms at Leeds Road in December 1955 and moved to Bradford City in March 1968, retiring three years later to take up a career in teaching. He returned to Valley Parade in 1984 as the club's liaison officer.

* Atkins' eldest daughter, Jill, was a member of the Great Britain hockey team that finished fourth in the 1988 Olympic Games.

ATTENDANCES

- The record attendance at Leeds Road was 67,037: Huddersfield v. Arsenal, FA Cup 6th round, 27 February 1932.
- The highest League attendance at Leeds Road was 52,479 v. Blackpool (Division One) on 7 April 1951
- The record attendance at The Alfred McAlpine Stadium is 23,678 v. Liverpool, FA Cup 3rd round, 12 December 1999.
- The lowest crowd for a competitive game at Leeds Road (excluding wartime football) was 1,069 for the Huddersfield v. Doncaster, Autoglass Trophy 1st round tie on 28 September 1993.
- The lowest League crowd at Leeds Road was 1,624 for the visit of Torquay on 30 April 1979 (Division Four).
- The lowest attendance for a senior match at The Alfred McAlpine Stadium has been 3,570 v. Halifax, LDV Vans Trophy, 1st round, 15 October 2001.
- The biggest crowd for a League Cup-tie at Leeds Road was 27,312 v. Arsenal, semi-final, 1st leg, 6 February 1968.

- Huddersfield have played in front of 60,000 plus crowd on 16 occasions (15 in the FA Cup, one in the League).
- The biggest League crowd for a Huddersfield game, home or away, has been 60,149 v. Newcastle, St James' Park, Division Two, on 15 April 1947.
- Huddersfield's average home League attendance for 1953-54 was a club record 31,810 (aggregate 647,002 for 21 matches).
- The average League attendance for the first season at The Alfred McAlpine Stadium (1994-95) was 11,666.
- The lowest average League attendance for a season at Leeds Road was a meagre 3,649 in 1978-79 (aggregate 83,929 for 23 games).
- Huddersfield's average post WW2 home League attendance (1946-47 to 2003-04 inclusive) is almost 12,250, while the club's all-time average home League crowd (1910 to 2004) is a fraction over 12,650.
- When Huddersfield won the First Division championship in 1923-24, their average home League attendance was 17,551. When they on it again the following season it was 17,878 and in 1925-26 when they completed the hat-trick, the average was only 19,571. During those three successful campaigns the average League crowd at Leeds Road (63 games played) was 18,333.
- Torquay United's record attendance (at Plainmoor) is 21,908 v. Huddersfield, FA Cup, 29 January 1955.

AUTOGLASS TROPHY: Huddersfield's full record in this competition is:

Venue	P	W	D	L	F	A
Home	9	6	3	0	23	6
Away	9	3	3	3	8	12
Totals	18	9	6	3	31	18

Huddersfield first entered the AGT in 1991-92 and after winning 1-0 at Wigan, drawing 1-1 at home with both Scarborough and Blackpool and beating Bury 2-1 at Gigg Lane, they were eliminated in Northern Section semi-final by Burnley who won 2-0 at Turf Moor in front of 10,775 spectators.

Re-entering the competition the following season, the Terriers once more did extremely well before losing again in the Northern Section semi-final.

After drawing 0-0 at Bradford City, thrashing Halifax 5-0 at Leeds Road (a hat-trick here for Iain Dunn) they ran up two successive 3-0 home victories over Doncaster and Bolton before going out 5-2 away to Wigan.

Huddersfield went one better in 1993-94 and qualified for the Wembley final.

They beat Doncaster 3-1 (h), drew 1-1 at Rotherham, defeated Preston 5-4 on penalties (after 0-0 draw), got past Crewe Alexandra 3-2 (after extra-time), won 1-0 at Stockport and then dismissed Carlisle 4-3 on aggregate, winning 4-1 at home but losing 2-0 away. Sadly, after a hard fought encounter with Swansea which finished 1-1 after extra-time, the Terriers lost the penalty shoot-out by 3-1.

A crowd of 47,773 saw the final when the Terriers fielded this team: Francis; Billy, Cowan; Starbuck, Scully, Mitchell; Logan, P Robinson, Booth, Bullock (Dunn) and Baldry. Richard Logan scored in normal time.

B

BAINES, Stephen John: Defender: 132 apps. 12 goals Born: Newark, 23 June 1954
Steve Baines signed professional forms for Nottingham Forest in July 1972. After two
League outings he moved to Huddersfield in July 1975 and did well at Leeds Road before
moving to Bradford City for £18,000 in March 1978, switching to Walsall in July 1980 for
£50,000 (fixed by an independent tribunal). After a loan spell with Bury, Steve became
player-coach at Scunthorpe (July 1982), helping the Iron gain promotion to the Third
Division. Twelve months (July 1983) later he joined Chesterfield for £50,000 and as
assistant-manager at Saltergate collected a Fourth Division championship medal in 1985.
His 441st and last appearance came in November 1986. Later with Matlock Town, he
started refereeing in 1988 and reached the Football League Panel in 1995.

BALDERSTONE, John Christopher: Midfield: 131 apps. 25 goals Born: Paddock,
Huddersfield, 16 November 1940. Died: 6 March 2000
Chris Balderstone signed for Huddersfield in July 1956 and left for Carlisle in June 1965.
He skippered the Cumbrians in the 1970 League Cup semi-final and netted 68 times
during his time at Brunton Park before assisting Doncaster (from July 1975), Queen of
the South and Enderby Town. One of the few sportsmen to combined soccer with
cricket, he was a middle-order batsmen, he played for Yorkshire (briefly) and
Leicestershire for whom he scored over 10,000 runs and captured more than 250
wickets. In fact, so keen was he at both ball games, on 15 September 1975 he played
for Leicestershire against Derbyshire in the afternoon and for Doncaster against
Brentford in the evening. Balderstone later became a first-class umpire.

BALDRY, Simon: Midfield: 166 apps. 10 Goals Born: Huddersfield, 12 February 1976,
Signed by Huddersfield as a teenager, Baldry turned professional in July 1994 and over
the next nine years (up to August 2003 when he joined Notts County) amassed over
160 appearances. He is the club record holder for most substitute appearances: 69.
Affected by injuries as a 'Terrier', in September 1998 he was loaned out to Bury to
regain match fitness.

BANKS, Ian Frederick: Midfield: 87 apps. 18 goals Born: Mexborough, 9 January 1961.
Between 1977 and 1995 gritty midfielder Ian Banks amassed almost 700 appearances,
scoring 102 goals. He started his career with Barnsley, turning professional at Oakwell in
January 1979 after serving his two-year apprenticeship. He then spent three years at
Leicester (from June 1983) before joining Huddersfield for £45,000 in September 1986.
From Leeds Road he moved to Bradford City for £180,000 in July 1988 and after that
served with WBA, Barnsley (again), Rotherham and Darlington, quitting League football in
May 1995. He surprisingly never won a winner's medal during his 18 years in the game.

BARKAS, Edward: Full-back: 131 apps. 4 goals Born: Wardley, Tyneside, 21 January 1901.
Died: Little Bromwich, Birmingham, April 1962.
Well-built, firm tackling defender Ned Barkas, the eldest of five brothers (four of whom

were professional footballers). Was a former miner, he played for Bedlington, South Shields and Hebburn Colliery before assisting Norwich (1920) and Bedlington Colliery. In January 1921 he moved to Huddersfield and over the next eight years made over 130 appearances, helping the Terriers win the First Division title three seasons running, gaining a championship medal in 1923-24 and 1925-26. An FA Cup runner-up with the Terriers in 1928, he received the same prize when skippering Birmingham against WBA in the 1931 final, having moved to St Andrew's for £4,000 in December 1928. After 288 outings for the Blues, he switched to Chelsea (May 1937) and was player-manager of Solihull Town during WW2 when working as a charge-hand. He was a tourist with the FA to Canada in 1926 - his only representative honour. Collectively, the Barkas brothers appeared in 1,125 League games between 1920 and 1949. Ned made the most (404), Sam 377, Tom 279 and Harry 45.

BARNETT, Gary Lloyd: Midfield: 130 apps. 17 goals Born: Stratford-upon-Avon, 11 March 1963
Before signing for Huddersfield for £30,000 in July 1990, Gary Barnett had served with Coventry, Oxford, Wimbledon and Fulham, scoring 31 goals in 182 League games for the latter club. He remained at Leeds Road until August 1993 when he moved to Leyton Orient. He was a Third Division championship winner with Fulham in 1984.

BARNSLEY: Huddersfield's record against the Tykes is:
Football League

Venue	P	W	D	L	F	A
Home	26	16	6	4	43	21
Away	26	8	4	14	36	47
Totals	52	24	10	18	79	68
FA Cup						
Home	2	0	1	1	4	5
Away	2	0	0	2	0	2
Totals	4	0	1	3	4	7
League Cup						
Home	2	2	0	0	4	1
Away	2	0	1	1	1	5
Totals	4	2	1	5	6	

Huddersfield first met Barnsley in a League game on 17 November 1910 (Division Two), winning 2-1 at Oakwell, Jim Richardson and Alex McCubbin the scorers.
The Terriers won the return game 2-0 to complete their first 'League' double.
Town beat Barnsley 6-0 (h) and 4-2 (a) in 1952-53, but the Tykes won 5-2 at Leeds Road in 1957-58. Huddersfield lost a thrilling 3rd round FA Cup-tie 4-3 at Oakwell in front of almost 40,000 spectators in January 1947. After winning their home leg 2-0, Huddersfield lost 4-0 in the return leg at Oakwell to crash out of the League Cup in the 2nd round in 1995-96.

BEASLEY, Albert Edward: Outside-left: 123 apps. 27 goals Born: Stourbridge, 27 July 1913. Died: Taunton hospital, 3 March 1986.
'Pat' Beasley joined Huddersfield for £750 in October 1936 and remained at the club until December 1945. He began his career with Stourbridge and switched to Arsenal in

May 1931. He made 89 appearances in five seasons with the Gunners, gaining two championship medals in the process before his transfer to Leeds Road. He played in the 1938 FA Cup final defeat by Preston and a year later scored on his international debut for England against Scotland at Hampden Park in front of 149,269 spectators. That summer he toured South Africa with the FA. After WW2, 'Pat' did well with Fulham as an inside-left and wing-half. Then, as player-manager, he took Bristol City to Third Division (S) title in 1955 and five years later was in charge of Birmingham when they reached the Fairs Cup final. His last club was Dover.

BEATON, Simon: Right-half: 118 apps. one goal Born: Inverness, 1888. Died: circa 1960 Beaton was associated with Huddersfield for four years, from May 1910 until May 1914 when surprisingly he announced his retirement at the age of 26. He played for Aston Villa, Newcastle and Middlesbrough before moving to Leeds Road for £75 in a deal that also involved Billy Hughes. Beaton appeared in Huddersfield's first-ever game in the Football League. He did not play for Villa or Newcastle at senior level.

BEECH, Christopher Stephen: Midfield: 79 apps. 15 goals Born: Blackpool, 16 September 1974. The energetic Chris Beech joined Huddersfield for £65,000 from Hartlepool in November 1998 and moved to Rochdale in July 2002. Starting his professional career at Blackpool, he transferred to Hartlepool in 1996 and reached the milestone of 300 appearances in 2003-04.

BERESFORD, David: Winger: 42 apps. 3 goals Born: Middleton, Lancs, 11 November 1976 The diminutive Beresford started his professional career with Oldham in 1994 and after a loan spell with Swansea joined Huddersfield for £350,000 in March 1997. During his four years at the club he also had loan spells with PNE and Port Vale. He signed for Hull in July 2001, switching to Plymouth in July 2002, helping the Pilgrims win the Third Division championship. Beresford played for England at Schoolboy and Youth team levels.

BILLY, Christopher Anthony: Central Midfield: 126 apps. 6 goals Born: Huddersfield, 2 January 1973 Chris Billy was another player who moved from Huddersfield to Plymouth, taking the road south in August 1995. Signing professional forms at Leeds Road in July 1991, four years later he had the pleasure of scoring the winning goal that beat Bristol Rovers 2-1 in the 1995 play-off final at Wembley. From Plymouth he switched to Notts County and later assisted Bury and Carlisle United, reaching the milestone of 500 career appearances in 2004.

BIRMINGHAM CITY: Huddersfield's record against the Blues is:
Football League

Venue	P	W	D	L	F	A
Home	46	19	18	9	71	38
Away	48	14	8	24	54	79
Totals	96	33	26	33	125	117
FA Cup						
Home	3	2	1	0	4	2
Away	3	1	0	2	3	4
Totals	6	3	1	2	7	6

Huddersfield's first League game against Blues took place in mid-December 1910 at St Andrew's. The home side won 2-1.

Huddersfield beat the Blues 7-1 in the return fixture at Leeds Road in April 1911 to claim their best League win of the season.

Two-and-a-half years later, in October 1913, the Terriers won 7-0 (Tom Elliott 3) and once again it was their best League victory of the season. The half-time score was 2-0.

Huddersfield beat the Blues 7-0 (h) and 4-1 (a) in 1913-14 and 4-0 (h) in December 1922, followed soon after by another double, 4-1 (h) and 3-1 (a) in 1925-26.

A week after slamming Derby 6-0 in November 1931, Huddersfield lost 5-0 away to the Blues. Huddersfield lost 6-1 at St Andrew's in December 1967 and the following season Geoff Vowden became the first substitute to score a hat-trick in a League game when he helped the Blues to a 5-1 victory (September 1968).

In the closing minutes of a League game against the Blues at St Andrew's on 5 January 1971, Huddersfield's goalkeeper Terry Poole was carried off with a broken leg. Steve Smith took over and almost immediately broke his thumb. The Terriers still won the game 2-0. Huddersfield met the Blues in the FA Cup in successive seasons of 1922-23 and 1923-24 and 1970-71 and 1971-72 Steve Bruce has been manager of both clubs.

BLACKMAN, Frederick: Full-back: 96 apps. Born: Kennington, 8 February 1884. Died: circa 1958 Blackman served with Woolwich Arsenal, Hastings & St Leonard's United and Brighton before joining Huddersfield in May 1911. He appeared in almost 100 competitive games for the Terriers before transferring to Leeds City in February 1914 for £1,200. After WW1 he moved to QPR. A Southern League championship winner with Brighton in 1910, he helped the Hove club beat Aston Villa in that year's FA Charity Shield.

BLACKBURN ROVERS: Huddersfield's record against the Rovers is:

Football League

Venue	P	W	D	L	F	A
Home	34	13	9	12	47	39
Away	34	7	12	15	43	61
Totals	68	20	21	27	90	100

FA Cup

Home	2	1	1	0	6	1
Away	2	1	1	0	3	2
Neutral	1	0	0	1	1	3
Totals	5	2	2	1	10	6

League Cup

Home	2	0	2	0	2	2
Away	2	0	1	1	3	4
Totals	4	0	3	1	5	6

Others

Home	1	0	0	1	1	2

The first Huddersfield-Blackburn League game took place on 5 February 1921 (Division One) when a crowd of 19,800 witnessed a 0-0 draw at Leeds Road. A week later Huddersfield won 2-1 at Ewood Park. After losing 4-2 at Ewood Park on Christmas Day 1926, Huddersfield won the return fixture 48 hours later by 5-0. They also won 5-2 at Blackburn in February 1930

Alf Lythgoe scored five goals when Huddersfield beat Blackburn 6-0 (h) in April 1935. In a 3rd round FA Cup replay in February 1922 Ernie Islip and Billy Smith both scored twice when Huddersfield beat Rovers 5-0 at Leeds Road after a 1-1 draw.

Blackburn defeated Huddersfield 3-1 in the 1928 FA Cup final and in 1980-81 knocked Rovers out of the League Cup in the 1st round on the away goal rule. The Lancashire club also won a 2nd round League Cup-tie 5-4 on aggregate in 1993-94.

BLACKPOOL: Huddersfield's record against the Seasiders is:

Football League

Venue	P	W	D	L	F	A
Home	33	18	7	8	71	36
Away	33	5	12	16	38	61
Totals	66	23	19	24	109	97

FA Cup

Venue	P	W	D	L	F	A
Home	2	1	0	1	2	3
Away	2	0	0	2	0	3
Totals	4	1	0	3	2	6

Others

Venue	P	W	D	L	F	A
Home	2	1	1	0	3	2
Away	1	0	0	1	1	3
Totals	3	1	1	1	4	5

The first League game between the clubs took place at Leeds Road on 4 February 1911 (Division Two) when a crowd of 6,000 witnessed the 2-2 draw. The following the month the teams drew 1-1 at Bloomfield Road.

Huddersfield's best League win in 1914-15 was against Blackpool, Ernie Islip scoring a hat-trick in a 5-0 home victory on Boxing Day. In December 1930 Huddersfield claimed what still remains as their best-ever League win when they whipped Blackpool 10-1 at Leeds Road, Joe Robson (3) and George McLean (4) leading the goal-rush in front of 11,932 spectators. Huddersfield lost their first League game after WW2, going down 3-1 at home to Blackpool. Playing their first game in the top flight since April 1956, Huddersfield beat Blackpool 3-0 at home in August 1970 before a crowed of 22,787, Steve Smith (2) and Frank Worthington (penalty) scoring the goals.

Huddersfield's last League game at Leeds Road was against Blackpool on 30 April 1994. A crowd of 16,159 saw the Terriers win 2-1 with Phil Starbuck netting the last and winning goal in the 61st minute Blackpool - courtesy of a 56-yard goal from full-back Tom Garrett - beat Huddersfield 1-0 at Bloomfield Road in the 4th round of the FA Cup, on their way to winning the trophy in 1953. They had knocked the Terriers out the competition at the same stage 20 years earlier (2-0). Blackpool beat Huddersfield with a sudden death goal in the LDV vans trophy in 2001-02 (game was tied at 3-3 after both legs had been completed in normal playing time).

BOLTON WANDERERS: Huddersfield's record against the Trotters/Whites is:

Football League

Venue	P	W	D	L	F	A
Home	42	24	8	10	59	38
Away	42	7	10	25	42	86
Totals	84	31	18	35	101	124

FA Cup

Home	2	0	1	1	1	2
Away	3	0	0	3	0	7
Neutral	1	0	0	1	1	3
Totals	6	0	1	5	2	12

League Cup

Home	2	0	0	2	0	5
Away	1	0	0	1	1	2
Totals	3	0	0	3	1	7

Other

Home	1	1	0	0	3	0

The first League game between Huddersfield and Bolton was staged at Burnden Park in December 1910 (Division Two). A crowd of 8,000 saw the Wanderers win 3-1. Huddersfield's first League win over Bolton followed in October 1921 when they triumphed 3-0 at Leeds Road in front of 16,200 spectators.

When Huddersfield defeated Bolton 3-0 on 12 April 1926 they clinched their third League championship - and there were still two games to play.

Huddersfield lost 6-1 at Bolton on Christmas Day 1925, their heaviest reverse of the season. Five years later Town crashed 7-1 at Burnden Park.

In season 1950-51 Bolton won both League games 4-0.

Bolton beat Huddersfield 3-1 in the 1929 FA Cup semi-final at Anfield.

Huddersfield lost 5-1 on aggregate to Bolton in a 1st round League Cup-tie in 1990-91.

Two players who both served with Huddersfield, scored 42 goals between them for Bolton in 1978-79. They were Frank Worthington (26) and Alan Gowling (16).

BOOT, Edmund: Wing-half: 325 apps. 5 goals Born: Laughton Common, Rotherham, 13 October 1915. Signed in March 1937 from Sheffield United (with Bobby Barclay) Boot appeared in more than 560 senior games for Huddersfield (239 during WW2). He played in the 1938 FA Cup final and retired as a senior player in 1953 and after a spell as reserve team player-coach, he became the club's fifth post-war manager, appointed in January 1960 and remaining in office until 1964. He played for Aughton and Denaby United and had trials with Sheffield Wednesday before moving to Bramall Lane in 1934 (see under Managers).

BOOTH, Andrew David: Striker: 286 apps. 100 goals Born: Huddersfield, 6 November 1973 Andy Booth played his part in helping the Terriers gain promotion to the Second Division in 2004. He was an apprentice at Leeds Road before signing professional in July 1992. After scoring over 60 goals in four seasons, he was transferred to Sheffield Wednesday for a record fee of £2.7 million and spent almost five years at Hillsborough, also having a spell on loan with Spurs, before returning to the Terriers in March 2001 for £200,000. Capped three times by

England at Under-21 level, Booth has now netted over a century of goals in almost 300 senior games for the Terriers.

BOTT, Wilfred: Winger: 115 apps. 26 goals Born: Featherstone near Pontefract April 1907 Bott started out with Edlington Colliery Welfare, moving to Doncaster in March 1927. After his £1,000 move to Huddersfield in March 1931 he scored a goal every four-and-a-half games for the Terriers up to December 1934. Able to play in either flank but preferring the left, on leaving Leeds Road he signed for Newcastle for £1,000 plus Tommy Lang, and scored a hat-trick on his debut for the Magpies. He then assisted QPR, Colchester and Lancaster Town, while also guesting in WW2 for Aldershot, Brighton, Chelsea and QPR. He returned to Colchester in 1945. In his career Bott appeared in 343 League games and scored 102 goals

BRADFORD CITY: Huddersfield's record against the Bantams is:
Football League

Venue	P	W	D	L	F	A
Home	18	7	6	5	29	20
Away	18	5	7	6	24	33
Totals	36	12	13	11	53	53

FA Cup

Venue	P	W	D	L	F	A
Home	1	1	0	0	2	1

League Cup

Venue	P	W	D	L	F	A
Home	1	1	0	0	2	1
Away	1	0	1	0	1	1
Totals	2	1	1	0	3	2

Others

Venue	P	W	D	L	F	A
Away	3	1	2	0	3	2

Huddersfield first met City in the League in 1920-21 (Division One) and they completed the double, winning 1-0 at home and 2-0 away, Fred Lunn scoring in both matches. The Terriers won 4-0 at Bradford in April 1922 and there were hat-tricks heroes in first Brain Stanton and then Duncan Shearer when Huddersfield won home League games v. the Bantams by 6-3 and 5-2 in January 1983 and December 1986 respectively. Huddersfield beat City on their way to the 1930 FA Cup final and won a 1st round League Cup-tie 3-2 on aggregate in 1997-98.

BRADFORD PARK AVENUE: Huddersfield's record against Park Avenue is:
Football League

Venue	P	W	D	L	F	A
Home	5	2	2	1	5	2
Away	5	1	1	3	5	8
Totals	10	3	3	4	10	10

FA Cup

Venue	P	W	D	L	F	A
Away	1	1	0	0	1	0

League Cup

Venue	P	W	D	L	F	A
Away	1	0	0	1	1	3

Huddersfield's first game at their Leeds Road round was a friendly against Park Avenue on 2 September 1908. A crowd of around 1,000 saw Town, playing in salmon pink

jerseys, win 2-1, Jimmy Freeborough (own-goal) and Richard Morris the scorers.
The winning team was: W J Crinson; R Trenhan, R Ray, W Hooton, F Walker, P Hartley, J Shackleton, J Morris, W S Cookson, R Morris and C Flowitt. Fred Walker was the team manager. Bradford also provided the opposition in Huddersfield's first League game on 3 September 1910. Harry Hamilton scored the only goal of the game to give the Terriers a 1-0 victory in front of 16,000 fans at Park Avenue.
Frank Mann scored the only goal in the FA Cup 2nd round clash at Park Avenue in 1920-21. Park Avenue beat Huddersfield in the 2nd round of the League Cup in 1962-63.

BRAY, Ian Michael: Left-back: 104 apps. one goal Born: Neath, 6 December 1962
Ian Bray made over 100 appearances for Hereford before joining Huddersfield in July 1985. He spent five years at Leeds Road, up to July 1990 when he signed for Bury

BRENTFORD: Huddersfield's record against the Bees is:
Football League

Venue	P	W	D	L	F	A
Home	20	8	5	7	25	24
Away	20	6	5	9	18	23
Totals	40	14	10	16	43	47

FA Cup

Home	1	1	0	0	5	1
Away	2	1	0	1	2	6
Totals	3	2	0	1	7	7

Play-offs

Home	1	0	1	0	1	1
Away	1	0	1	0	1	1*

* Huddersfield won 4-3 on penalties
Huddersfield won their first League game against Brentford by 2-1 at Griffin Park in September 1935 (Division One).
On their way to the 1920 FA Cup final, Huddersfield beat the Bees 5-1 in the 1st round at Leeds Road. Huddersfield defeated Brentford 4-3 on penalties (after two 1-1 draws) to reach the Second Division play-off final in 1994-95

BRIGHTON & HOVE ALBION: Huddersfield's record against the Seagulls is:
Football League

Venue	P	W	D	L	F	A
Home	15	7	1	7	20	16
Away	15	2	4	9	17	27
Totals	30	9	5	16	37	43

FA Cup

Home	1	1	0	0	2	0
Away	1	0	1	0	0	0
Totals	1	1	1	0	2	0

League Cup

Home	1	1	0	0	1	0
Away	1	0	0	1	0	2
Totals	2	1	0	1	1	2

The first Huddersfield-Brighton League encounter was played at Leeds Road in September 1958 (Division 2) when 13,244 fans saw the Terriers win 3-2, Les Massie netting the vital goal. In November 1985 Brighton won a thrilling League game in Hove by 4-3. Huddersfield beat Albion in a 2nd round replay on their way to winning the FA Cup in 1922. Albion beat Town 2-1 on aggregate in a 2nd round League Cup-tie in 1981-82.

BRISTOL CITY: Huddersfield's record against the Robins is:
Football League

Venue	P	W	D	L	F	A
Home	21	12	2	7	44	21
Away	21	7	6	8	25	29
Totals	42	19	8	15	69	50
FA Cup						
Home	1	0	0	1	0	2
Neutral	1	1	0	0	2	1
Totals	2	1	0	1	2	3

A crowd of 5,000 at Ashton Gate in December 1911 saw Huddersfield lose their first League game against City by 3-2. City then completed the double with a 2-1 victory at Leeds Road. Frank Mann scored a hat-trick when Huddersfield recorded their first League win over City - 5-0 at home in April 1913. Two years later Huddersfield won a home League game 5-3 (April 1915), beat City 6-2 (h) and 3-2 (a) in 1959-60, won 5-0 (h) in May 1982 and lost 6-1 at Ashton Gate in April 1989
A crowd of 35,463 saw Huddersfield beat City 2-1 in the 1920 FA Cup semi-final at Stamford Bridge. Sam Taylor scored both goals.

BRISTOL ROVERS: Huddersfield's record against the Pirates is:
Football League

Venue	P	W	D	L	F	A
Home	14	6	3	5	22	16
Away	14	1	7	6	13	25
Totals	28	7	10	11	35	41
FA Cup						
Home	1	1	0	0	2	0
Play-offs						
Neutral	1	1	0	0	2	1

Dave Hickson scored both Huddersfield's goals when they registered their first League win over Rovers by 2-1 in September 1956 (Division Two). Soon after the return fixture at Eastville saw Rovers win 4-0.
Huddersfield's heaviest defeat against Rovers is 5-1 (a) in October 1988.
The Terriers gained their FA Cup win in the 3rd round in January 1953.
Huddersfield beat Rovers 2-1 in the 1995 play-off final at Wembley in front of 56,175 spectators, Chris Billy scoring the winning goal in the 81st minute.

BROWN, Allan Winston: Centre-half: 60 apps. Born: Corbridge, 26 August 1914. Died: Biddecombe, 9 March 1996.
After making over 160 senior appearances as a player with Huddersfield, Burnley and Notts County, Allan Brown became an excellent manager, discovering some fine young

talent. He assisted his local club Corbridge United and Spen Black & White before signing professional forms at Leeds Road in April 1933. He was then transferred to Turf Moor (February 1946) and later spent six seasons with Notts County up to August 1954 when he became manager of Burnley. He was briefly a coach with Sheffield Wednesday and then managed Sunderland from 1957-64, at Hillsborough 1964-68 and back at Sunderland 1968-72. Later coached in Norway and was scout for Plymouth. A Football League representative and FA Cup runner-up with Burnley in 1947, he then took Sunderland back into the First Division in 1964 and two years later was an FA Cup runner-up with the Owls (beaten by Everton).

* His cousin, Austen Campbell, also played for Huddersfield.

BROWN, George: Centre-forward: 229 apps. 159 goals Born: Mickley, Northumberland, 22 June 1903. Died: 10 June 1948

Brown had a fine career, scoring 298 goals in 473 appearances in all competitions. Starting out with Mickley Juniors, he then assisted Mickley Colliery before having a trial with Huddersfield in March 1921. That proved successful and the following month signed professional forms at Leeds Road. A clever dribbler, his eye for snapping up the half-chance, allied to his power and accuracy with his shooting (especially his right foot rockets) earned him the nicknamed of 'Bomber' and over the next eight years scored a record number of goals (159) for the Terriers. A key member of the attack when three League championships were won in the mid-1920s, he also equalled the club's scoring record of 35 goals in a season in 1925-26. He missed the 1922 FA Cup final victory over Preston but played in the losing Final of 1928. Capped eight times by England as a 'Terrier', he also represented the Football League and later added one more cap to his collection as an Aston Villa player. Signed for £5,000 in August 1929, he netted 89 times in 126 outings for the Midland club and later played for Burnley (from October 1934), Leeds United (September 1935) and Darlington (player-manager, October 1936 to his retirement in October 1938). A guest for Sutton Town and Shirley during WW2, he later became a licensee in the Aston and Shirley districts of Birmingham.

* Brown's uncle, Joe Spence, played for Manchester United and England.

BROWN, Malcolm: Defender: 403 apps. 23 goals Born: Salford, 13 December 1956

Brown had two spells with Huddersfield whom he served for almost 10 years between May 1977 and February 1989. He was a professional with Bury before moving to Leeds Road, going on to help the Terriers win the Fourth Division championship in 1980 and gain promotion again three years later. He moved to Newcastle for £100,000 in July 1983 and returned to Leeds Road for £45,000 in June 1985, having made 45 appearances for the Magpies. After leaving the Terriers for second time, he joined Rochdale, later assisting Stockport before returning to Spotland in 1991 following promotion to the Fourth Division with County.

Brown holds the record for consecutive League appearances for the Terriers, totalling 226 between 1978 and 1983.

BROWN, Nathaniel Levi: Wing-back: 66 apps. Born: Sheffield, 16 June 1981
Nat Brown, 6ft 2in tall and weighing 12st 6lbs, joined Huddersfield as a youngster and turned professional in July 1999. He developed fast and became an accomplished player who helped the Terriers gain back to back promotions in 2003 and 2004 while taking his total number of senior appearance past the 65 mark. He can also play as an emergency striker.

BULLOCK, Darren John: Midfield: 156 apps. 20 goals Born: Worcester, 12 February 1969.
A hard tackler, busy and totally committed, Darren Bullock joined Huddersfield from Nuneaton Borough for £550,000 in November 1993 and went on to give the Terriers wonderful service over the next three-and-a-half years before transferring to Swindon for £400,000 in February 1997. Two years later he joined Bury for £150,000 and after a loan spell with Sheffield United, he dropped out of the League to sign for Worcester in October 2002.

BULLOCK, Frederick Edwin: Left-Back: 215 apps. Born: Hounslow, Middlesex, 11 July 1886. Died: 10 November, 1922
Sturdy defender Fred Bullock was first-choice in the Huddersfield line-up for practically seven years, from December 1910 to May 1921 when he retired after failing to recover from a cartilage operation. He played for his local club, Hounslow Town and then Ilford and captained England against Ireland in an Amateur international in Belfast before joining the Terriers as a full-time professional. A soldier in the Footballers' Battalion of the Middlesex Regiment during WW1, after playing in the 1920 FA Cup final and helping Huddersfield climb out of the Second Division, he received a benefit payment of £753 and subsequently became licensee in Huddersfield. Bullock committed suicide at the age of 36.

BURKE, David Ian: Defender: 223 apps. 3 goals Born: Liverpool, 6 August 1960
England Youth international David Burke made over 75 appearances for Bolton before joining Huddersfield in June 1981 on a free transfer. He proved a wonderful signing and went on to play in more than 200 first-class games for the Terriers before transferring to Crystal Palace for £78,000 in January 1988.
He helped the Terriers win promotion in 1983 and the following season was the only ever-present in the side. In a home League game against Fulham in March 1985, Burke broke his left leg, the injury requiring a bone graft and the insertion of a steel plate. A civil act prosecution followed in the High Court whereby Burke sued the Fulham defender Jeff Hopkins for damages. Regaining full fitness, he helped Palace gain promotion from the Second Division. A second spell at Bolton followed from 1990 and after assisting Blackpool, he quit top-class football in 1995 with well over 500 senior appearances under his belt.

BURNETT, Wayne: Midfield: 59 apps. one goal Born: Lambeth, 4 September 1971
Burnett was creative, gritty and determined. He played for Leyton Orient, Blackburn (briefly), Rotherham, Plymouth and Bolton before joining Huddersfield in September 1996. He had already appeared in over 140 competitive games at that time added almost 60 more to his tally up January 1998 when he transferred to Grimsby for £100,000. He moved to Grays Athletic in September 2002.

BURNLEY: Huddersfield's record against the Clarets is:

Football League

Venue	P	W	D	L	F	A
Home	28	14	4	10	37	23
Away	28	8	6	14	34	43
Totals	56	22	10	24	71	66

FA Cup

	P	W	D	L	F	A
Home	2	1	0	1	4	4
Away	5	1	1	3	4	9
Totals	7	2	1	4	8	13

League Cup

	P	W	D	L	F	A
Home	1	0	0	1	0	1

Other

	P	W	D	L	F	A
Away	1	0	0	1	0	2

Huddersfield's first home game in the Football League was against Burnley on 10 September 1910. A crowd of 7,371 saw the visitors win 1-0. Burnley completed the double over the Terriers that season before Town collected their first win in February 1913 by 1-0 at home. The first team to complete a League double over Huddersfield was Burnley in 1910-11. The Clarets won 1-0 at Leeds Road, 2-1 at Turf Moor.
Over the Christmas period of 1924 Huddersfield beat Burnley 5-1 (a) and 2-0 (h)
Alex Jackson scored a hat-trick in Huddersfield's 7-1 home win in November 1928.
Town did the double over the Clarets in 1956-57, winning 2-0 (h) and 5-0 (a).
The first of the seven FA Cup games was played in January 1915 when Burnley won a 1st round encounter 3-1 at Turf Moor. The last was in the 3rd round in January 1972 when the Terriers won 1-0 at Burnley.
Burnley beat Huddersfield 2-0 at Turf Moor in the Autoglass Trophy semi-final in 1992 and in 2002-03 won 1-0 in a 2nd round League Cup-tie at The Alfred McAlpine Stadium.

BURRELL, Gerald: Outside-right: 61 apps. 9 goals Born: Belfast, 6 September 1926
Burrell played for Dundee before joining Huddersfield from St Mirren in December 1953, replacing Alistair Gunn on the right-wing. He held his position until the end of the 1954-55 season but after playing second fiddle to Jackie Marriott while languishing in the reserves, he was transferred to Chesterfield in June 1956 and spent two seasons at Saltergate.

BURY: Huddersfield's record against the Shakers is:

Football League

Venue	P	W	D	L	F	A
Home	27	19	3	5	54	21
Away	27	9	9	9	41	38
Totals	54	28	12	14	95	59

FA Cup

	P	W	D	L	F	A
Home	1	1	0	0	3	1
Away	2	1	1	0	2	1
Totals	3	2	1	0	5	2

League Cup

	P	W	D	L	F	A
Away	1	1	0	0	2	0

Others

Away   2   1   0   1   3   3

Huddersfield started the 1912-13 season with a 4-0 home win over Bury - the first League meeting between the clubs.

Jack Cock scored four goals in Huddersfield's 5-0 home win over Bury in September 1919.

On 1 April 1989, Huddersfield beat Bury 6-0 at Gigg Lane. It was their highest winning margin for almost 62 years, since their 7-1 away success against Sheffield United on 12 November 1927. In April 1990, Bury gained sweet revenge with a 6-0 win at Gigg Lane. Huddersfield beat the Shakers 4-2 (h), 4-2 (a) and 4-1 (h) in the space of two-and-half years: 1966-68.

Huddersfield eclipsed Bury 3-1 (h) en route to the 1930 FA Cup final.

BUTLER, Michael Anthony: Forward: 87 apps. 25 goals Born: Barnsley, 27 January 1951
Mike Butler played for Worsborough Bridge before becoming a professional at Oakwell in July 1973. He scored 57 goals in 120 League games for the Tykes who then transferred him to Huddersfield in March 1976, recruited to partner Rod Belfitt up front. He did a good job during his time at Leeds Road before moving south to Bournemouth July 1978. Butler ended his League career with Bury, retiring in May 1982 with some 400 appearances to his credit.

BUTT, Leonard: Inside-forward: 70 apps. 11 goals Born: Wimslow, Cheshire, 26 August 1910. Died: 1994
Butt's professional career spanned 20 years. He played initially for Ashton National and Wimslow Albion before joining Stockport in August 1928. A spell with Macclesfield preceded his move to Huddersfield in May 1935. He spent eighteen months at Leeds Road, up to January 1937 when he switched to Blackburn (with Jock Wightman). He remained at Ewood Park for ten years, helping Rovers win the Second Division championship in 1939 and finish runners-up in the 1940 WW2 Cup final at Wembley. He then assisted York and Mansfield before retiring in 1928.

BYRNE, Michael: Forward: 60 apps. 11 goals Born: Dublin, 14 January 1960
Byrne was signed from Shamrock Rovers in September 1988. He had two useful seasons at Leeds Road before returning to Shamrock in September 1990.

C

CAMPBELL, Austen Fenwick: Wing-half: 212 apps. 6 goals Born: Hamsterley, County Durham, 5 May 1901. Died: Blackburn, 1981.

Austen Campbell won the FA Cup with Blackburn (v. Huddersfield) in 1928 and was a beaten finalist with Huddersfield (v. Arsenal) two years later. A curly-haired, hard-shooting untiring footballer who loved to dribble with the ball, he played for Spen Black & White and Leadgate Park before starting his career with Coventry during the first season after WW1. In June 1921 he returned to Leadgate Park only to re-enter League action with Blackburn in February 1923. Six years later he was signed by Huddersfield and spent six years at Leeds Road before enjoying his last season with Hull (November 1935-May 1936) prior to going into coaching. An England international, capped eight times between 1929-32, he was uncommonly fast for a left-half, was trenchant in the tackle and stylish in all he did. A very fine player, Campbell also represented the Football League on five occasions and toured Canada with the FA in 1931. He was the cousin of Huddersfield defender Allan Winston Brown (q.v).

CAMPBELL, Robert McFaul: Forward: 41 apps. 13 goals Born: Belfast, 13 September 1956
The much-travelled Bobby Campbell had two spells with Huddersfield - April 1975 to July 1977 and September to October 1978. He represented his country at Youth team level and later gained two full caps, while playing club football for Aston Villa, Halifax, Sheffield United, Bradford City (two spells), Derby and Wigan between 1974 and 1988. He also assisted Vancouver Whitecaps (NASL) and Brisbane City (Australia). Campbell scored 179 goals in 476 League games including 121 in 274 outings for Bradford City.

CAMBRIDGE UNITED: Huddersfield's record against United is:
Football League

Venue	P	W	D	L	F	A
Home	9	6	2	1	19	9
Away	9	4	5	0	15	9
Totals	18	10	7	1	34	18

The first League game between Huddersfield and Cambridge, in September 1973 (Division Three) ended in a 2-1 home win for the Terriers, Alan Gowling and Roger Hoy the scorers.

CAPTAINS:
- Fred Walker was Huddersfield's first recognised team captain in 1908.
- Charlie Morris followed Walker in 1910.
- Sam Wadsworth skippered both Huddersfield and England in the 1920s
- Clem Stephenson skippered Huddersfield to three successive League titles in the 1920s.

Among the other players who have skippered the Terriers over the years we have (in A-Z order) Ned Barkas, Fred Blackburn, Eddie Boot, George Brown, Austen Campbell, Trevor Cherry (Division Two champions, 1970), Fred Fayers, Roy Goodall, Terry Gray,

George Hepplewhite, Bob Hesford, Don McEvoy, Alex Mutch, Efe Sodje, Steve Smith, Ron Staniforth, Sam Wadsworth, Tom Wilson, Alf Young.
Austen Campbell also skippered Huddersfield's second XI for many years.

CARDIFF CITY: Huddersfield's record against the Bluebirds is:
Football League

Venue	P	W	D	L	F	A
Home	32	21	7	4	62	21
Away	32	8	11	13	31	48
Totals	64	29	18	17	93	69

Huddersfield failed to score in their first two League games with Cardiff in season 1921-22, drawing 0-0 away and losing 1-0 at home. The following season Town completed the double, winning both matches 1-0.
In October 1927, Bob Kelly scored a hat-trick as Huddersfield beat Cardiff, the FA Cup holders, 8-2. This was the Terriers' biggest League win at that time.
Mark Lillis scored four times when Cardiff were defeated 4-0 at Leeds Road in October 1982, and this scoreline was repeated in April 1984, again at Leeds Road.
After suffering five successive defeats and failing to score, Huddersfield bounced back to beat Cardiff 5-1 at Leeds Road in March 1990, Craig Maskell netting a fourtimer.

CARLISLE UNITED: Huddersfield's record against the Cumbrians is:
Football League

Venue	P	W	D	L	F	A
Home	12	6	6	0	18	9
Away	12	2	5	5	8	12
Totals	24	8	11	5	26	21
FA Cup						
Home	1	0	0	1	0	1
Away	2	1	1	0	5	4
Totals	3	1	1	1	5	5
League Cup						
Home	3	2	1	0	6	2
Away	3	0	2	1	4	5
Totals	6	2	3	1	10	7
Others						
Home	1	1	0	0	4	1
Away	2	0	0	2	0	4
Totals	3	1	0	2	4	5

Tony Leighton netted twice from the penalty spot as Huddersfield beat Carlisle 2-0 at Leeds Road in the first League meeting between the clubs in December 1965.
Huddersfield beat Carlisle 3-2 in the 3rd round of the FA Cup in January 1982. Peter Fletcher scored a hat-trick.
Huddersfield beat Carlisle 4-3 on aggregate in the semi-final of the AGT (N) in 1994. A decade later the Cumbrians won 2-0 (h) in the 1st round of the LDV Vans Trophy but at the end of that season (2004) they lost their Football League status after 76 years

CARR, William Edward: Half-back: 100 apps. one goal Born: Framwellgate Moor, County Durham, 7 March 1905. Died: 1989

Bill Carr was a Huddersfield player for more than eight years, playing in only six games in the first four. Initially with Horden Colliery, he joined the Terriers from Horden Athletic in April 1926 and left for Southend in October 1934. He missed the 1930 FA Cup final, having failed to gain a first team place. He made almost 100 League appearances for Southend.

CATTLIN, Christopher John: Left-back: 70 apps. 2 goals Born: Milnrow, 25 June 1946

A former Burnley amateur, Chris Cattlin signed as a professional for Huddersfield in August 1964, becoming Derek Parkin's full-back partner in 1966-67. A strong kicker with good balance, he held his position until halfway through the following campaign when Billy Legg took over the number '3' shirt. In March 1968, Cattlin moved to Coventry for whom he made almost 250 appearances in eight years before joining Brighton whom he later managed (1983-86), signing Dean Saunders for the price of a train ticket (£18). He now owns property including a hotel in Brighton.

CAVANAGH, Thomas Henry: Inside-forward/wing-half: 98 apps. 29 goals Born: Liverpool, 29 June 1928

During his 12-year playing career, 1949-61, Tommy Cavanagh made 302 League appearances while serving with six different League clubs: PNE, Stockport, Huddersfield (May 1952-May 1956), Doncaster, Bristol City and Carlisle. He guested for Preston during WW2 before signing full-time at the age of 21. He followed manager Andy Beattie to Stockport and then played his part in bringing First Division football back to Leeds Road in 1952-53 when he scored 10 goals in 21 League games. On leaving Carlisle he became player-manager of Cheltenham, as trainer then manager of Brentford and first team coach at Nottingham Forest before teaming up with Tommy Docherty at Hull (July 1971). When the 'Doc' took over as boss at Manchester United, Cavanagh went with him. He later had a spell as assistant to manager Dave Sexton at Old Trafford and was for a while trainer of the Northern Ireland national team and assistant-boss at Newcastle. In 1983 Cavanagh took charge of BK Rosenborg (Norway) and six years later he was back in England as a part-time coach with Wigan.

CECERE, Michele Joseph: Midfield: 71 apps. 13 goals Born: Chester, 4 January 1968

Mike Cecere assisted six different League clubs during his career - Oldham (from 1986), Huddersfield (signed for £100,000 in November 1988), Stockport (on loan), Walsall (a £25,000 buy from Leeds Road in August 1990), Exeter and finally Rochdale (July-December 1996)., he scored over 70 goals, having best spell with Walsall for whom he netted 34 times in 141 games

CHAIRMEN: Here are some the Chairmen of Huddersfield: J M Asquith, Ian Ayre, J Chadwick, Ken Davy, Frank Drabble, T S Fisher, N G Graham FRCS, DG Heady, S Kinder OBE., K S Longbottom, Barry Rubery and David Taylor

CHAPMAN, Leslie: Midfield: 158 apps. 12 goals
Born: Oldham, 27 September 1948
Chapman spent over 23 years in football during which time he amassed almost 850 appearances. He was associated, in turn, with Huddersfield (amateur), Oldham (professional, January 1967), Huddersfield (signed for £20,000, plus David Shaw, September 1969), Oldham (£10,000, December 1974), Stockport (May 1979), Bradford City (£10,000, February 1980), Rochdale (June 1983), Stockport (as player-manager, October 1985 to July 1986) and finally PNE (August 1986 as player/assistant-manager, then manager from January 1990 to September 1992). He also starred for San Jose Earthquakes (1978) and in 1995-96 was reserve team trainer at Manchester City. Chapman played his best football at Boundary Park, scoring 22 goals in 292 games, was a

Second Division winner with the Terriers in 1970. Chapman twice suffered relegation (1973, 1975) and as a manager steered Preston clear of the Third Division trapdoor.

CHARITY SHIELD: Huddersfield played for the Charity Shield in May 1922, beating Liverpool 1-0 at Old Trafford before a crowd of almost 20,000. Tom Wilson scored the deciding goal in the second half.

CHARLTON ATHLETIC: Huddersfield's record against the Addicks is:
Football League

Venue	P	W	D	L	F	A
Home	35	16	9	10	61	36
Away	35	9	5	21	45	67
Totals	70	25	14	31	106	103

FA Cup

Venue	P	W	D	L	F	A
Home	1	0	1	0	2	2
Away	2	1	0	1	1	1
Totals	3	1	1	1	3	3

Huddersfield lost their first-ever League game against Charlton, going down 2-1 at home in December 1936. The London club doubled up over the Terriers that season before Huddersfield won their first game 4-0 at Leeds Road in February 1939
In 1955-56, Huddersfield lost 4-1 at Charlton yet won 4-0 at home
One of the greatest comebacks in Football League history took place at The Valley, home of Charlton, on 21 December 1957. That afternoon, Huddersfield, undefeated in four matches, were the visitors for a Second Division encounter which attracted a pre-Christmas crowd of 12,535, Charlton's sixth lowest in eleven years. But those who

stayed away missed a terrific contest that contained 13 goals and plenty of action at both ends of the field.

Charlton lost defender Derek Ufton with a dislocated shoulder in the 17th minute (he had also been injured in the first game of the season between the two clubs) and they fell behind to Len Massie's goal in the 27th minute. Alex Bain then pounced to make it 2-0 on 35 minutes.

Johnny Summers, who was to become the Valiants' hero, reduced the deficit two minutes into the second half only for the alert Bain to score again soon afterwards (3-1). Bill McGarry converted a penalty in the 51st minute (4-1) and Bob Ledger netted a fifth for the Terriers eleven minutes later. At this juncture Charlton were struggling but they were given a lifeline within 50 seconds of Ledger's goal when John 'Buck' Ryan scored. Almost straight from the kick-off Summers made it 5-3 and the same player then scored three times in eight minutes (73, 78 and 81) to fire the London club in front at 6-5. Amazing stuff. Huddersfield were shell-shocked but somehow they raised their game and when Stan Howard's shot was deflected in by John Hewie for a dramatic equaliser with just four minutes remaining, it looked as if a point had been secured! Not so - Charlton had other ideas and with time running out up popped Ryan to claim the winning goal with 45 seconds remaining.

Summers' five goals were all scored with his right foot and he had changed his boots for a new pair at half-time. Charlton had never before (or since) scored seven goals during the second half of a competitive game and the scoreline of 7-6 in unique in Football League history.

On the opening day of the season, at Leeds Road, Huddersfield came back from 3-0 down at half-time to earn a 3-3 draw, Ken Taylor grabbing an 87th minute equaliser. Huddersfield and Charlton met again in the 3rd round of the FA Cup a month after that epic 13-goal thriller and this time the Addicks won 1-0 after a 2-2 draw at Leeds Road. The four matches between the clubs in 1957-58 produced 24 goals.

In 1967-68, the Terriers lost 4-2 at Charlton but won the return game 4-1 and in October 1969 the Addicks were beaten 4-0 at Leeds Road.

CHARLTON, Simon Thomas: Left-back: 157 apps. 2 goals Born: Huddersfield, 25 October 1974

England Youth international Simon Charlton signed professional forms for Huddersfield in July 1989 and established himself in the Terriers' first team in 1990-91, going on to accumulate a fine record at Leeds Road before transferring to Southampton for £250,000 in June 1993. He played in 114 Premiership games for Saints and 72 for Birmingham, before signing for Bolton in July 2000, linking up with former Huddersfield defender Sam Allardyce, who was manager at The Reebok Stadium. In July 2004, Charlton signed for Premiership newcomers Norwich City.

CHELSEA: Huddersfield's record against the Blues is:
Football League

Venue	P	W	D	L	F	A
Home	28	17	1	10	55	35
Away	28	8	7	13	30	47
Totals	56	25	8	23	85	82

FA Cup

Home	2	0	1	1	2	3
Away	2	1	0	1	2	3
Totals	4	1	1	2	4	6

League Cup

Away	2	1	0	1	1	2

March 1911 saw the first League game between Huddersfield and Chelsea that went in favour of the London club by 2-0 at Stamford Bridge. The following month Huddersfield gained revenge with a 3-1 victory at Leeds Road.

Huddersfield's biggest League win over Chelsea was achieved in September 1933 when a crowd of 7,508 saw then gain an impressive 6-1 victory at Leeds Road.

Huddersfield completed the double over Chelsea in 1947-48, winning 3-1 (h) and 4-2 (a). The following season Chelsea did the double, winning 4-3 at Leeds Road and 5-0 at Stamford Bridge.

A crowd of 36,407 saw Chelsea beat Huddersfield 2-1 in a 3rd round FA Cup-tie at Leeds Road on their way to reaching the 1967 final.

Both League Cup games were in the 3rd round, Chelsea winning in 1976-77 and Huddersfield (against Premiership opponents) in 1999-2000.

CHELTENHAM TOWN: Huddersfield's record against the Robins is:

Football League

Venue	P	W	D	L	F	A
Home	2	0	2	0	3	3
Away	2	0	1	1	1	2
Totals	4	0	3	1	4	5

The first League game between the Terriers and the Robins was played in November 2002 and resulted in a 1-0 win for newcomers Cheltenham at Whaddon Road.

After drawing 1-1 at Cheltenham on the final day of the 2003-04 League season, the Terriers missed out on automatic promotion (pipped at the post by Torquay) and therefore had to go on and earn their place back in the Second Division via the play-offs.

CHERRY, Trevor John: Defender: 216 apps. 17 goals Born: Huddersfield, 23 February 1948

Trevor Cherry was a junior at Leeds Road before turning professional in July 1962. He formed a superb defensive partnership alongside Roy Ellam and skippered the Terriers to the Second Division championship in 1970.

In June 1972, he and his team-mate Ellan, were both transferred to Leeds for £100,000 and £30,000 respectively. Cherry stayed the distance at Elland Road and while occupying a variety of positions including midfield, he helped Leeds win the League title and finish runners-up in both the FA Cup and European Cup-winner's Cup competitions.

He also gained 27 England caps, having the ill-luck to be sent-off against Argentina in 1977. In December 1982, after 460 senior appearances for Leeds he joined Bradford City as player-manager in a £10,000 deal, collecting the Bells Whisky manager of the season award after guiding the Bantams to promotion in 1985. Controversially sacked in January 1987, he became marketing director of a sports equipment company and also worked on local radio. In later years he was appointed as a director of Huddersfield.

CHESTER: Huddersfield's record against the Seals is:

Football League

Venue	P	W	D	L	F	A
Home	8	4	2	2	16	8
Away	8	4	1	3	10	10
Totals	16	8	3	5	26	18

FA Cup

	P	W	D	L	F	A
Home	1	1	0	0	1	0
Away	1	0	0	1	2	3
Totals	2	1	0	1	3	3

In October 1981 Huddersfield beat Chester 2-0 away in the first League meeting between the two clubs.

In May 1990 Chester were defeated 4-0 at Leeds Road. The first of the two FA Cup-ties took place in the 2nd round at Chester in December 1973 and ended with the home side winning 3-2.

CHESTERFIELD: Huddersfield's record against the Spireites is:

Football League

Venue	P	W	D	L	F	A
Home	8	5	3	0	14	3
Away	8	2	2	4	6	9
Totals	16	7	5	4	20	12

FA Cup

	P	W	D	L	F	A
Away	3	3	0	0	10	0

Huddersfield and Chesterfield met for the first time in the Football League in 1973-74 (Division Three). The Terriers won both games: 1-0 at home, 2-0 away.

Almost 16,000 spectators saw George Brown score four times when Huddersfield beat Chesterfield 4-0 at The Recreation Ground in a 3rd round FA Cup-tie in January 1929.

CHIVERS, Francis Cornelius: Utility player: 54 apps. 17 goals Born: Drybrook, 7 April 1909. Killed in action: 1942

Frank Chivers played for Goldthorpe United before joining Barnsley in 1930. Scorer of 16 goals in 79 League games for the Tykes, he moved to Huddersfield in January 1936 and had two decent years at Leeds Road before moving to Blackburn in March 1938.

CHRISTMAS DAY: The last time Huddersfield played on Christmas Day was in 1958, when they defeated Charlton 1-0 at Leeds Road in a Second Division game, Stan Howard scoring the only goal in front of 14,295 spectators - despite there being no major public transport.

Huddersfield's first Christmas Day match was at home to Glossop in the League in 1911 (won 3-1) and after that they played a further 35 games on December 25, finishing with this record:

P	W	D	L	F	A	Pts
36	14	11	11	64	45	39

Fact File

- Biggest win of the 14 was 7-1 over Rotherham County (h) in 1919 (Division Two).

- Heaviest defeat was 4-1 away to Aston Villa (Division One) in 1935.
- Jack Swann (3) and Frank Mann (3) v Rotherham in 1919, Charlie Wilson (4) at Burnley in 1924, Arthur Claverley (3) v. Leeds in 1943 and Edward Carr (3) at Blackburn in 1945, were the only Terriers players to score a hat-trick on Christmas Day.
- Biggest home attendance for a Christmas Day game was 28,510 v. Swansea Town in 1952 (won 3-0) and the lowest, 5,000 v. Rotherham County in 1919.
- A crowd of 53,950 saw the Spurs v. Huddersfield League game at White Hart Lane in December 1933.
- Huddersfield's best run of undefeated Christmas Day games was six, achieved twice: 1942-48 and 1951-58. They lost only one of their last 13 Christmas Day fixtures.

CLARKE, Dennis: Full-back: 194 apps. 4 goals Born: Stockton, 18 January 1948
Clarke was the first substitute to be used in an FA Cup final, coming on at the end of normal time for WBA in their 1968 clash with Everton. He duly collected a winner's medal to go with the League Cup runners-up prize he received twelve months earlier. He was never a regular in the Baggies' line-up and was subsequently transferred to Huddersfield for £25,000 in January 1969. He bedded in splendidly at Leeds Road and was a regular for four seasons, helping the terriers win the Second Division title in 1970 as an ever-present. Moving back to the Midlands with Birmingham in June 1973, he was forced to retire through injury in May 1975. He later worked in ice-cream and fabrics before becoming a partner in a building company.

CLARKE, Timothy Joseph: Goalkeeper: 91 apps. Born: Stourbridge, 16 September 1968
Tim Clarke played for Halesowen Town and Coventry before joining Huddersfield for £15,000 in July 1991. An imposing goalkeeper, 6ft 3ins tall and 13st 7lbs in weight, he took high crosses with ease but was suspect on the ground. He took over from Lee Martin at Leeds Road before losing his place to Steve Francis in 1993. After a loan spell with Rochdale and a brief sojourn with Altrincham, Clarke signed for Shrewsbury in October 1993. He later assisted Witton Albion (1996), York and Scunthorpe, gaining a runners-up medal in the AWS final with the 'Shrews' in 1996 and helping the 'Iron' reach the play-offs three years later. He moved to Kidderminster Harriers in September 1999, having appeared in 250 games in eight years.

COACHES: The following have all held coaching positions with Huddersfield: ex-Charlton Athletic, Blackpool, Watford and Hull defender Dennis Booth, full-back Martyn Booty, future manager Mick Buxton, Henry Cockburn (1950s Manchester United and England wing-half), John Deehan (the former Aston Villa, WBA, Ipswich and England Under-21 international striker), 1970s Terriers' star Terry Dolan, 1920s/30s Leeds Road favourite Roy Goodall, future managers Ian Greaves, Eoin Hand and John Haselden, former Leeds, Manchester United and Scottish international World Cup striker Joe Jordan and ex-Bury, St Johnstone and Sheffield Wednesday goalkeeper Roy MacLaren, future manager Ted Magner, 1950s left-winger Vic Metcalfe, 1970s Swindon and Luton winger David Moss, the former Aberdeen and Sunderland outside-left George Mulhall, inside-forward Jimmy Robson who scored for Burnley in the 1962 FA Cup final, 'Terrier' Steve Smith, Aston Villa's League championship and 1982 European Cup final hero Peter Withe and

Huddersfield's 1938 Cup final centre-half Alf Young
Other coaches (at reserve, youth & intermediate levels) include: Kevin Blackwell, ex-Huddersfield players Eddie Boot, Mark Lillis, David Moss and Gerry Murphy

Fact File.
- Withe was Huddersfield's first official player-coach.
- On 21 November 1981, Huddersfield were forced to include Steve Smith at left-back in their 1st round FA Cup-tie at Workington because of injuries, illness and suspensions. He was coach to the juniors and had not played for four years. The game ended 1-1.

COCK, John Gilbert: Centre-forward: 18 apps. 9 goals Born: Hayle, Cornwall, 14 November 1893. Died: April 1966
Jack Cock was Huddersfield's first England international, capped against Ireland in 1919. He was also the first Terriers' player to score four goals in a League game, doing so against Bury in September 1919. Soon afterwards he was sold to Chelsea for a record fee of £2,500.
Cock played in London for West Kensington United, Forest Gate, Old Kingstonian and Brentford as amateur before joining Huddersfield in the May 1914. Perfectly proportioned, he was physically strong and was a fine athlete, fast and lethal in front of goal, being able to use both feet and his head to great effect. From Chelsea he moved to Everton (January 1923) and thereafter served, in turn, with Plymouth, Millwall, Folkestone and Walton FC (Surrey). He then became manager of Millwall in November 1944, a position he held until August 1948 when he retired to become a licensee in New Cross, London. A Third Division (S) championship winner with Millwall in 1928, Cock gained one more cap v. Scotland in 1920, having been awarded the Military Medal during WW1.

CODDINGTON, John William: Defender: 356 apps. 118 goals Born: Worksop, 16 December 1937
John Coddington played for Worksop Boys' Club and joined Huddersfield shortly after leaving his Shirebrook school (where one of his fellow pupils was Ray Wilson, q.v). He made his League debut away to Manchester United in October 1955 (aged 17) and turned professional in June 1958 after completing his national service). Dominant, strong and reliable, Coddington gained a regular place in the side in 1958-59 and was a first team regular right up until the end of 1966-67 when he moved to Blackburn for £20,000. Later employed as chief scout by Bradford City, in February 1973 he linked up with the League of Ireland club Drogheda before joining the coaching staff at Middlesbrough. A victim of the economy cuts at Ayresome Park, Coddington later ran the Ship Inn pub in Easton and in August 1985 was persuaded to return to Middlesbrough as first team coach, being replaced by Bruce Rioch six months later.

COLCHESTER UNITED: Huddersfield's record against the 'U's' is:
Football League

Venue	P	W	D	L	F	A
Home	5	3	2	0	8	4
Away	5	1	1	3	8	12
Totals	10	4	3	3	16	16

FA Cup

Away	1	0	0	1	0	1

League Cup

Home	1	0	1	0	1	1
Away	1	1	0	0	2	0
Totals	2	1	1	0	3	1

Just over 5,200 fans saw Huddersfield win their first League game 3-2 at home v. Colchester in November 1974. The result was reversed with the teams met at Layer Road later in the season.

Huddersfield suffered a humiliating FA Cup defeat at the hands of Southern League side Colchester at Layer Road in January 1948, losing 1-0 in front of a 16,000 crowd.

Huddersfield knocked United out of the League Cup in the 2nd round in 1996-97.

COLLINS, Simon: Midfield/defender: 70 apps. 5 goals Born: Pontefract, 16 December 1973. Signed as a professional by Huddersfield in July 1992 (after two years as a trainee) Collins performed competently over the next five years before transferring to Plymouth for £60,000 in March 1997. Initially a midfielder he developed into a powerful central defender and went on playing in the Football League with Macclesfield and Shrewsbury (on loan) until July 2001 when he moved down the ladder with Frickley Athletic, having amassed well over 200 appearances at club level.

COLOURS: Huddersfield players wore salmon pink jerseys for their first-ever game in 1908 (a friendly v. Bradford Park Avenue). Soon afterwards the team wore white shirts with a blue neck-band and from 1919 onwards traditional blue and white striped shirts, white shorts, with various sock designs including blue and white hoops, all white, white with blue trim, white with single blue hoop, have been the chosen club colours. Over the years the team, like all other League clubs, have to change colours and for most of the time between 1908 and WW1, the opponents (home or away) did Huddersfield a favour by either loaning them a change strip or changing the colours of their own shirts. Things got better after the hostilities and from 1919 to the 1960s, Huddersfield's second strip was simply white shirts and black shorts with black and white socks. Since then several change strips have been worn including (in order):

- black & red striped shirts, black shorts with red stripe, black socks with red turnover yellow shirts, green shorts, yellow socks
- all yellow (various times)
- all white
- yellow shorts, blue shorts, yellow socks
- yellow & black squared, black shorts, yellow socks
- red & black striped shirts, black shorts, black socks/blue & white hoop on turnover

red & black hooped shirts, black shorts, black socks
- white shirts, black sleeves, black shorts, white socks.
- yellow shirts, purple shorts, yellow socks.
- ecru shirts with single jade & navy band with jade & navy blue sleeves, ecru shorts with jade & navy blue trim, ecru, jade & navy blue hooped socks/all yellow
- red & black striped shirts, black shorts with red stripe down side, black socks with red turnover, cream shirt with horizontal blue stripe, blue sleeves, cream shorts with blue trim, blue & cream striped socks
- red shirts, blue shorts, red socks
- black shirts, black shorts, with royal blue trim, black socks with royal blue turnover.

COMEBACKS:
- Huddersfield were 4-2 down in a League game at Manchester United in November 1947 but fought back to earn a 4-4 draw.
- The Terriers were 4-1 behind at half-time in a League game at Bury in September 1991 but a splendid second 45 minutes saw them grab a 4-4 draw.
- Huddersfield trailed Charlton 3-0 at half-time in their home Second Division match in August 1957. They fought back to draw 3-3.
- Charlton (down to 10 men) were trailing Huddersfield 5-1 in the return game that season (21 December 1957). Final score: 7-6 to the London club (see Charlton Athletic).
- In a 1st round 1st leg League Cup encounter at Rotherham in August 1987, Huddersfield were 3-1 down after 72 minutes but fought back to earn a 4-4 draw, only for the Millermen to win the second leg 3-1.

CONWELL, Anthony: Full-back: 112 apps. 2 goals Born: Bradford, 17 January 1932
Conwell was signed from Sheffield Wednesday with Jackie Marriott in a deal that took Ron Staniforth and Roy Shiner to Hillsborough in July 1955. A strong, forceful defender with good pace, he was as huge favourite with the Leeds Road supporters and spent four years at the club before transferring to Derby for £6,000 in June 1959. He turned professional at Hillsborough at the age of 17 but struggled to get into the first XI, making under 50 senior appearances. He played in over 100 games for the Rams and did well with Doncaster prior to his retirement in May 1964.

COOK, George: Forward: 91 apps. 35 goals Born: Evenwood, County Durham, February 1895. Died: Colwyn Bay, 31 December 1980.
Cook had a wonderful career that spanned 23 years. He began locally with Evenwood Juniors (1912-14) and after a spell with Trindle Juniors joined the Royal Field Artillery (from 1916). After WW1 he signed amateur forms for Bishop Auckland (August 1919) and turned professional with Rotherham County in May 1922, transferring to Huddersfield in March 1923. After four years at Leeds Road Cook moved south to Aston Villa (February 1927) before assisting Spurs from June 1929 to April 1931, Brentford in season 1931-32, Colwyn Bay for two years and finally Rhyl, retiring in April 1935. An accomplished footballer, Cook won many honours in the game. He made his mark with Bishop Auckland whom he twice helped win the FA Amateur Cup (1921 & 1922). His performances around this time attracted many scouts and it was Rotherham who enticed him to turn professional. As George Brown's strike-partner, he gained three League championship medals with the

Terriers before joining Villa (Brown followed him later). However, with the arrival of 'Pongo' Waring, Cook struggled to get into the side in his second season and subsequently moved to White Hart Lane. Aged 34 when he joined Spurs, he still gave the London club excellent service, notching 30 goals in 73 games.

COOPER, Graham: Winger: 87 apps. 13 goals Born: Huddersfield, 22 May 1962
Cooper was 21 when he joined the Terriers from Emley in March 1984. He remained at Leeds Road for four years before transferring to Wrexham in July 1988. He later played for York (loan) and Halifax, quitting League football in May 1992.

CORK, David: Midfield/forward: 125 apps. 28 goals Born: Doncaster, 28 October 1962
Cork represented Doncaster Schools and was a trialist with Doncaster before rejecting an offer from Manchester United to join Arsenal as an apprentice in July 1978, turning professional two years later. He moved to Huddersfield in July 1985, signed by Mick Buxton and played splendidly for three seasons before losing his way. He was loaned out to WBA (September-October 1988), had a trial with Norwich the following month and then signed as a non-contract player with Scunthorpe in February 1989. He rounded off his career with Darlington (July 1989-May 1992), helping the Quakers regain their Football League status as Conference champions in 1990.

CORNER-KICK:
- Huddersfield winger Billy Smith was the first player to score a goal direct from a corner playing against Arsenal on 11 October 1924...the year this rule was introduced.
- Eddie Baily (Spurs) took a corner against Everton at White Hart Lane on 2 April 1952. The ball struck the referee and bounced back to Baily who chipped a pass to Len Duquemin to head the game's only goal. Despite Huddersfield's appeal, the result was allowed to stand and Spurs duly gained promotion while the Terriers were relegated.

COVENTRY CITY: Huddersfield's record against the Sky Blues is:
Football League

Venue	P	W	D	L	F	A
Home	6	4	0	2	11	5
Away	6	3	1	2	9	5
Totals	12	7	1	4	20	10
FA Cup						
Home	1	0	1	0	3	3
Away	1	1	0	0	2	1
Totals	2	1	1	0	5	4
League Cup						
Home	1	0	0	1	0	2

Huddersfield won their first two League matches against Coventry in 1919-20 by 2-0 at Highfield Road and 5-0 at Leeds Road.
Huddersfield beat City 2-1 after extra-time at Highfield Road in a 3rd round FA Cup replay in January 1955. Jim Glazzard and Jimmy Watson scored in both matches.

COWAN, Thomas: Left-back: 165 apps. 10 goals Born: Belshill, Glasgow, 28 August 1969

Cowan played for Netherdale Boys' Club before starting his senior career with Clyde in July 1888. In February 1989 he moved into the bigtime with Glasgow Rangers but failed to establish himself at Ibrox Park and in August 1991, a £350,000 deal took him to Sheffield United. A loan spell at Stoke preceded his transfer to Huddersfield for £150,000 in March 1994. He remained a 'Terrier' for five years before switching his allegiance to Burnley for £20,000 in March 1999. In July 2000 he diverted to Cambridge United after a loan spell and following a similar deal with Peterborough, he signed for York in July 2002, moving to Dundee in August 2003 and Carlisle in November 2003. Cowan has now appeared in more than 400 club games.

COWLING, David Roy: Outside-left: 393 apps. 48 goals Born: Doncaster, 27 November 1958 Dave Cowling was an apprentice with Mansfield before joining Huddersfield on a free transfer in July 1977, signing as a full-time professional a month later. A smart, old-fashioned type of winger, he gained a regular place in the side in 1978-79 and the following season was a key member of the Fourth Division championship winning team, starring in 39 games and scoring 10 goals. Then in 1982-83 he did the business on the flank when promotion was gained from the Third Division, Cowling missing only one game this time. After losing his form he was loaned out to Scunthorpe and Reading, before signing for the latter club on a permanent basis in March 1988. In July 1989, he was reunited with his former boss Mick Buxton at Scunthorpe and he

had the pleasure of scoring the Iron's first goal at their new £2.5 million Glanford Park stadium. When he quit competitive football in 1991, Cowling had almost 600 club appearances safely under his belt. In 1997, he had a spell as manager of Doncaster Rovers.

COX, Brian Roy: Goalkeeper: 250 apps. Born: Sheffield, 7 May 1961, Recruited on a two-month loan deal from Sheffield Wednesday in March 1982, Brian Cox had no hesitation in signing for Huddersfield on a permanent basis for just £10,000 in readiness for the new season. And what a signing he turned out to be! Over the six years he amassed 250 senior appearances for the Terriers, helping the team gain promotion from the Third Division in 1983. After holding off several candidates for the number one spot, he was eventually replaced between the posts by young Lee Martin and in July 1988 moved to Mansfield for £25,000, signed by former Huddersfield boss Ian Greaves. In August 1990 he joined Hartlepool and pulled out of League football at the end of that season. Cox made his League debut for the Owls as a 16 year-old apprentice.

CRAIG, Benjamin: Full-back: 106 apps. Born Leadgate, County Durham, 6 December 1915. Died: January 1982. Able to occupy both full-back positions, Craig signed for Huddersfield in January 1934. He stayed at Leeds Road until his £4,000 transfer to Newcastle in November 1938 and then spent the rest of his life with the St James' Park club, serving as a player, assistant-coach and physiotherapist. Craig played his early football with Medomsley Juniors, Leadgate FC, Ouston Juniors and Eden Colliery before joining the Terriers. After playing in the 1938 FA Cup final, he was replaced in the side by Bill Hayes and within six months left Leeds Road. He guested for Chelsea during WW2 and helped Newcastle win the Second Division title before retiring as a player in July 1950, having appeared in 122 games for the Geordies.

CREWE ALEXANDRA: Huddersfield's record against the Alex is:

Football League

Venue	P	W	D	L	F	A
Home	13	7	3	3	20	7
Away	13	4	6	3	21	18
Totals	26	11	9	6	41	25

League Cup

Home	1	1	0	0	2	1
Away	1	1	0	0	3	1
Totals	2	2	0	0	5	2

Other

Home	1	1	0	0	3	2

In January 1976 Huddersfield won their first League game against Crewe 1-0 at Gresty Road. Later in the season they completed the double with a 2-0 scoreline at Leeds Road. Bob Newton scored in both matches.
Huddersfield beat the Alex 5-2 on aggregate in a 1st round League-Cup in 1979-80 and 3-2 after extra-time in an Autoglass Trophy game in 1993-94

CRICKETER-FOOTBALLERS:

- Willie Watson and Ken Taylor were both born in the West Riding of Yorkshire, played football for Huddersfield and county cricket for Yorkshire while also appearing in Test

Matches for England as opening batsmen and both later coached in South Africa. Taylor scored over 13,000 first-class runs and took 129 wickets while Watson amassed 25,670 runs (average 39.86), claimed 295 catches and played in 23 Tests.
- Arnie Sidebottom played for England v. Australia in 1985 and also starred in 122 County matches for Yorkshire. His son later played for England in Test Matches.
- Huddersfield's 1938 winger Joe Hulme played in 223 Country matches for Middlesex (1929-39) as a middle-order batsman. He scored 8,103 runs (average of 26.56). He also took 36 wickets at 40.00 each and held 110 catches. His highest score was 143.
- Tony Leighton played for Leicestershire CCC's second XI.
- Goalkeeper Billy Mercer played for Hull CC (1914-24)
- Winger Mike Hellawell played in one County match for Warwickshire.
- Charlie Slade played cricket for Bradley Mills and Lockwood CC (Yorkshire).

CRYSTAL PALACE: Huddersfield's record against the Eagles is:
Football League

Venue	P	W	D	L	F	A
Home	18	6	6	6	27	17
Away	18	3	10	5	18	20
Totals	36	9	16	11	45	37
FA Cup						
Home	1	1	0	0	5	2
Away	1	0	0	1	0	4
Totals	2	1	0	1	5	6

Huddersfield lost their first League game by 3-0 to Palace at Selhurst Park in November 1964 but won the first home game in March 1965 by 2-0. George Brown scored a hat-trick when Palace were defeated 5-2 in a 5th round FA Cup-tie at Leeds Road in January 1929. The 4-0 Cup defeat was suffered at Selhurst Park in the 4th round in January 1990.

D

DALTON, Paul: Left-winger: 116 apps. 27 goals Born: Middlesbrough, 25 April 1967, Dalton served Huddersfield for almost five years, August 1995 to March 2000. He played for Brandon as a youngster before joining Manchester United for £35,000 in May 1988. He failed to make the grade at Old Trafford and in March 1989 joined Hartlepool for £20,000. He became a star at Victoria Park, scoring 43 goals in 177 games for the 'Pool who transferred him to Plymouth for £275,000 in June 1992. He continued to produce the goods for the Pilgrims, netting 32 goals in 116 games up to his departure to Huddersfield. A strong player, predominantly left-footed, Dalton had a loan spell with Carlisle (December 1999), being released by the Terriers four months later to sign for Gateshead.

DARLINGTON: Huddersfield's record against the Quakers is:

Football League

Venue	P	W	D	L	F	A
Home	7	5	1	1	12	8
Away	7	4	1	2	12	8
Totals	14	9	2	3	24	1

FA Cup

Home	1	0	0	1	0	1
Away	1	0	1	0	1	1
Totals	2	0	1	1	1	2

League Cup

Home	2	2	0	0	6	0
Away	1	0	0	1	0	1
Totals	3	2	0	1	6	1

In November 1975 Huddersfield met Darlington for the first time in a League game. They won 1-0 at Leeds Road, Steve Smith the scorer in front of 4,133 spectators. Later that season the double was completed with a 3-0 victory at The Feethams. The two FA Cup games were played in 1979-80.

DAVIE, William Clark: Inside-forward: 118 apps. 16 goals Born: Paisley, 7 January 1927 Willie Davie started as a professional in January 1946 with St Mirren. In December 1950 he moved to Luton for £10,000, helping the Hatters stave off relegation for a second time before joining Huddersfield for £22,500 in December 1951 - the fee a record for both clubs. He immediately slotted into the Terriers' front-line and played a vital part in helping the team gain promotion to the First Division in 1952-53, scoring five goals in 31 League games as partner to Vic Metcalfe on the left-wing. After five-and-a-half years at Leeds Road, Davie left to join Third Division (S) club Walsall in July 1957. He left the Saddlers for Bath City in June 1958.

DEFEATS:
- Huddersfield's biggest League defeat to date is 10-1 at Manchester City (Division 2) on 7 November 1987. There were also heavy defeat at Middlesbrough (by 8-0) on 30 September 1950 and 7-1 at home by Wolves on 29 September 1951.
- The Terriers suffered two heavy Third Division defeats by 6-0 at Oldham on 20 April 1974 and Bury on 16 April 1990.
- The Terriers' heaviest defeat in the FA Cup is 6-0 at Sunderland, 3rd round, on 7 January 1950.
- A 5-0 home defeat by Arsenal in the 2nd round, 1st leg on 21 September 1993 has been Huddersfield's heaviest in the League Cup. The Terriers also lost 5-1 at Middlesbrough in a 3rd round tie on 23 October 1997 and 4-0 in a 2nd round replay at Manchester City on 11 September 1968.
- The Terriers lost a club record 12 home League games during their Second Division season of 1987-88.
- The team suffered 17 away defeats in the League in 1974-75 (Division 3)
- In season 1987-88, the Terriers suffered a record 28 League defeats.
- In 1982-83, for the only time in the club's history, not one home League game was lost (Division 3). Huddersfield duly gained promotion by finishing in third position.

- In 1924-25 (Division 1) the Terriers lost only two of their 21 away League games.
- In that same season (1924-25) only five defeats were suffered in 42 home and away League games.
- On four occasions, in 1934-35 (Division 1), 1960-61 (Division 1), 1977-78 (Division 4) and 1987-88 (Division 2) the Terriers had a run of four consecutive home League defeats.
- Also on four occasions - between April and November 1912 (Division 2) and in seasons 1914-15 (Division 2), 1946-47 (Division 1) and 1987-88 (Division 2) - the Terriers suffered nine consecutive away League defeats.
- Between 6 December 1913 and 1 January 1914 (Division 2) and 8 October and 19 November 1955 (Division 1) the Terriers suffered seven consecutive League defeats.
- There was a run of six straight defeats at the start of the 1992-93 season and if the 2nd leg of the play-off semi-final (v Peterborough) from the previous season is added, then the winless run was also seven.
- Huddersfield lost a League game by 5-0 at Portsmouth on 3 November 1934; a week later they beat Liverpool 8-0 (h).

DEFENSIVE RECORDS:
- The team conceded a record 100 League goals in that season 1987-88.
- The Terriers conceded in 29 consecutive away League games during 1973 and 1975 and conceded in 27 in consecutive home and away League fixtures in 1974-75.
- In seasons 1922-23 and 1975-76, the Terriers' defence played out 10 League games without conceding a goal.
- In that 1922-23 season, Huddersfield's defence kept a clean sheet in 23 of 42 League games completed.
- They managed only two clean sheets in 21 home League games in 1950-51 and failed to keep a single one in 1974-75, while keeping a total of six blank sheets (at home and away) in 1960-61, 1974-75 and 1987-88.
- Huddersfield went eight consecutive home League games with conceding a goal between 14 April and 27 October 1923 while their best away record of consecutive blank sheets is three - achieved many times.
- In 1964-65, the Terriers went eight consecutive home and away League games without conceding.
- Huddersfield conceded 19 goals in a total of four League games during October 1946, losing 6-1, 5-0, 4-1 and 4-1.
- The team scored only eight times in 21 League games during the second-half of the 1971-72 season, having netted 19 in the first 21.
- They let in 17 goals in four League games during November and December 1955.
- Huddersfield conceded 21 goals in five games during October and November 1955.

DENT, John George: Centre-forward: 53 apps. 22 goals Born: Spennymoor, County Durham, 31 January 1903. Died: West Bridgford, Notts, September 1979.
John Dent played for Spennymoor Rangers and Tudhoe United before signing for Durham City in August 1923. Two years later he signed for Tow Law Town and was transferred to Huddersfield in June 1926. He remained at Leeds Road until October 1929 when he joined Nottingham Forest, later assisting Kidderminster Harriers (1937-39). He served in the RAF during WW2 and also played for West Bridgford Cricket Club. Honest,

thrustful and courageous, Dent scored 26 goals in 47 games for Durham, averaged a goal a game for Tow Law, did very well with Huddersfield and played even better for Forest for whom he netted 122 times in 207 games including five hat-tricks

DERBY COUNTY: Huddersfield's record against the Rams is:
Football League

Venue	P	W	D	L	F	A
Home	40	22	13	5	69	29
Away	40	4	9	27	49	87
Totals	80	26	22	32	118	116
FA Cup						
Home	1	0	1	0	2	2
Away	1	0	0	1	1	3
Totals	2	0	1	1	3	5
League Cup						
Home	1	1	0	0	2	1
Away	1	0	0	1	1	2
Totals	2	1	0	1	3	3

Huddersfield played out their first draw in the Football League when they shared the points at 1-1 with Derby at the Baseball Ground in October 1910. Later that season the Rams won 3-0 at Leeds Road.

Eight goals were shared at 4-4 when Huddersfield visited Derby for a League game in April 1927 and in December 1930, a week after beating Blackpool 10-1 and fielding the same team, the Terriers lost 4-1 at Derby.

Dave Mangnall bagged five goals to set a new individual club scoring record when Huddersfield hammered Derby 6-0 at Leeds Road in November 1931.

Huddersfield beat the FA Cup holders Derby 5-2 in a home League game in September 1946.

The two 5th round FA Cup games took place in 1998-99, while away League Cup-tie took place in September 1975 and the home one in the 1st round in August 2003.

DID YOU KNOW?

* Former Labour Prime Minister Harold Wilson, an avid Huddersfield supporter, used to carry a picture of the 1922 FA Cup winning team around with him in his inside pocket.

DINSDALE, Peter: Utility Player: 239 apps. 10 goals Born: Bradford, 19 October 1938. Died: British Columbia, Canada, 5 June 2004.

Preferring the left-half berth, Dinsdale would, if required, occupy any other outfield position. He was certainly one of Huddersfield's unsung heroes, serving the club for 11 years during which time he appeared in almost 240 matches, being twice an ever-present. He played for Yorkshire Amateurs before joining the Terriers in January 1956, initially on a part-time basis. After completing his national service he established himself in the League side in 1959-60 and remained first choice for five years. In August 1967 he left Leeds Road for Bradford Park Avenue but never settled at the club and after only 11 appearances teamed up with Bobby Robson's Vancouver Royals, soon to become one of the founder members of the NASL with Ferenc Puskas in their ranks. In October 1968, Dinsdale was appointed coach of the Canadian national team preparing for the 1970 Mexico World Cup finals but after only nine months in charge he took over the manager's job at Vancouver Spartans. Returning in June 1970, he become coach at Brighton, staying there for two years until replaced by the former England and Ipswich star Ray Crawford. He later emigrated to Canada where he died aged 65.

DIRECTORS MINUTES
- The first Board of Directors of Huddersfield Town FC in 1908 comprised: Messrs J H Crowther (Chairman), J Cotton, D Dickinson, W L Hardcastle, A B Hirst, F Obbotson, G Jenkins and L Bath Jones, who were later joined by Messrs SS Lockwood, A Moore and N Robinson.
- Huddersfield Director Dick Parker was almost 90 when he died in 1974. At the time he was the game's longest-serving Director, appointed by the club in 1920.
- Former Leeds United and England international Trevor Cherry was a director of Huddersfield in the 1990s/early 2000s.

DOBSON, Colin: Forward: 175 apps. 52 goals
Born: Eston near Middlesbrough, 9 May 1940
Dobson was a slightly built but highly effective forward who and played for South Bank before joining the groundstaff at Sheffield Wednesday as a 15 year-old, turning professional in November 1961 - after completing his ship-building apprenticeship. He scored 52 goals in 193 appearances for the Owls while also gaining an England Under-23 cap. After losing his place in the team during the club's 1966 FA Cup run, Dobson was subsequently sold to Huddersfield for £20,500 in August.1966. He was then the Terriers top-scorer in each of his first two seasons at Leeds Road and in 1969-70 played a vital role when the Second Division championship was won. In January 1972, when on loan to Brighton, he fractured a leg but recovered to join Bristol Rovers in July of that year, quickly helping the Pirates win promotion from the Third Division. After coaching the reserves he left Eastville in May 1976 to become youth coach at Coventry. He then managed a club in the Middle East before returning in June 1986 to take over as reserve and youth team coach at Villa Park, resigning after a year.

DOHERTY, Peter Dermont: Inside-forward: 87 apps. 36 goals Born: Magherafelt, 5 June 1913. Died: April 1990.
It was once said that Peter Doherty, the flame-haired inside-forward, was the best player ever produced by Ireland. Yes indeed he was a fine footballer who could tackle, dribble, shoot and head the ball with the best, his passing was accurate and precise and he had one of the most astute tactical brains in football. He was, without doubt, one of the great footballers over a period of 20 years, 1932-52. He played for Coleraine

and Glentoran before Blackpool brought his talents to the English game in 1933, two years after he had helped Glentoran win the Irish Cup. In February 1936 he was sold to Manchester City for £10,000 – just £1,000 short of the overall transfer record. He scored 79 goals in 130 games in four full seasons at Maine Road helping City win the League title in 1937 before WW2 disrupted his career as it did many others. During the hostilities Doherty guested for several clubs. In fact, the war denied him greater international reward – 16 full caps was far fewer than he deserved. After moving to Derby in December 1945, Doherty collected an FA Cup winner's medal that same season and then he inspired both Huddersfield (signed for £10,000 in December 1946) and Doncaster (from June 1949). As player-manager he helped Rovers win the Third Division (N) title in 1950. He made over 400 League appearances in total. He was then the manager of the Northern Ireland team that reached the quarter-finals of the 1958 World Cup in Sweden and after that coached and/or scouted for several clubs including Aston Villa, Blackpool, Bristol City, Notts County, Preston and Sunderland.

DOLAN, Terence Peter: Midfield: 186 apps. 16 goals Born: Bradford, 11 June 1950
Terry Dolan was an amateur with Bradford City before signing professional forms for rivals Park Avenue in April 1969. Soon after, Park Avenue had lost their Football League status and he moved to Huddersfield for £2,000 in October 1970. He went on to serve the Terriers until August 1976 when he moved Bradford City for £10,000, helping the Bantams win the Third Division title in his first season at Valley Parade. In August 1981 a free transfer took him to Rochdale and when he retired as a player the following year, Dolan had appeared in 448 League games. He continued in football with non-League sides Thackley and Harrogate Town and also worked as a coach at Valley Parade before becoming Bradford City's manager in January 1987, leaving in January 1989. He then took charge at Rochdale (March 1989), guiding them to the 5th round of the FA Cup for the first time in the club's history. From 1991 to 1997, he was managed Hull City, taking the Tigers into the Second Division and out again during that time.

the light at the end of the tunnel

DONCASTER ROVERS: Huddersfield's record against the Rovers is:

Football League

Venue	P	W	D	L	F	A
Home	11	7	1	3	24	12
Away	11	5	2	4	19	18
Totals	22	12	3	7	43	30

FA Cup

Away	3	2	0	1	6	3

League Cup

Home	2	0	2	0	2	2
Away	2	2	0	0	3	1
Totals	4	2	2	0	5	3

Others

Home	3	2	1	0	8	3

The first League game between Huddersfield and the Rovers ended in a 1-1 draw at Belle Vue in September 1952. Eight days later the Terriers won the return fixture 3-1 at Leeds Road when the crowd topped 26,500.

In 1977-78, Huddersfield beat Rovers 4-1 at home but lost 4-3 away and in March 1983 they triumphed 4-0 at Belle Vue to record their best League win of the 12.

Huddersfield beat Rovers 4-1 at Belle Vue in a 1st round FA Cup-tie in November 1994 and eliminated them from the League Cup in 1982-83 and 1989-90.

DONIS, Georgios: Winger: 25 apps. Born: Athens, Greece, 22 October 1969
Greek international Donis (24 caps) was Huddersfield manager Steve Bruce's first signing in June 1999. The 'flying' winger played in 25 first-class games for the Terriers before his release in May 2001. Prior to entering the Football League with Blackburn in July 1996, Donis had played for Panathinaikos. He returned to his homeland in September 1997 when he joined AEK Athens but started a second spell in England with Sheffield United in March 1999 and rounded things off with a disappointing two seasons at Huddersfield.

DOUBLES:
- Huddersfield completed a club record nine doubles in season 1919-20, winning both League games against Barnsley, Clapton Orient, Coventry, Hull, Lincoln, Nottingham Forest, Rotherham County, Stoke and Wolves.
- They had six doubles completed against them in 1950-51, 1974-75 and 1987-88. On several occasions the Terriers have failed to claim a double and have not conceded a double during the course of a League season.

DOYLE, Stephen Charles: Midfield: 187 apps. 6 goals Born: Port Talbot, 2 June 1958
Steve Doyle was a regular in the Huddersfield side for four seasons: 1982-86. He became a professional with PNE in June 1975 and made over 220 senior appearances during his time at Deepdale. He had trials with both Newcastle and the Terriers before transferring to Leeds Road in September 1982, having helped the Lilywhites gain promotion to the Second Division in 1978. A Welsh Under-21 international (three caps), Doyle was a very popular and extremely capable player and it was perhaps a surprise when he left the club in September 1986, Sunderland paying £50,000 down with a further £325,000 to follow for his services. As the midfield general, he helped the

Wearsiders regain their Second Division status at the first attempt (1988) before going on to assist Hull (signed for £75,000) and Rochdale, finally pulling out of top-class football with over 700 appearances under his belt (626 in the Football League). In April 1994, he became player-manager of Chorley.

DRAWS:

- The most home draws in season by Huddersfield is 9 in 1972-73
- The most away draws in a season is 11 in 1926-27
- The most draws (home and away) in a League season is 17 in 1926-27 and 1972-73.
- The fewest home draws in a season is one in 1927-28
- The fewest away League draws in a season is also one on 1911-12 and 1988-89
- The lowest number of drawn games (home and away) in a League season is 6 in 1971-72 and 1987-88
- During May and then August and September 1977, the Terriers drew six consecutive home League games (three 0-0, three 1-1).
- During the first half of the 1926-27 season (between August and October) the Terriers drew six consecutive away League games.
- In March and April 1987, six consecutive League games (home and away) all ended in draws (three of them 2-2).
- During a 20-match home spell during seasons 1913-14 and 1914-15, the Terriers went 20 League games without playing out a single draw and from 20 November 1937 to 15 October 1938, a total of 18 away games failed to produce a draw.
- The Terriers went 23 League games (home and away) without registering a draw between 3 February and 5 October 1912.
- Huddersfield's highest scoring draw in major League and Cup football is 5-5 versus Spurs (a) on 19 September 1925 (Division One).
- The Terriers have also played out three 4-4 draws in League games against Derby (a) in April 1927 and at Manchester United in November 1947 and a League Cup game at Rotherham in August 1987.

DYSON, Jonathan Paul: Defender: 261 apps. 9 goals Born: Mirfield, 18 December 1971 Jon Dyson joined Huddersfield as a trainee in May 1988, turning professional in March 1990. He then served the club honestly and effectively until his release in May 2002 but owing to injury problems was re-engaged on a short-term contract just after the start of the new season. He left the club in January 2003 for Conference side Nuneaton Borough.

E

EDWARDS, Robert: Full-back/midfield: 180 apps. 18 goals Born: Manchester, 23 February 1970
After making almost 200 senior appearances for Crewe Alexandra, the versatile Edwards joined Huddersfield in March 1996 for £150,000, transferring to Chesterfield for £20,000 in September 2000 and then returning to The McAlpine Stadium in August 2003. He has now topped 450 club appearances and helped the Terriers clinch promotion in 2004. Joining the apprentice ranks at Gresty Road in 1986, he signed professional under manager Dario Gradi in July 1988.

ELLAM, Roy: Defender: 261 apps. 11 goals Born: Hemsworth, 13 January 1943
Ellam served Huddersfield superbly well for six-and-a-half years, January 1966 to August 1972, before transferring to Leeds United with Trevor Cherry. He returned for a second spell with the Terriers in 1974-75 and after assisting both Philadelphia Atoms and Washington Diplomats, rounded off his career in non-League football with Mossley and Gainsborough Trinity, managing the latter until February 1980. He later became mine host of the Nelson Inn in Thornhill Lees near Dewsbury. Ellam played for Bradford City prior to joining Huddersfield in exchange for Derek Stokes. He was an ever present at the heart of the Terriers defence when the Second Division championship was won in 1970.

ELLIOTT, Thomas William: Forward: 75 apps. 20 goals Born: Annfield Plain, 5 April 1890
Signed from South Shields in May 1912, Tom Elliott played for Huddersfield until December 1919 when he moved to Grimsby. He later assisted Nottingham Forest, Brentford, Durham and Crewe Alexandra, retiring in 1925 with over 200 appearances behind him. Elliott started his career with West Stanley before signing as a professional with Gainsborough Trinity in 1910, switching to South Shields a year later. A player who thrived on hard work, he was a strong runner with a powerful right-foot shot.

EVERTON: Huddersfield's record against the Merseysiders is:
Football League

Venue	P	W	D	L	F	A
Home	28	13	7	8	42	27
Away	28	8	6	14	39	53
Totals	56	21	13	22	81	80

League Cup

Home	1	0	1	0	1	1
Away	1	0	0	1	1	2
Totals	2	0	1	1	2	3

The first two League games between Huddersfield and Everton were played in October 1920. The Merseysiders won 1-0 at Leeds Road and were then held to a 0-0 draw at Goodison Park.
In April 1922, just before Huddersfield's the FA Cup final showdown with Preston,

Everton doubled up in the League, winning 6-2 at Goodison Park and 2-1 at Leeds Road.

Terriers' striker Jim Glazzard headed home four goals (all from crosses by left-winger Vic Metcalfe) when Everton were thrashed 8-2 in a Second Division game at Leeds Road in April 1953. Twenty-four hours earlier the Merseysiders had won 2-1 at Goodison Park.

The Merseysiders beat Huddersfield in the 2nd round of the League Cup in 1998-99.

EXETER CITY: Huddersfield's record against the Grecians is:

Football League

Venue	P	W	D	L	F	A
Home	9	2	4	3	8	5
Away	9	5	1	3	17	16
Totals	18	7	5	6	25	21

Huddersfield lost their first ever League game against Exeter in December 1975 by 1-0 at Leeds Road. Later in the season the Grecians won 4-1 at St James' Park to complete the double which they repeated the following season.

Huddersfield claimed their first win over the Devon club in October 1980, taking the points with a 4-1 success at Leeds Road when Steve Kindon scored a hat-trick.

In April 1981 Exeter were defeated 5-0 at Leeds Road and two years later Huddersfield won 4-3 at St James' Park.

F

FACEY, Delroy Michael: Forward: 82 apps. 15 goals Born: Huddersfield, 22 April 1980
Delroy Facey started his career with the Terriers, signing professional in May 1997. Over the next five years, as a fast, direct and powerful striker, he produced some useful performances, occupying virtually every position in the front-line. In July 2002 he was transferred to Bolton but was unable to hold down a first team place at The Reebok Stadium and in 2002 and 2004 was loaned out to Bradford City and WBA respectively, helping the latter club clinch promotion to the Premiership. In June 2004 he joined Hull.

FAMILY CONNECTIONS:
- Defender Billy Watson (1912-28) was followed to Leeds Road by his sons Albert (1935-48) and Willie (1937-46).
- Brothers Jeff and Ken Taylor played for the Terriers in the 1940s/50s.
- Clem Stephenson managed Huddersfield before from 1929-42 and his brother George Ternent from 1947-52. Both played for Aston Villa while another Stephenson brother,
- James, also played for Villa as well as Sunderland and Watford.
- Former 'Terrier' Austen Campbell was the cousin of Huddersfield defender Alan W Brown
- The uncle of Terriers' 1920s striker George Brown was Joe Spence (Manchester United and England).
- George McLean's brother, David, a Scottish international, scored 346 League goals between 1907 and 1928 while playing for Forfar, Celtic, PNE, Sheffield Wednesday,

Third Lanark, Rangers, Bradford Park Avenue and Dundee
- Collectively, the four Barkas brothers appeared in 1,125 League games between 1920 and 1949. Ned (ex-Norwich, Huddersfield, Birmingham and Chelsea) made the most (404), followed by Sam (ex-Bradford City and Manchester City) 377, then Tom (Bradford City, Halifax, Rochdale, Stockport and Carlisle) 279 and Harry (South Shields, Gateshead and Liverpool) 45.
- Bobby Laverick, the brother of Huddersfield midfielder Mick, played for Chelsea, Everton, Brighton and Coventry between 1955 and 1963.
- Levi Redfern's brother, Les, played for Wolves, Southend and Crewe in the 1930s.
- Huddersfield left-back Phil Sandercock started his career with his brother Ken at Torquay.
- John Richardson, brother of Huddersfield's Jimmy, played for Oldham.
- The Worthington brothers: Frank (Huddersfield), Bob (Notts County) and David (Grimsby) were all ever present with their respective clubs in 1970-71.
- Terry Poole's younger brother, Andy, also a goalkeeper, played for Mansfield, Northampton, Wolves, Port Vale and Gillingham.
- Conway, son of the legendary Billy Smith, played for Huddersfield as a youngster.
- Malcolm Levitt, cousin of Terriers' Derek Hawksworth, played for Bradford City.
- Terriers' defender Arnie Sidebottom and his son both played Test Cricket for England.
- Ken and Jeff Taylor were brothers who both played for Huddersfield while Ken's son, Nicholas, like his father, also played cricket for Yorkshire as well as Surrey

FAYERS, Frederick L: Centre-half: 164 apps. 18 goals Born: Kings Lynn, 29 January 1890. Died: Huddersfield, February 1954.

Although slightly built and barely 5ft 5ins tall, weighing 11st, 'Tiny' Fayers was still a solid defender, afraid of no one who gave Huddersfield wonderful service for five seasons leading up to WW1. He represented the Hertfordshire FA and won seven England amateur caps when registered with Southern League side Watford. And it was during an international match against Wales at Leeds Road in February 1910 that Huddersfield spotted the undoubted talents of Fayers, signing him for the start of the next season. He became skipper of the side but after the war (August 1919) moved to Stockport, switching to Manchester City in May 1920 and finally making his debut in the top flight against Liverpool, aged 30. In May 1923, he was appointed Halifax's first player-coach.

FEARNLEY, Henry: Goalkeeper: 103 apps. Born: Penistone, 16 June 1935

Fearnley spent twelve years with Huddersfield, from June 1951-October 1963, but was only a regular in the first team in 1956-57, 1960-61 and 1961-62. In between times, Jack Wheeler, Harry Mills, Sandy Kennon and Ray Wood all kept goal and it was frustrating for Fearnley to see so many other 'keepers pushing for the number one position. Nevertheless he was still a fine custodian, despite having a nightmare debut when he conceded six goals against Newcastle and suffered a head injury. He joined Huddersfield as a 16 year-old from Penistone Juniors and signed as a part-time professional in December 1952. Rewarded with a benefit in 1958, Fearnley left Leeds Road for Oxford in a £3,500 deal and after helping the manor Ground club gain promotion he was transferred to Doncaster in February 1966, almost immediately gaining a Fourth Division championship medal. He retired in 1967 with 202 League appearances in his locker.

FESTIVAL OF BRITAIN: Huddersfield beat the Dutch club PSV Eindhoven 4-1 and Stade Rennais from France 5-1 in two Festival of Britain matches at Leeds Road in May 1951. Albert Nightingale scored twice against PSV and Harry Hassall and Jim Glazzard both claimed braces against Rennais.

FA CUP COMPETITION: Huddersfield's record in the FA Cup competition:

Venue	P	W	D	L	F	A
Home	112	62	23	27	240	122
Away	134	48	29	57	158	178
Totals	246	110	52	84	398	300

* Away record includes games played on a neutral ground, semi-finals and finals.

FA Cup Honours
Winners:

1922	beat Preston North End 1-0	Stamford Bridge	Att. 53,710

Runners-up:

1920	lost to Aston Villa 1-0 (aet)	Stamford Bridge	Att. 50,018
1928	lost to Blackburn Rovers 3-1	Wembley	Att. 92,041
1930	lost to Arsenal 2-0	Wembley.	Att. 92,488
1938	lost to Preston North End 1-0 (aet)	Wembley.	Att. 93,357

FA Cup Talk:
- Jack Foster scored Huddersfield's first FA Cup goal, in a record 11-0 away win in the preliminary round at Heckmondwike on 18 September 1909 - the club's first game in the competition. Foster finished up with four to his name in that tie.
- Huddersfield's biggest home FA Cup win is 7-0 v. Rothwell WR on 16 October 1909 when Foster scored a hat-trick.
- Huddersfield scored a record 32 goals in the FA Cup in season 1909-10. They took their total up to 46 in ten with another 14 in four Cup matches the following season.
- Billy Smith scored Huddersfield's winning goal in the 1922 FA Cup final from the penalty spot and Alex Jackson netted (to no avail) in the 1928 final.
- The team's heaviest defeat in the competition is 6-0 at Sunderland in a 3rd round tie on 7 January 1950.
- The heaviest home defeat is 4-2 v. Norwich in a 3rd round replay on 21 January 1987.
- A record Leeds Road crowd of 67,037 attended the Huddersfield v. Arsenal, 6th round tie on 6 February 1932 (won 1-0 by the Gunners).
- A deflected goal off Huddersfield defender Tom Wilson gave Aston Villa victory in the 1920 FA Cup final.
- Jack Roscamp gave Blackburn the lead after just 40 seconds against Huddersfield in the 1928 FA Cup final. He shoulder-charged goalkeeper Billy Mercer and as the ball squirted loose he calmly slotted it into the net.
- During the 1930 FA Cup final v. Arsenal, the giant German Graf Zeppelin airship passed over Wembley Stadium, dipping as to salute the crowd before passing on.
- After centre-half Alf Young was ruled to have tripped George Mutch inside the area (when the offence was clearly outside) the Preston winger scored from the penalty spot in the very last minute of extra-time to deny Huddersfield a replay in the 1938 FA Cup final.

- Stoke ousted the Terriers from the competition in February 1971, winning a 4th round 2nd replay 1-0 at Old Trafford in front of almost 40,000 spectators.
- Clem Stephenson played in four FA Cup finals at three venues and was later manager in two other finals. He was a member of the Aston Villa team at the Crystal Palace in 1913 (v. Sunderland) and at Stamford Bridge in 1920 (v. Huddersfield). Then he played for Huddersfield against Aston Villa at Stamford Bridge in 1922 and at Wembley against Blackburn in 1928. As manager of Huddersfield he took the club back to Wembley in 1930 (v. Arsenal) and again in 193(v. Preston). His first three finals were won, the last three lost, and this after being 'auctioned off' when Leeds City were disbanded in 1919.
- Bob Barclay played in two FA Cup finals for different clubs in three seasons and lost them both, with Sheffield United v. Arsenal in 1936 and with Huddersfield v. PNE in 1938.
- After missing both the 1932 and 1936 FA Cup finals with Arsenal, Pat Beasley finally made it with Huddersfield in 1938.
- Clem Stephenson - later to join Huddersfield - dreamed that his team at the time (Aston Villa) would win the 1913 FA Cup final against Sunderland and that left-half Tommy Barber would head the winning goal. That's what precisely happened!

FA YOUTH CUP: Huddersfield first entered the Youth Cup in 1952. They have reached the final once and the semi-finals twice.

This is the club's record in the competition (to 2004):

Venue	P	W	D	L	F	A
Home	73	35	12	26	149	103
Away	70	29	13	28	132	107
Totals	143	64	25	54	281	210

Fact File

- Huddersfield reached the final in 1973-74 after defeating Doncaster (a) 5-0, Bradford City (a) 2-0, Burnley (a) 2-1 after a 1-1 draw, Charlton 1-0 (home) after a 2-2 draw, Manchester United (h) 2-0 and WBA 2-1 on aggregate in the semi-final (1-0 away, 1-1 at home). In the final they were beaten 2-1 on aggregate by Spurs, drawing 1-1 at White Hart Lane but losing 1-0 at Leeds Road.
- The following season (1974-75) Huddersfield were defeated 4-0 on aggregate in the semi-final by Ipswich (losing 1-0 at home, 3-0 away). They had earlier knocked out Manchester City (a) 3-1, Derby (a) 1-0 after a 0-0 draw, Leeds (a) 2-1 and Everton (a) 2-1.
- Biggest win: 11-0 v. Chadderton (h) in 1989-90
- Heaviest defeats: 6-0 v. Bolton Wds (h) 1954-55 and Everton (a) 1962-63
- Hull were defeated 8-7 on penalties (after a 2-2 draw) in 2002-03
- Huddersfield's early home games were staged at Beck Lane, Heckmondwike.
- The away game at Blackpool in 1964-65 was reduced to 40 minutes each-way due to fog. Huddersfield lost the first round tie 2-1.
- Wrexham failed to field a team for their second round tie in 1954-55 and withdrew from the competition, handing Huddersfield a walkover.

FIRSTS:

- The first game played by Huddersfield was a friendly against Bradford on 2 September 1908. A crowd of around 1,000 saw this team in action: W J Crinson; R Trenam, R Ray; W Hooton, F Walker, P Hartley; J Shackleton, J Morris, WS Cookson, R Morris and C Flowitt. An own-goal by Bradford defender Jimmy Freeborough and a strike by Welsh international Richard Morris gave Huddersfield a 2-1 victory.
- Huddersfield's first competitive game was played on 5 September 1908 when they travelled to South Shields Adelaide for a North-Eastern League fixture. A crowd of 5,000 saw the home side win 2-0.
- A week later, on Saturday 12 September 1908, Huddersfield won their first competitive match, beating Workington 2-0 (a) with goals from Richard Morris (the first) and Jack Wallace.
- On 18 September 1909, Huddersfield played their first FA Cup-tie, away to Heckmondwike in the 1st preliminary round. They won 11-0 which is still the club's best-ever win. Jack Foster (4), Ernest Kenworthy (2), Walter Stacey (4) and Bill McCreadie scored the goals in front of 2,000 spectators.
- Huddersfield suffered their first defeat in the FA Cup on 25 November 1909 when, following a 2-2 home draw they were beaten 2-1 by Rotherham Town in a 4th qualifying round replay.
- Huddersfield's first-ever game in the Football League (Division 2) took place on 3 September 1910. It was a Yorkshire derby at Bradford Park Avenue and in front of 16,000 spectators, won 1-0, the historic goal coming from centre-forward Harry Hamilton. The team was Mutch; Taylor, Morris; Beaton, Hall, Bartlett; Blackburn, Wood, Hamilton, McCubbin and Jee.
- A week later on 10 September, Huddersfield played (and lost) their first home League game, going down 1-0 to Burnley before a crowd of 7,371.
- A crowd of 7,500 witnessed Huddersfield's first home League win, 3-2 over Leeds City on 24 September 1910.
- Huddersfield's first game in the First Division of the Football League was against PNE at Deepdale on 28 August 1920. They won 1-0, Sammy Taylor scored the goal and the attendance was 26,000.
- The first home game in the top flight followed on 30 September when Burnley were defeated 1-0, thanks to a Billy Smith goal in front of 22,500 spectators.
- In the summer of 1921, Huddersfield went on their first overseas tour, playing friendly matches in Paris, France.
- Huddersfield were the first club to finish runners-up in both the Football League championship and FA Cup final in the same season (1919-20).
- The Leeds United v. Huddersfield League game at Elland Road on 19 March 1927 was the first to be broadcast live on radio, featured on the Leeds-Bradford Station of the BBC. The result was a 1-1 draw.
- In 1928, Huddersfield winger Alex Jackson became the first FA Cup finalists to finish on the losing side after earlier scoring for Scotland at Wembley! Two years later he scored nine of Huddersfield's 11 goals on the way to the final and finished up a loser for a second time.
- On 12 October 1960, Huddersfield played their first game in the League Cup competition, losing 4-1 to Aston Villa in Birmingham.
- Huddersfield were the first club to win the Football League championship three

seasons running: 1923-24, 1924-25 and 1925-26. Arsenal (1932-35), Liverpool (1981-84) and Manchester United (1998-2001) have since joined the club.

FLETCHER, Peter: Forward: 115 apps. 45 goals Born: Manchester, 2 December 1953
Fletcher joined the apprentice ranks at Old Trafford as a 15 year-old and turned professional with United in December 1970. With so many talented players around at that time he made only seven League appearances for the Reds before transferring to Hull in May 1974, moving to Stockport two years later and onto Huddersfield in July 1978. He remained at Leeds Road until July 1982, when he retired with a League record of 54 goals in 193 outings.

FLOODLIGHTS: The first floodlit game staged at Leeds Road was the 3rd round FA Cup replay between Huddersfield and Wolves on 11 January 1961. A crowd of 46,155 saw the Terriers win 2-1 with goals from Derek Stokes and Mike O'Grady who was later to play for the Molineux club.

FOGG, William Henry: Wing-half: 69 apps. 3 goals Born: Birkenhead, 9 March 1903, Died: July 1966
A Huddersfield player from May 1928 to August 1933, Billy Fogg was a strong, totally committed footballer who had an occasional game at centre-forward, scoring his first two goals for the club from that position in October 1929 against Middlesborough and Sheffield Wednesday. Unfortunately he missed the 1930 FA Cup final through injury, having played in all the previous rounds. He was still awarded a medal. He played for Wirral Railways, Tranmere and Bangor City before joining the Terriers for £20. On leaving Leeds Road, Fogg signed for Clapton Orient, later assisting New Brighton until retiring in May 1937. A fine golfer, he won the Merseyside Professional Footballers' Golf Handicap Challenge Cup in 1936.

FOOTBALL JUBILEE: The Football League celebrated its 50th anniversary in 1938 and to mark the occasion the League Benevolent Fund launched. Clubs all over the country played against another from close by Jubilee Fund matches, the proceeds from each game going into the fund.
Huddersfield met Leeds at Elland Road in August 1938 and the following year played them at Leeds Road. A crowd of 7,352 witnessed the 1-1 draw in 1938 while 4,630 spectators saw the Terriers race to a 5-0 win twelve months later when Billy Price and Jimmy Isaac both scored twice. These two matches were classed as friendlies.

FOOTBALL LEAGUE HONOURS:
League champions: 1923-24, 1924-25, 1925-26
Runners-up: 1926-27, 1927-28, 1933-34
Division Two champions: 1969-70
Runners-up: 1919-20, 1952-53
Promoted from Division Two: 1994-95 (via play-offs)
Promoted from Division Three: 2003-04 (via play-offs)
Division Four champions: 1979-80

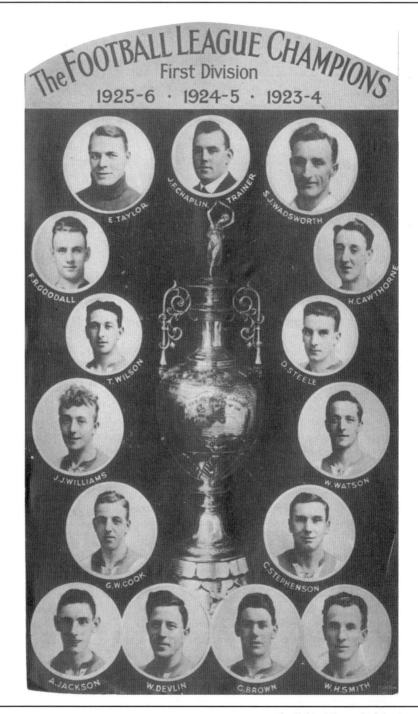

The FOOTBALL LEAGUE CHAMPIONS

First Division

1925-6 · 1924-5 · 1923-4

E. TAYLOR

J.F.CHAPLIN, TRAINER

S.J.WADSWORTH

F.R.GOODALL

H. CAWTHORNE

T. WILSON

D. STEELE

J.J.WILLIAMS

W. WATSON

G.W.COOK

C.STEPHENSON

A.JACKSON

W.DEVLIN

G.BROWN

W.H.SMITH

Football League Fact File

- Huddersfield have completed 83 seasons of League football.
- Huddersfield applied for entry to the Football League (Division Two) on 28 April 1910. Some six weeks later, on 13 June, at London's Imperial Hotel, the club received 26 votes and were duly elected along with Birmingham (30 votes) with Grimsby (17) missing out.
- First League game played on 9 September 1910 v. Bradford Park Avenue (a) won 1-0 with a goal from Harry Hamilton.
- Registered first home League win on 24 September 1910, beating Leeds City 3-2.
- In 1922-23 Huddersfield finished third in the First Division. They then completed a hat-trick of League championship triumphs and were runners-up in 1926-27 and 1927-28.
- Since the competition started in September 1888 (up to the end of the 2003-04 season) more than 167,500 games have been played in the Football League/Premiership and over 475,000 goals have been scored.
- Huddersfield's most common scoreline (home or away) is 2-1.

FOOTBALL LEAGUE CUP: Huddersfield's record in the Football League Cup: 1960 to 2004 inclusive:

Venue	P	W	D	L	F	A
Home	61	27	17	17	87	74
Away	71	21	16	34	89	118
Neutral	1	1	0	0	2	1
Totals	133	49	33	51	178	193.

NB: Penalty shoot-outs not included.

- Huddersfield's first League Cup-tie took place on 12 October 1960, away to Aston Villa. A crowd of 17,057 saw the home side win 4-1, John Milner scoring for the Terriers. Villa went on to defeat Rotherham 3-2 in the two-legged final.
- Huddersfield's first win in the competition was achieved on 25 September 1961 when they beat Carlisle 3-0 in a 1st round replay before a crowd of 8,880 at Leeds Road.
- In season 1967-68, Huddersfield reached the semi-final stage after beating Wolves, Norwich, West Ham and Fulham, They met Arsenal for a place in the final but lost 6-3 on aggregate after suffering a 3-2 defeat before 40,079 spectators at Highbury and a 2-1 reverse at Leeds Road when the crowd was 27,312
- After 2-2 and 3-3 draws, Huddersfield beat Plymouth 2-1 (at Villa Park) in a 2nd round 2nd replay in October 1963.
- Another three-game League Cup-tie took place in 1974-75 when Leeds beat Huddersfield in a 2nd rd, 2nd replay, 2-1 in the October, after two 1-1 draws.
- The only other occasion that Huddersfield have been taken to three games in any one round of the League Cup was in August 1977 when they overcame Carlisle 2-1 (h) after playing out 1-1 and 2-2 draws at Leeds Road and Brunton Park respectively.
- Huddersfield suffered their heaviest League Cup defeat at the hands of Arsenal in September 1993. The Gunners won 5-0 at Leeds Road in a 2nd round, 1st leg encounter, in front of 14,275 spectators. Ian Wright scored a hat-trick
- Huddersfield's biggest League Cup win has been 5-1 v. Mansfield (h), 1st round 2nd leg, 13 September 1983. Mark Lillis scored twice in front of 5,190 fans. The first

leg had also ended in a victory by 2-1 at Field Mill.

- Huddersfield produced an excellent display when beating Sunderland (two Divisions higher) 4-2 at The Stadium of Light in the 2nd round of the competition in September 2003.

FOOTBALLING NOMADS: Frank Worthington was associated with 22 different football clubs during his 28 years in the game: 1964-92.
Edwin 'Terry' Curran served with 16 clubs during his soccer career and, in fact, prior to becoming a footballer he had 10 different jobs, five of them in 18 months.

FORMATION OF CLUB: Huddersfield Football Club was officially formed in 1908.
An initial meeting was held at the Imperial Hotel on 26 January 1906 and was attended largely by members of the Huddersfield & District FA. The main item on the agenda was to discuss the feasibility of establishing a football team deep in the heart of a Rugby League stronghold. However, nothing really materialised and as a result a second meeting followed just under a fortnight later on 7 February when the following attended: Mr David Dickinson (President of the Huddersfield & District FA), three doctors, Messrs Coward, Kennedy and Whitehead, Rev. R Garrett Johnson, Messrs JHR Appleyard, E Barrett, F Bates, JH Blackwell, D France, LH Gill, J Hall, CEW Halles, WL Hardcastle, AB Hirst, S Holland, J Kaye, A Lagard, G Milner, HA Nelson, H Noble jnr, FW Reedor, F Robinson, N Robinson, WG Scott, E Shaw, J Spittle, G Wileaton, H Worthington and Sergeant-Major Topps. Mrs J Hall took the notes.
A provisional committee was elected (mainly comprising members of local FA officials) and after a lengthy discussions it was suggested that at least a capital of £5,000 would have to be found to start up a football club.
At this juncture several wealthy local men-folk were approached including Huddersfield businessman John Hilton Crowther, an Old Rossalian whose family owned a woollen mill. Crowther was certainly enthusiastic and along with members of his family, including Mr D Stoner Crowther, offered financial backing.
Some progress was made, albeit slow at first, and after serious negotiations had taken place with regards to securing a ground (a piece of land in Leeds Road) the Huddersfield Association Ground Company was formed. The chairman was local solicitor Amos Brook Hirst who was backed all the way by Sergeant-Major Topps
On 19 June 1908, a scheme was officially drawn up to form a limited liability company and this was duly submitted to the authorities. Mr WL Hardcastle (who a year earlier had been elected President of the Huddersfield & District FA) presided over the negotiations and at another meeting - on 25 June 1908, at the Albert Hotel, Huddersfield AFC was officially founded.
The committee proposed that £2,000 (required as capital) should be raised by selling £1 shares. This was forthcoming and with everything in place and all bodies eager and ready to go into action, Huddersfield gained entry to the North-Eastern League. Within two seasons a place was secured in the Football League (Division 2) and in 1920 First Division football came to Leeds Road...just 12 years after formation.

FOSTER, Jack: Forward: 5 apps. 11 goals Born: Rawmarsh, 18 November 1877. Died: 1946.
Signed from Southampton in May 1909, Foster spent just one season with Huddersfield during which time he scored 27 goals, including 11 in the FA Cup. Indeed, he netted the

club's first goal in the latter competition v. Heckmondwike in September 1909.
Foster was later assistant-trainer at Leeds Road, then head trainer and also acted as assistant-manager. He was in charge of Huddersfield's second team that twice won the Central League in the mid-1920s. Initially with Rotherham Church Institute, he then assisted Thornhill United, Blackpool (1901), Rotherham, Stockport (briefly), Watford (1906), Sunderland (December 1907) and West Ham (May 1908) before teaming up with Southampton (March 1909).

FRANCIS, Stephen Stuart: Goalkeeper: 227 apps. After 88 appearances for Chelsea and 259 for Reading, the experienced Francis joined Huddersfield for £150,000 in August 1993. He remained at the club until January 1999 when, after losing his place to Nico Vaesen, he joined Northampton, retiring at the end of that season. Born Billericay, May 1964, Francis gained England honours at Youth team level and was twice a winner at Wembley with Chelsea in 1986 (FMC) and Reading in 1988 (Simod Cup).

FULHAM: Huddersfield's record against the Cottagers is:

Football League

Venue	P	W	D	L	F	A
Home	28	17	5	6	51	29
Away	28	5	8	15	28	44
Totals	56	22	13	21	79	73

FA Cup

Home	1	1	0	0	3	0
Away	1	1	0	0	3	2
Totals	2	2	0	0	6	2

League Cup

Home	1	1	0	0	2	1
Away	1	0	1	0	1	1
Totals	2	1	1	0	3	2

Boxing Day 1910 saw the first Huddersfield-Fulham League game and it went in favour of the Londoners who won 2-1 at Craven Cottage before a crowd of 20,000. The Cottagers completed the double over the Terriers that season before losing for the first time 2-0 at Leeds Road in September 1911. Two years later Fulham lost 5-1 on Huddersfield soil
The next big scoreline appeared in May 1981 when the Terriers won 4-2 at home
Huddersfield beat Fulham 3-2 in a 3rd round FA Cup-tie at Craven Cottage in January 1976.

FULL MEMBERS CUP: Huddersfield entered the FMC in 1986-87 but despite a Duncan Shearer goal, were knocked out in the first round, beaten 2-1 at home by Blackburn in front of 1,947 fans.

G

GAMES: Like all other clubs, Huddersfield played three Football League games at the start of the ill-fated 1939-40 season, the details being:

26 August	v. Blackpool	(h) 0-1		Att. 15,588
30 August	v. Sunderland	(a) 2-1 (Gorman og, Price)		Att. 16,600
2 September	v. Brentford	(a) 0-1		Att. 13,000

These games were later declared null and void.
* Huddersfield played ten League games in 26 days during April 1979.
* They played 16 matches in 56 days during March and April 1990, completed the same number of games in 57 days during March and April 1978 and played nine North-Eastern League games in 20 days at the end of the 1908-09 season.
* Owing to the arctic weather conditions, not one single football match was staged for two months and three days from 30 December 1962 to 1 March 1963.
* Only two games were played in 24 days during January and February 1947.

GARNER, Paul: Left-back: 106 apps. 2 goals Born: Edlington near Doncaster, 1 December 1955 Garner was with Huddersfield when they were relegated from the Second Division in 1973 and from the Third in 1975. He then joined Sheffield United who, a year later, were relegated from the First. He then went down into the Third Division with the Blades in 1979 and slipped into the Fourth in 1981. Eventually after five relegation campaigns, Garner's luck changed and in 1982 he helped Sheffield United win promotion from the Fourth Division and followed up two years later with promotion from the Third. He signed for Huddersfield as a junior and turned professional in December 1972. A runner-up in the FA Youth Cup final two years later he moved to Bramall Lane in December 1975 (after a loan spell) and during his nine years with the Blades he donned nine different jerseys while making 301 appearances. After assisting Gillingham on loan, he switched to Mansfield in September 1984 and retired through injury five years later, having helped the Stags gain promotion from the Fourth Division in 1986 and win the Freight Rover Trophy in 1987. He later bought his own milk round in Renishaw, Sheffield.

GATE RECEIPTS:
* There were record gate receipts at The Alfred McAlpine Stadium of £243,081 for the Huddersfield v. Liverpool, FA Cup 3rd round tie on 12 December 1999.
* The previous record at 'The McAlpine' was £155,149 v. Wimbledon. FA Cup 5th round, 17 February 1996
* The Huddersfield v. Southampton League Cup-tie on 20 September 1994 realised gate receipts of £110,850.
* Record gate receipts for a competitive game at Leeds Road was £89,081 v. Arsenal, League Cup, 2nd round, 1st leg, 21 September 1993. This beat the £81,490, banked from the Third Division play-off semi-final, 2nd leg, against Peterborough, 14 May 1992. Prior to that the record stood at £65,485 v. Manchester City, FA Cup 3rd round replay, 25 January 1988.
* £50,000+ was taken for the first time at Leeds Road (involving Huddersfield) on 7

May 1984 when the League clash with Newcastle United produced £52,607.
- When the Leeds Road record attendance of 67,037 was set for the Huddersfield v. Arsenal, FA Cup-tie in February 1932, the gate receipts amounted to a then record £4,892. This stood for more than 19 years, until March 1951 when the FA Cup semifinal replay between Newcastle United and Wolves produced receipts of £7,625.
- Huddersfield's home FA Cup-tie v. Barnsley in mid-February 1957, then realised receipts of £7,814.
- The first time more than £4,000 was taken at a Huddersfield home game was in March 1920 when £4,005 was banked from the FA Cup-tie with Liverpool.
- £5,260 was taken at the gate when Arsenal met Grimsby Town in the FA Cup semifinal at Leeds Road in March 1936.
- The first time the £2,500 receipts barrier was broken for a League game at Leeds Road was in April 1927 when the monies from the Newcastle United fixture reached £2.538.

GIBSON, Brian: Right-back: 171 apps. one goal Born: Huddersfield, 22 February 1928
Despite spending eleven years at Leeds Road, Gibson was never always a first-choice selection, having his best spells in the League side during the 1955-56 and 1956-57 seasons. He was 23 when signed by manager George Stephenson from Paddock's Athletic in May 1951. With Ron Staniforth and Laurie Kelly the established full-back pairing, Ray Wilson then arrived on the scene and with Tony Conwell also pressing for a place, Gibson had to work hard at his game to guarantee first-team football. Retiring in April 1962, he later returned to the club to work in the pools office.

GILLINGHAM: Huddersfield's record against the Gills is:
Football League

Venue	P	W	D	L	F	A
Home	6	3	1	2	9	8
Away	6	2	1	3	10	10
Totals	12	5	2	5	19	18
FA Cup						
Home	1	1	0	0	2	1
Away	1	0	1	0	0	0
Totals	2	1	1	0	2	1

Huddersfield lost their first League game with Gillingham, going down 2-0 at home in December 1974. The Kent side then completed the double with a 3-2 win later in the season. The Terriers registered their first victory in September 1980, winning 1-0 at Leeds Road. Huddersfield knocked the Gills out of the FA Cup in the 2nd round in 1992-93.

GILLIVER, Allan Henry: Centre-forward: 53 apps. 22 goals Born: Swallownest, 3 August 1944,
Allan Gilliver's professional career spanned 18 years: August 1961 to May 1979. During that time he played for Huddersfield (signed initially as a junior in 1959), Blackburn (transferred from Leeds Road in June 1966), Rotherham, Brighton, Lincoln, Bradford City, Stockport, Boston United and Bradford City (non-contract), later becoming stadium manager at Valley Parade. He scored over 100 goals (95 in the League) in more than 350 club appearances.

GLAZZARD, James: Centre-forward: 321 apps. 154 goals Born: Normanton, 23 April 1923. Died: 1996 (pictured opposite, goalscorers)
After a moderate start, Glazzard - known by everyone as 'Gentleman Jim' - developed into a wonderfully gifted centre-forward, brilliant in the air, explosive on the ground and always a difficult opponent to handle. He made his name with the Altoffs Colliery team before signing amateur forms for Huddersfield in July 1943, turning professional three months later. He gained some first team experience during the second part of the war before scoring on his League debut on the opening day of the 1946-47 campaign, in a 3-1 home defeat by Blackpool. Leading marksman that season, he went through a tough time before returning to form during the latter stages of the 1951-52. He then rattled in 31 goals (in League and Cup) as the Terriers gained promotion to the top flight in 1952-53, netting with four headers from crosses by left-winger Vic Metcalfe in an 8-2 home win over Everton. Playing against international-class defenders virtually every week, he continued to plague defences and rattled in another 29 in 1953-54, claiming 32 the following season and 11 more in 1955-56. In August 1956, having done Huddersfield proud, he joined Everton for £4,000 but failed to fit in at Goodison Park and quickly switched to Mansfield, retiring in September 1957. Glazzard gained only one representative honour, playing for England 'B' against Germany 'B' in March 1954.

GLOSSOP: Huddersfield's record against Glossop is:
Football League

Venue	P	W	D	L	F	A
Home	5	4	0	1	12	3
Away	5	2	1	2	10	12
Totals	10	6	1	3	22	15

Huddersfield crashed to a 5-2 away defeat in their first League encounter with Glossop in November 1910. They made up later in the season with a 1-0 home victory. Huddersfield defeated Glossop 6-0 in March 1913 - their best League win of the campaign.

GOALS:
(For and against, scored and conceded)
- The Terriers scored a record 101 League goals in Division Four in 1979-80.
  In 1979-80, the Terriers netted 61 home League goals and in 1925-26 scored a record 42 away goals.
- During March and April 1913, the Terriers scored 23 goals in five consecutive home League games - 6,2,5,5,5.
- Only 12 goals were scored in 21 home League games at Leeds Road in 1971-72.
- The lowest number of away League goals (15) in a season were scored in 1971-72, 1972-73 and 1974-75.
- Just 27 goals were scored in 42 League games in that 1971-72 campaign.
- During the 1931-32 season (from 5 December) the Terriers scored in 21 consecutive League games. They netted in 19 consecutive games: 1919-21 and 1927-28.
- The Terriers scored in 24 consecutive away League games: 1961-63 and in 21 games (home and away) in 1931-32.
- The Terriers failed to score in any of seven consecutive League games played between 29 January and 11 March 1972.
- The Terriers conceded only nine League goals at home in 1923-24, having let in 17 in

their 21 away games the previous season...both club records.
- The fewest number of goals conceded in a League season (home & away) is 32 in 1922-23.
- A total of 40 were conceded at home in season 1950-51 and in 1987-88 the Terriers gave away 62 on their travels in 1987-88.
- Visiting teams scored in 12 consecutive League games at Leeds Road in 1950-51, during 1963 and 1965 and 1974-75.
- The Terriers kept 14 blank sheets in their 23 home League games of 1980-81.
- The Terriers failed to score in 12 home League games in 1971-72 and in 12 away games in 1974-75 - both records.
- In season 1971-72 the team did not score a goal in 23 of their 42 League matches.
- The Terriers scored in 20 of their 21 home League games in each of seasons 1927-28, 1930-31, and 1931-32.
- The Terriers went seven League games without scoring between 22 January and 21 March 1972.

GOALSCORERS: Huddersfield's top ten leading scorers in all major competitions.

159	George Brown	1921-29
154	Jim Glazzard (right)	1946-56
126	Billy Smith	1913-34
108	Les Massie	1956-66
100	Andy Booth*	1992-
90	Vic Metcalfe	1946-57
89	Alex Jackson	1925-31
75	Frank Mann	1912-23
73	Dave Mangnall	1929-34
69	Derek Stokes	1960-65

*Two spells at the club, still adding to the total

Goal Talk
- George Brown scored all his League goals in the First Division while Les Massie netted all of his in Division Two.
- Dave Mangnall scored in nine consecutive League games for Huddersfield between 2 January and 5 March 1932. During this same period he also scored in four consecutive FA Cup games.
- Sam Taylor scored 20 goals in the 16 League matches played in 1919-20 and another four in six FA Cup games (making it 24 in 22).
- Ken Willingham is believed to have scored the fastest goal for Huddersfield - netting 10 seconds into the home League game against Sunderland on 14 December 1935.
- Only two players have scored five goals in a League game for Huddersfield: Dave Mangnall v. Derby (Division One) on 21 November 1931 and Alf Lythgoe v. Blackburn (Division One) on 13 April 1935.
- Jim Glazzard headed four goals for Huddersfield in an 8-2 home League win over Everton on 7 April 1953 - and all came from centres by left-winger Vic Metcalfe.
- Huddersfield's Joe Lee conceded five 'own goals' during his time with the club.
- Five goals were scored in a 10-minute spell (60-70) during Huddersfield's 5-5 League

draw with Spurs at White Hart Lane in September 1925.

- Huddersfield received six own goals in League games during the 1951-52 season - a club record. They accepted five in 1958-59 and 1981-82.
- Newcastle defenders Joe Harvey and Alf McMichael conceded own-goals in their side's 4-2 home win over Huddersfield in October 1951.
- After failing to score in five consecutive League games, losing four of them by a single goal, Huddersfield suddenly hit top form and beat Cardiff 5-1 at Ninian Park in March 1990.
- In 16 League games played between 12 January and 29 April 1972, Huddersfield scored only four times (two of them own-goals).
- The fastest goal scored by a Huddersfield player came 10 seconds into the League game with Sunderland in December 1935. It was scored by Ken Willingham who later moved to Roker Park

GOALKEEPERS:

- William J Crinson was Huddersfield's first recognised goalkeeper, playing in 26 North-Eastern League games in 1908-09.
- Hugh Turner (q.v) has made most first-class appearances for the Terriers - 394 including 364 in the Football League. He is sixth in the club's all-time list of appearance-makers.
- Huddersfield used three goalkeepers in their away 3rd round FA Cup-tie at Shrewsbury in January 1981 and all conceded a goal in a 3-0 defeat. They were Andy Rankin, Steve Kindon and Mark Lillis.

GOODALL, Frederick Roy: Full-back: 440 apps. 21 goals Born: Dronfield, 31 December 1902. Died: Shipley, January 1982.

Roy Goodall was a Huddersfield player for 26 years. He joined the club from Dronfield Woodhouse in January 1921 and left Leeds Road to become trainer at Nottingham Forest in May 1937. Never overawed by the big occasion, he developed into a great full-back, a master of positional tactics, and besides being a regular in the Terriers' line-up, he also starred in 25 internationals for England between 1926-34. Fast and a solid tackler, he loved the shoulder charge and often sent his opponent flying with one of his almighty clean and fair challenges. He played alongside Sam Wadsworth for both club and country for many seasons and was Huddersfield's penalty expert. After Wadsworth had left, Goodall continued to star despite having an assortment of different partners. A League championship winner on three occasions, he also appeared in the 1928 and 1930 losing FA Cup finals. He also represented the Football League eight times and also played for the FA and in May 1924 he was reprimanded by the club for 'misleading the management' in respect of an injury received when riding a motor cycle!

After his duties with Forest, Goodall (left) went on to manage Mansfield (August 1945-June 1949). He then returned to Leeds Road and worked on the training staff before taking charge of the youth team in his last season in football (1964-65). He served the club to 42 years.

GORRE, Dean: Midfield: 64 apps. 7 goals Born: Surinam, 10 September 1970
Dutch Under-21 international Gorre was signed for £330,000 from Ajax Amsterdam in September 1999, having previously played for SVV Dordrecht, Feyenoord and Groningen. He made over 200 League and Cup appearances in his homeland and went on to give the Terriers good value for money with some impressive displays in centre-midfield. He left the club for Barnsley in July 2001 for £50,000 and was released by the Tykes in May 2004.

GOWLING, Alan Edwin: Forward/midfield: 139 apps. 61 goals Born: Stockport, 16 March 1949
Alan Gowling represented Stockport, Cheshire & England Grammar Schools before joining Manchester United as an amateur in August 1965, turning professional in August 1967. After scoring 21 goals in 86 games for the Reds he moved to Huddersfield for £60,000 in June 1972 and spent three years at Leeds Road before switching to Newcastle for £70,000 in August 1975. He then diverted south to Bolton for £120,000, in March 1978 before spending 1982-83 with Preston after which he retired with 480 League appearances under his belt (139 goals)..
A tall, angular striker, who had an awkward style which confounded defenders Gowling was converted into a highly effective attacking midfielder by manager Frank O'Farrell at Old Trafford having been signed while studying for an economics degree at Manchester University. A member of the Great Britain soccer team in the Mexico Olympics, Gowling later succeeded Gordon Taylor as Chairman of the PFA (November 1980) and thereafter was deeply involved as general-manager of a Buxton-based chemical company while also working as a soccer summariser on Bolton matches for local radio.

GRAVESEND & NORTHFLEET: Huddersfield beat Gravesend 2-1 at home in the 1st round of the FA Cup in November 2001.

GRAY, Ian: Goalkeeper: 30 apps. Born: Manchester, 25 February 1975.
Career: Oldham Athletic (trainee, April 1991, professional July 1993), Rochdale (loan, November-December 1994, signed July 1995), Stockport County (£200,000, July 1997), Rotherham United (free transfer, July 2000), Huddersfield Town (free, August 2003). Tall, well built and agile, Ian Gray quickly established himself as the Terriers' number one goalkeeper. Now back to full fitness after missing the second half of the 2003-04 campaign with a hand injury.

GRAY, Kevin John: Full-back/defender: 269 apps. 6 goals Born: Sheffield, 7 January 1972
Kevin Gray (right) joined Mansfield as a trainee in 1988 and turned professional in July 1990. He made over 170 appearances for the Stags before transferring to Huddersfield in July 1994. A six-footer, weighing 14st, he gave the terriers splendid service over the next eight years, having almost 270 games as a string tackling, totally committed defender. He had a loan spell with Stockport prior to leaving the Terriers for Tranmere on a free transfer in July 2002.

GRAY, Terence Ian: Utility Player: 181 apps. 41 goals Born: Bradford, 3 June 1954.
An England junior tennis player at Wimbledon at the age of 15, Terry Gray also played
for the English Grammar Schools at football before joining Chelsea as an amateur. He
didn't make the grade at Stamford Bridge and was with Leeds Ashley Road when he
won two England Youth caps. After an unsuccessful trial with Wolves, he was spotted
by Huddersfield and joined the club as a professional in August 1972. He played in the
Second, Third and Fourth Divisions for the Terriers and prior to leaving for Southend in
a £10,000 deal in June 1979, he had skippered the first team. A Fourth Division
championship medal with the Shrimpers, he left Roots Hall for Bradford City in July
1982 and after a spell with PNE, he had trials with Rochdale before joining Northern
Counties (East) League side Ossett Town in 1986.

GRIMSBY TOWN: Huddersfield's record against the Mariners is:

Football League

Venue	P	W	D	L	F	A
Home	34	16	9	9	47	35
Away	34	5	12	17	37	59
Totals	68	21	21	26	84	94

FA Cup

Home	1	1	0	0	3	1
Away	1	0	0	1	0	1
Totals	2	1	0	1	3	2

League Cup

Home	1	0	0	1	1	4
Away	1	0	0	1	0	1
Totals	2	0	0	2	1	5

Others

Away	2	1	1	0	6	4

Huddersfield's first League game with the Mariners resulted in a 2-1 away win in
November 1911. They completed the double that season when winning 2-0 at Leeds
Road.
Huddersfield drew 0-0 at Grimsby in their last pre-WW1 League game (April 1915).
During a week in September 1947, the Mariners lost 5-1 at Leeds Road and then gained
revenge with a 3-1 victory at Blundell Park.
Huddersfield's heaviest reverse against the mariners is 5-1 (a) in January 1985.
Huddersfield's home FA Cup win over the Mariners was accomplished in the 3rd round
in January 1990 in front of almost 10,000 spectators.
The Terriers lost 5-1 on aggregate to Grimsby in a 2nd round League cup-tie in 1979-80.

GROUNDS
Leeds Road: from 1908 to 1994
Address: Leeds Road, Huddersfield, HD1 6PE
Highest capacity: 67,100 (for seasons 1931-33)
Pitch measurements (at the time of closure): 115 yards long x 76 yards wide
Huddersfield has always been a rugby stronghold, in 1895 the Northern Union (later the
Rugby League) was 'born' there. In 1907, a group of soccer stalwarts purchased the
Leeds Road recreation fields to form a football club. When Huddersfield AFC was

created in 1908 the ground had no facilities. Playing first in the North-Eastern League (1908-09) then the Midland League (1909-10), Huddersfield engaged football stadium expert Archibald Leitch to design a ground on the site. He proposed a pitch-length grandstand with his trademark gable frontage, with standing terraces to accommodate 34,000 spectators. Immediately the club applied to join the Football League, who always looked to encroach into rugby strongholds. Town was accepted for the 1910-11 season, the inaugural League match taking place on 10 September when Burnley were the visitors for a Second Division fixture. A new roof was fitted in 1920 and 12 years later a record crowd packed into the ground to watch an FA Cup-tie against Arsenal. A fire destroyed most of the main stand in April 1950, a replacement being built. In 1955 a roof was erected over the north side of the ground and then an electronic scoreboard was assembled on the Dalton bank terrace while floodlights were installed in 1960 (switched on early in 1961). In later years the ground showed its age, the capacity being considerably reduced as a result of more stringent safety standards having to be met. It was no surprise when Leeds Road closed and the brand new Alfred McAlpine Stadium opened in 1994.

Fact File

- Huddersfield's first match at Leeds Road was a friendly against Bradford Park Avenue on 2 September 1908 and resulted in a 2-1 victory for the Terriers.
- The last match at Leeds Road was a Second Division League encounter against Blackpool on 30 April 1994 when a crowd of 16,195 saw the Terriers win 2-1, Phil Starbuck having the pleasure of scoring the last (and winning) goal.
- The first League game was staged on 3 September 1910 when Bradford Park Avenue were defeated 1-0.
- Biggest crowd at ground: 67,037 v. Arsenal, FA Cup 6th round, 27 February 1932.
- Biggest League crowd: 52,479 v. Blackpool, Division One, 7 April 1951
- Lowest League crowd: 1,624 v. Torquay, Division 4, 30 April 1979
- Lowest attendance (for a competitive game, excluding wartime football): 1,069 v. Doncaster, Autoglass Trophy 1st round, 28 September 1993.
- Biggest win on ground: 10-1 v. Blackpool, League, 13 December 1930
- Heaviest defeat: 7-1 v. Wolves, League, 29 September 1951
- Huddersfield played 1,556 League games at Leeds Road (including one play-off).
- Following a fire at Valley Parade, Bradford City played six 'home' League football games at Leeds Road during the 1985-86 season.
- Manchester United played Charlton in a 5th round FA Cup-tie at Leeds Road in February 1948 (Old Trafford had been bombed by German planes during WW2). A crowd of 33,312 saw United win 2-0.
- In all, a total of 100 teams played in 1,562 League games at Leeds Road.
- In 1994, Leeds Road was sold to developers and today it is the site of a retail park accommodating what is believed to be one of the largest DIY superstores in Europe.

The Alfred McAlpine Stadium: from 1994 (now known as the Galpharm Stadium)
Address: Leeds Road, Huddersfield, HD1 6PX
Tel: 01484 484 100
Fax: 01484 484 101
Ticket office: 01484 484 123
Club Shop: 01484 484 144

Capacity (at 2004): 24,500

Pitch measurements: 116 yards long x 76 yards wide

Following the publication of the Taylor Report, Huddersfield in common with most League clubs, was left with the problem - modify the old ground or build afresh. In reality, with the capacity of Leeds Road being continuously reduced for safety reasons and the ancient ground visibly crumbling, there was only one answer - relocate. Fortunately, all the interested parties were enthralled by the plans for a completely new type of stadium which would accommodate not only the town's football club but also the local Rugby League club which was close to bankruptcy. The Kirklees Metropolitan Council, the clubs themselves the architects and the sponsors achieved a harmony of purpose rarely found in football stadium planning. Everyone sang from the same hymn sheet as the necessary funds poured in, all and sundry seemingly inspired by the exciting project. The council provided a suitable site, also on Leeds Road, on land already earmarked for development. The appointed contractors, Alfred McAlpine, got to work quickly as the old ground was bulldozed flat, building the futuristic design which would win the prestigious Royal Institute of British Architects' Building of the Year Award in 1995. The elegantly curved 'banana-shaped' stands give the stadium its distinctive look, as well as providing all spectators with an excellent view of the pitch. The now mandatory executive boxes were all snapped up immediately and the ground was officially opened on 20 August 1994 with a Second Division game against Wycombe Wanderers. Only three of the four stands were built at this time with almost 20,000 seats in place, but with an open end complex due to be completed by 1996, the stadium's capacity would eventually rise to 24,500.

Huddersfield (as a town) can be justifiably proud of its achievements with both football and rugby thriving as a result. If only all such ventures could be conducted so well with such sensational results!

Fact File

- The ground stands close to the River Colne. Initially it consisted of a two-tier 8,281 seater west stand and a 7,329 seater east stand, further development saw a 4,053 seater stand constructed on the south side with a fourth stand on the north side completed later.
- A crowd of 13,334 saw the first game which Wycombe won 1-0.
- The biggest attendance so far at the ground is 23,678 v. Liverpool, FA Cup 3rd round, 12 December 1999.
- The biggest League crowd is 20,741 v. Sunderland, 21 October 1998
- The lowest attendance so far at the stadium has been 3,570 v. Halifax, LDV Vans Trophy, 1st round, 15 October 2001.
- Biggest win at the stadium: 7-1 v. Crystal Palace, League, 28 August 1999.
- Heaviest defeat: 4-0 v. Port Vale, League, 3 May 1998
- Over 230 League games (including play-offs) have now been played at the stadium featuring more than 70 teams.

GUNN, Alistair Robert: Outside-right: 85 apps. 11 goals Born: Broughty Ferry, 2 November 1924.

Signed from Dundee in January 1951, right-winger Alistair Gunn served Huddersfield well for three-and-a-half years before his transfer to Bournemouth in June 1954. He spent only one season at Dean Court before drifting into non-League football.

H

HALF-TIME SCORES:
- Huddersfield led Liverpool 4-0 at half-time in a home League game in November 1934. Final score: 8-0.
- The Terriers were also four goals to the good against Everton in a League game at Leeds Road in April 1953. Final score: 8-2.
- Huddersfield led Blackpool 3-1 at half-time of a Second Division encounter at Leeds Road in December 1930. The final score was 10-1. This is the only time the Terriers have scored seven goals in the second-half of a League game and the second time in major competitions.
- Huddersfield were 4-0 up at half-time in their first-ever FA Cup-tie away to Heckmondwike in September 1909. They went on to win the game 11-0 and the haul of seven second-half goals was not repeated for 21 years.
- Huddersfield trailed Barnsley 6-0 at half-time in a League game at Oakwell on 27 November 1998. Final score: 7-1.

HALIFAX TOWN: Huddersfield's record against the Shaymen is:

Football League

Venue	P	W	D	L	F	A
Home	6	4	1	1	15	4
Away	6	1	3	2	5	6
Totals	12	5	4	3	20	10

League Cup

Home	1	1	0	0	3	1
Away	1	0	1	0	2	2
Totals	2	1	1	0	5	3

Other

Home	1	1	0	0	5	0

The first Yorkshire League derby between Huddersfield and Halifax took place at Leeds Road on Boxing day 1973 when a crowd of 11,514 (the best of the season) saw the Terriers win 4-0 (Alan Gowling scoring twice). The return clash at The Shay finished goalless.

Huddersfield's best win over Halifax is 5-0 (h) in April 1980.

Halifax lost 5-3 on aggregate in a 1st round League Cup-tie in 1986-87 and crashed 5-0 in an Autoglass Trophy game in 1992-93.

HANVEY, Keith: Central Defender: 235 apps. 15 goals Born: Manchester City , 18 January 1952 Hanvey was an apprentice at Maine Road before turning professional with Manchester City in August 1971. Having failed to make the first team he moved to Swansea in July 1972 (after a loan spell) and a year later returned to Lancashire with Rochdale. He made over 120 League appearances for the Spotland club and then had 54 outings in the same competition with Grimsby (from February 1977). In July 1978 he was recruited by Huddersfield for £14,000 and spent six years at Leeds Road during which time he gave some excellent performances, helping the Terriers rise from the

Fourth to the Second Division in double-quick time. He returned to Rochdale in July 1984 and retired from football the following May. From June 1986 he was appointed chairman of Huddersfield's 'Junior Terriers' organisation and then became a vital member of the commercial and promotions department. In 1990, Hanvey (as Commercial Executive) started masterminding the club's imminent move to their new ground.

HARDWICK, Steven: Goalkeeper: 132 apps. Born: Mansfield, 6 September 1956
When Huddersfield signed former England Youth international Hardwick from Oxford on a free transfer in July 1988, he had already appeared in more than 500 competitive games, having made his League debut for Chesterfield 14 years earlier. He signed professional forms at Saltergate as a 17 year-old and in December 1976 was sold to Newcastle for £80,000. There followed in February 1983, a £20,000 move to Oxford for whom he played 195 games before joining the Terriers. With Lee Martin ready to take over the goalkeeping position, Hardwick left Leeds Road in the summer of 1991

HART, Peter Osborne: Defender/midfield: 229 apps. 8 goals Born: Mexborough, 14 August 1957
Peter Hart joined Huddersfield as an apprentice and tuned professional in August 1974, having already made his League debut as a 16 year-old against Southend the previous March and skippering the Terriers youngsters in the FA Youth Cup final. He was successfully converted from a defender into a midfielder and in 1980 captained the Terriers to the Fourth Division championship, being one of three ever presents in the side. A model of consistency, Hart moved to Walsall for £70,000 shortly after that championship triumph and he went on to give the Saddlers great service over the next decade, amassing 474 senior appearances and receiving a testimonial (v. West Brom) in 1990. Since retiring Hart has become a popular preacher of the gospel, specialising in addresses to young people in which he uses his footballing background to good effect.

HARTLEPOOL UNITED: Huddersfield's record against the 'Pool is:
Football League

Venue	P	W	D	L	F	A
Home	8	7	1	0	18	4
Away	8	2	3	3	9	9
Totals	16	9	4	3	27	13
FA Cup						
Home	1	1	0	0	3	1
Away	1	1	0	0	2	0
Totals	2	2	0	0	5	1
League Cup						
Home	1	1	0	0	2	0
Away	1	1	0	0	2	1
Totals	2	2	0	0	4	1
Others						
Home	2	0	1	1	1	4
Away	1	0	0	1	0	1
Totals	3	0	1	2	1	5

Huddersfield met Hartlepool for the first time in a League game in November 1975 (Division Four). The Terriers won 2-0 at Leeds Road and later in the season drew 1-1 at Victoria Park.

Huddersfield doubled up over the 'Pool in 1976-77, winning 4-1 (h) and 1-0 (a).

Eddie Quigley scored twice in Huddersfield's 3-1 home win in the FA Cup in January 1966 and 'Pool were defeated 4-1 on aggregate in a 1st round League Cup-tie in 1976-77.

HASSALL, Harold William: Wing-half/inside-forward: 78 apps. 26 goals Born: Tyldersley, 4 March 1929

While a member of the Astley & Tyldesley Collieries team, Harry Hassall was playing for Mossley Common when Huddersfield signed him as a full-time professional in September 1946. He developed fast and made his League debut two years later. He gained the first of his five England caps in 1951, scoring against Scotland in a 3-2 defeat. In January of the following year Hassall was transferred to Bolton for £27,000 and became a member of the Trotters' all international forward-line, collecting a runners-up medal after Bolton had lost the 1953 FA Cup final to Blackpool. On New Year's Day 1955, Hassall sustained a serious knee injury playing against Chelsea, thus ending his professional career. He was awarded a benefit match that drew a 20,000 crowd to Burnden Park. Afterwards he qualified as a teacher, adding a Physical Education certificate and post graduate diploma in management studies to his C.V. In 1958 he was appointed manager-coach of the England Youth team and in 1966, with three other coaches, Hassall was asked by FIFA to report and later submit all findings regarding tactics and general play on certain World Cup games. In December of that year he became a lecturer on physical education at Padgate College of Higher Education as well as becoming a member of a study team that helped emerging countries with all aspects of football. Later Hassall was appointed general secretary of the Amateur Swimming Association, working mainly from his home in Bolton.

* During his Huddersfield days, Hassall had the distinction of saving a penalty from the Preston and England winger Tom Finney when he went into goal following an injury to Harry Mills

HAT-TRICK HEROES: Over the years, Huddersfield players, between them have scored over 140 hat-tricks in major competitive games (more than 80 coming in the Football League).

- Billy Price scored a club record 16 hat-tricks for Huddersfield - one in the FA Cup, 15 in WW2. He claimed four v. Leeds and his tally included a seven, a five and three fours.
- George Brown scored a record 12 'peacetime' hat-tricks for Huddersfield (10 in the League, two in the FA Cup) and they all came against different clubs.
- Charlie Wilson hit six hat-tricks for the Terriers, all in the First Division, including

- three against Arsenal, two in successive League games - first at Highbury on 15 December 1923 (won 3-1) and then at Leeds Road a week later (won 6-1).
- Les Massie repeated Wilson's feat in 1965-66 - scoring trebles in both League games against Middlesbrough (in wins of 6-0 at home and 3-1 away).
- Alex Jackson holds the club record for most trebles scored by a winger - six - including three in four games during November/December 1928.
- Three of Brian Stanton's four goals in a 6-3 home League win over Bradford City on 1 January 1986, came in the space of just six minutes - probably the fastest hat-trick by a non-forward for the Terriers.
- Jim Glazzard netted six hat-tricks against different clubs in the 1950s.
- Dave Mangnall's haul of five hat-tricks included a five and one four, with four trebles coming in the 1931-32 season.
- The club's first hat-trick hero was James Wallace against Sunderland RR (a) in a North-Eastern League game in December 1908.
- Bill McCreadie netted the first in the Midland League v. Castleford Town (a) in December 1909 and Jack Foster notched the first in the FA Cup against Heckmondwike in September 1909. Walter Stacey also hit a treble in this same game.
- There have been three other instances when two different Huddersfield players have scored hat-tricks in the same game - Ernie Islip and Billy Smith against PNE (h) in April 1922 (won 6-0), Joe Robson and George McLean v. Blackpool (h) in December 1930 (won 10-1) and Allan Gilliver and Les Massie v. Middlesbrough (h) in August 1965 (won 6-0).
- Huddersfield's first Football League hat-trick was secured by Jim Richardson against Birmingham (h) in December 1911 and the first in the League Cup was obtained by Duncan Shearer v. Rotherham (a) in August 1987.
- For only the fifth time in Football League history, three players netted hat-tricks for Manchester City in their 10-1 home win over Huddersfield in November 1987. They were Tony Adcock, Paul Simpson and David White.

HAWKSWORTH, Derek Marshall: Outside-left: 59 apps. 14 goals Born: Bradford, 16 July 1927
Predominantly right-footed, Derek Hawksworth preferred the left flank and was a regular scorer throughout his career. He was an amateur with both Bradford Park and Huddersfield before entering the RAF. On demob he joined Bradford City as a professional in October 1946 and moved to Sheffield United for £12,000 in December 1950. He scored 103 goals in 286 appearances for the Blades and helped them win the Second Division title as well as playing for England 'B' against France 'B' in 1952 before returning to Leeds Road in an exchange deal involving Ron Simpson plus £6,000 in May 1958. He spent just under two years at Leeds Road, leaving for Lincoln in February 11960 for £3,000. Hawksworth had a second spell with Bradford City and Nelson before retiring in May 1964 to run a newsagent's shop. His cousin, Malcolm Levitt, also played for Bradford City.

HAYES, William Edward: Right-back: 195 apps. 5 goals Born: Cork, 7 November 1915
One of the few players to serve Huddersfield in League and Cup football before, during and after WW2, Bill Hayes was brought up in Sheffield. He represented England

Schoolboys and later gained four caps full caps for Northern Ireland (1937-38) and two more for the Republic of Ireland v. England and Portugal in 1946-47. As tough as they come, he signed for the Terriers as an amateur in June 1932 from St Vincent's (Sheffield) turning professional in April 1933. He had to wait until August 1934 for his League debut (v. Derby) and it was not until 1938 that he finally established himself in the side. He played regularly during WW2 and remained at Leeds Road until February 1950 when he moved to Burnley, retiring three months later.

HEARY, Thomas: Midfield: 109 apps. Born: Dublin, 14 February 1978
Heary signed for Huddersfield as an apprentice in 1994 and turned professional two years later. Capped by the Republic of Ireland at Schoolboy, Youth and Under-21 levels, he was released by the club in May 2003.

HELLAWELL, Michael Stephen: Outside-right: 54 apps. one goal Born: Keighley, Yorkshire, 30 June 1938
Fast and direct, Mike Hellawell enjoyed hugging the touchline. He began his career with Huddersfield but failed to make the grade at Leeds Road, switching to QPR via Salts FC in August 1955. He then moved to Birmingham in May 1957 as a replacement for Gordon Astall and scored 33 goals in 213 outings for Blues in eight years before transferring to Sunderland in January 1965. He returned to Huddersfield in September 1966 and rounded off his career with spells at Peterborough (from December 1968) and Bromsgrove Rovers (1969-71). A Fairs Cup finalist with Blues in 1960 and 1961, he gained a League Cup winner's medal in 1963 and won two England caps, and whilst with QPR represented the Third Division South. After hanging up his boots Hellawell ran a shop in Keighley for many years. Besides being a fine footballer he was also a talented cricketer and represented Warwickshire in the County Championship.

HEPPLEWHITE, George: Centre-half: 165 apps. 3 goals Born: Edmondsley, 5 September 1919. Died: 1989.
Hepplewhite was signed in May 1939 from Horden Colliery Welfare, but owing to WW2 when he made just one appearance, he had to wait seven years before making his Football League debut against Preston in November 1946. With his no-nonsense approach, he developed into a rock-like centre-half, strong in all departments of defensive play. In March 1951 he was transferred to Preston for £9,000 but failed to fit in at Deepdale and moved to Bradford City in July 1953, retiring in February 1955 after making well over 250 club appearances. He later worked in his native North-East and in the 1960s was a scout for Newcastle.

HEREFORD UNITED: Huddersfield's record against the Bulls is:
Football League

Venue	P	W	D	L	F	A
Home	4	1	1	2	4	5
Away	4	2	1	1	5	5
Totals	8	3	2	3	9	10

In April 1972, Huddersfield were in the First Division and Hereford in the Southern League. In November 1973 they played each other in the Third Division, the Terriers having been relegated twice in successive seasons and Hereford having gained promotion in their first season of Football League membership. Huddersfield won 1-0 at Edgar Street but were held to a goalless draw at Leeds Road.

HESFORD, Robert Taylor: Goalkeeper: 220 apps. Born: Bolton, 13 April 1916. Died: Blackpool, June 1982.
Bob Hesford, 6ft 2ins tall and 13st in weight, a former pupil at Blackpool Grammar School, was a registered player with Huddersfield for 17 years. Signed from South Shore (Blackpool) as an amateur in May 1933, he turned professional four months later while studying at Leeds University, and went on to serve the club right through to May 1950 when he announced his retirement. He made almost 150 appearances, collecting an FA Cup runners-up medal in 1938, before wartime Military Service and then after the hostilities returned to League action having guested for a handful of clubs in the meantime. In February 1948 he fractured his ankle at Sunderland and never really recovered from that mishap. In May 1950 he quit Leeds Road and after a brief spell with Stalybridge Celtic he concentrated on being a teacher and worked in this field in Zambia. His eldest son, Iain, kept goal for Blackpool. Sheffield Wednesday, Fulham, Notts County, Sunderland, Hull and Maidstone United between 1977-92; another son, Robert, played for Bristol and England at Rugby Union while a third son, Steve, served with Warrington Rugby League club.

HILL, Brian: Outside-left: 101 apps. 7 goals Born: Mansfield, 15 December 1942
Hill joined Grimsby from Ollerton Colliery in July 1960, turning professional a month later. He made 180 appearances for the Mariners up to November 1966 when he signed for Huddersfield for £20,000. Over the next three years, mainly as Colin Dobson's left-wing partner, the pacy, lightweight and slim-looking Hill produced some excellent displays. However, in June 1969 he was sold to Blackburn for £32,500 and two years later skipped down the ladder to join Torquay, ending his career with Boston United in 1972-73. He was at Plainmoor with another Brian Hill and often both players lined up in the same team – a nightmare for reporters!

HIRST, SIR Amos Brook, OBE: Born: Yorkshire, 1879. Died: Yorkshire, 26 November 1955
Known affectionately as Huddersfield's 'Mr Football', Sir Amos Brook Hirst, OBE did great things for the club over the years and was a notable figure in local society. As Chairman of the FA, he accompanied several dignitaries to matches, including King George VI, the Duke of Edinburgh, Sir Winston Churchill, Clement Atlee, King Peter of Yugoslavia, the respective Kings of both Greece and Norway. The current Queen (then Princess Elizabeth) was also in his company when she attended her first football match - the England v. Scotland international at Wembley in April 1951.

HOLLAND, Christopher James: Midfield: 139 apps. 39 goals Born: Whalley, 11 September 1975
An England Youth and Under-21 international (capped 10 times in the latter category), Chris Holland started his career with PNE for whom he made just two appearances before joining Newcastle for £100,000 in January 1994. He struggled to come to terms with the surroundings at St James' Park and in September 1996 moved south to Birmingham for £600,000. He made 88 appearances for the Blues who then transferred him to Huddersfield for £150,000 in February 2000. Injuries effected his game over the

next four years but he battled on and helped the Terriers edge towards the play-offs before transferring to Boston United in March 2004.

HOLMES, Ian Michael: Right-half/midfield: 80 apps. 23 goals Born: Wombwell, 8 December 1950
Ian Holmes moved from York to Huddersfield in October 1977. He spent almost three complete seasons at Leeds Road before being released in June 1980, after losing his place in the side to Brian Stanton, his first club was Sheffield United where he signed as a professional in January 1968, switching to Bootham Crescent in July 1973.

HORNE, Barry: Midfield: 56 apps. one goal Born: St Asaph, 18 May 1962
Horne played for Rhyl before joining Wrexham in June 1984. He moved to Portsmouth for £60,000 in July 1987, switched to Southampton for £670,000 in March 1989, was signed by Everton for £675,000 in July 1992 before securing a £250,000 transfer to Birmingham in June 1996. At this juncture, Horne was already an established Welsh international (he went on to gain a total of 59 caps) and had won the FA Cup and Charity Shield with Everton in 1995 while also accumulating 550 club appearances. He spent two-and-a-half years at Huddersfield (October 1997 to March 2000) before switching to Sheffield Wednesday, later assisting Kidderminster Harriers, Walsall and Belper Town. He retired in 2003, having appeared in more than 750 games. An effective, hardworking player, he was never found wanting and always gave 100 per cent on the park.

HOTTE, Timothy Alwin: Forward: 16 apps. 4 goals Born: Bradford, 4 October 1963
Reserve forward Tim Hotte spent two years as an apprentice with Arsenal before becoming homesick. Moving back to Yorkshire, he joined the Terriers as a professional in September 1981 and stayed two seasons at Leeds Road before going on to play for Bradley Rangers, Harrogate Town, Frickley Colliery, Halifax Town, North Ferriby United, Hull City and York City. He was also approached by a Finnish club but was advised by the British Embassy not to go because two Brits had been taken hostage there, and when Halifax asked him to assist them they found out that he was classed as a Finnish citizen, even though he had never set foot in that country.

HOWARD, Stanley: Wing-forward: 64 apps. 13 goals Born: Chorley, 1 July 1934
Signed from Chorley in July 1952, Howard spent his first five seasons at Leeds Road in the reserves, finally making his senior debut on the right-wing in place of Kevin McHale against Liverpool at Anfield in August 1957 (Division Two). Over the next two years he did very well, occupying both flanks and in 1958-59 missed only two games. With other players ready to occupy the left-wing berth Howard was transferred to Bradford City June 1960, moving to Barrow in January 1961 before ending his League career with Halifax (1964-65).

HOWE, George: Right-back/right-half: 41 apps. Born: Wakefield, 10 January 1924. Died: November, 1971
Howe was recruited from Carlton United in May 1942 and had a handful of games for the Terriers during WW2 before making his League debut in February in 1947 against Everton at Goodison Park. He remained at Leeds Road, playing mainly as a reserve,

until June 1954 when he moved to York. As a reliable and consistent defender, he went on to give the Minstermen sterling service, appearing in 338 competitive matches (including the 1955 FA Cup semi-final) before retiring in May 1961. Later in life, Howe worked in the maintenance department at Pinderfields Hospital, Wakefield. He died suddenly, aged 47.

HOY, Robert: Winger: 165 apps. 20 goals Born: Halifax, 10 January 1950
Hoy joined Huddersfield as a 15 year-old and turned professional in November 1967 - having already celebrated his League debut with a goal against Birmingham at St Andrew's the previous April. A traditional old-fashioned winger, he won England Youth caps as a teenager and played a major part in helping the Terriers win the Second Division championship in 1969-70, scoring seven goals in 28 League outings. When the side started to stumble down the League ladder, Hoy found it hard to hold his place and in March 1975 was transferred to Blackburn Rovers for £5,000 plus Barry Endean. Things did not work out for Hoy at Ewood Park and in May 1976 he joined Halifax, later assisting York and Rochdale. In September 1983, following his release from Spotland, he had an unsuccessful trail with Bradford City, giving up the game soon afterwards, having amassed 273 League appearances.

HULL CITY: Huddersfield's record against the Tigers is:
Football League

Venue	P	W	D	L	F	A
Home	22	11	4	7	34	27
Away	22	7	6	9	28	32
Totals	44	18	10	16	62	59
FA Cup						
Home	1	1	0	0	3	1
Other						
Away	1	1	0	0	1	0

On 2 January 1911, Huddersfield and Hull met for the first time in the Football League and it was the Terriers who got the better of the Tigers, winning 2-0 at Leeds Road. The return fixture ended 2-2 at Anlaby Road.
In October 1912, following a 4-0 defeat at Burnley, Huddersfield turned things round by beating Hull 5-2 at Leeds Road. The Terriers also won 5-0 at Hull in April 1915 with Bert Smith claiming hat-trick. Sam Taylor scored five goals against the Tigers in five days during March 1920, helping Huddersfield win 2-0 at home and 4-1 away.
Hull lost 5-0 at Leeds Road in December 1980.
Huddersfield beat Hull 3-1 in a 3rd round on their way to the1938 FA Cup final.
Huddersfield defeated Hull 1-0 in the semi-final of the LDV Vans Trophy (N) in 2002.

HULME, Joseph: Outside-right: 10 apps. Born: Stafford, 26 August 1904. Died: Palmer's Green, London, 26 September 1991.
Hulme played in four FA Cup finals for Arsenal and one for Huddersfield. Indeed, his final appearance as a professional footballer was in the 1938 final against Preston. He played for the YMCA team before joining York in 1923, switching to Blackburn Rovers in February 1924 and onto Arsenal two years later. He spent 12 years at Highbury during which time he scored 107 goals in 333 League games and 17 in 39 FA Cup games as

the light at the end of the tunnel

well as netting once in two Charity Shield matches. A League championship winner in 1931, 1933 and 1935, he also gained nine England caps (4 goals) between 1927-33. He cost Huddersfield £1,500 when signed in January 1938, retiring three months later with 10 medals to his name. A police reserve during WW2, in February 1944 he was appointed assistant-secretary at Spurs and between October 1945 and May 1949 acted as team manager. After that he worked as a journalist with the Sunday People. Hulme also played in 223 country cricket matches for Middlesex (1929-39), scoring 8,103 runs for an average of 26.56, taking 36 wickets as an occasional bowler (at 40.00 each) and holding 110 catches. His highest score was 143.

HUTCHINGS, Christopher: Full-back/midfield: 131 apps. 10 goals Born: Winchester, 5 July 1957
A £28,000 signing from Brighton in December 1987, Hutchings spent two-and-half seasons at Leeds Road during which time he produced some fine performances, his all-action play when driving forward from the back or midfield, giving opponents plenty to think about. He started out with Southend, but surprisingly drifted into non-League football with Southall and Harrow Borough before returning to the League scene with Chelsea in July 1980, signed for £5,000 by manager Geoff Hurst. He made over 100 appearances during his time at Stamford Bridge and then played in 175 games for Brighton before his move to Leeds Road. On leaving the Terriers in August 1990, Hutchings switched to Walsall before rounding off his League career with Rotherham (1991-94). He accumulated a total of 468 League appearances for his five clubs. Hutchings was later manager of Bradford City (2000-01)
* Hutchings moved from Brighton to Chelsea shortly after he had been fined £250 for using insulting language to a policeman at the end of League game between the two clubs.

HUTT, Geoffrey: Full-back: 281 apps. 4 goals Born: Duffield, 28 September 1958
Hutt joined Huddersfield as an apprentice in April 1965 and turned professional in September 1967. He remained at Leeds Road for the next nine years before moving abroad to play for Haarlem FC (Holland) in June 1976 (after a loan spell with Blackburn).
He had made his League debut against Oxford in February 1969 and the following season helped the Terriers win the Second Division championship. Unfortunately he then suffered relegation three times in double quick time and in 1975 was playing in the Fourth Division in front of less than 2,000 spectators at Scunthorpe. After his spell in Holland he returned to have a couple of seasons with Halifax (1978-80). Later worked in the Customer Services Department at Tibbetts & Britten's, Huddersfield.

I

INTERNATIONAL TERRIERS: Over the years, certainly prior to 1970, several Huddersfield players gained full international honours for their country.
Listed here is a selection of Terriers who achieved honours.

Full Internationals

England: A Beasley (1), G Brown (8), F Bullock (1),
A Campbell (6), J Cock (1), R Goodall (25), H Hassall (4),
R Kelly (2), W McGarry (4), V Metcalfe (2), M O'Grady (1),
WH Smith (3), R Staniforth (8), C Stephenson (1), E Taylor (8),
H Turner (2), S Wadsworth (9), K Willingham (12),
R Wilson - right - (30), T Wilson (1), A Young (9).
Northern Ireland:/Ireland: H Baird (1), L Cumming (2),
P Doherty (4), C Gallogy (2), W Hayes (4), J McKenna (7),
J Macaulay (6), J Nicholson (31).
Republic of Ireland: W Hayes (2), M Meagan (12), P Saward (4)
Scotland: A Jackson (14), D Law (6), D Steele (3), J Watson (1)
Wales: M Browning (1), D Evans (1), J Jones (6), S Jenkins (15),
R Krzywicki (2), C Morris (1), I W Roberts (3), W Lewis (1)
Democratic Republic of Congo FM Ngonge (3)
Nigeria E Sodje (9)
Rest of Europe R Wilson (1)

International Talk Back:

- In June 1910, Charlie Morris became the first international player signed by Huddersfield. He went on to win three Welsh caps whilst at Leeds Road.
- Jack Cock was Huddersfield's first England international, scoring on his debut against Ireland in October 1919. He scored in his second international v. Scotland in April 1920 (won 5-4).
- In January 1911, Jimmy Macaulay became Huddersfield's first Irish international when he was capped against Wales.
- The club's first Scottish international was David Steele, capped against Ireland in March 1923.
- The first Huddersfield player to represent the Republic of Ireland was Bill Hayes v. England in September 1946.
- Denis Law is Scotland's joint leading scorer (with Kenny Dalglish) at senior international level. He netted 30 goals in 55 appearances for his country.
- Jimmy Nicholson (Northern Ireland) is Huddersfield's most-capped player, winning 31 of his total of 41 with the Terriers.
- Ray Wilson won 30 England caps as a Huddersfield player.
- Huddersfield, despite providing five players for the England v. Scotland game on 31 March 1928 - the famous Wembley Wizards occasion - they still managed to beat Bury 3-2 in a League game that same afternoon.
- Huddersfield winger Mike O'Grady scored twice on his England debut in a 3-1 win

over Northern Ireland in 1962. Nearly seven years later he won his second cap and scored once in a 5-0 win over France. That was his international career.

- Former Huddersfield star Denis Law scored four goals for Scotland against Northern Ireland at Hampden Park in November 1962 and four against Norway on the same ground twelve months later.
- The player with the most full caps to his name to have been registered with Huddersfield is David Phillips (Wales) who had 62 to his credit when he joined the Terriers in November 1997. Fellow countryman Barry Horne's tally was 59 when he joined the club that same month.

IPSWICH TOWN: Huddersfield's record against the Tractormen is:
Football League

Venue	P	W	D	L	F	A
Home	17	9	3	5	28	21
Away	17	2	2	13	16	41
Totals	36	11	5	18	44	62
FA Cup						
Away	1	0	0	1	0	1

In October 1957 (Division Two) Huddersfield beat Ipswich 3-0 at Leeds Road in the first League game between the clubs. Later that season Ipswich won 4-0 at Portman Road. Ipswich knocked Huddersfield out of the 1958-59 FA cup competition.

IRONS, Kenneth: Midfield: 169 apps. 13 goals Born: Liverpool, 4 November 1970. When he signed for Huddersfield for £450,000 in June 1999, central midfielder Irons had scored 67 goals in 430 senior games for Tranmere whom he had served since June 1987, turning professional in November 1989. An accurate passer of the ball, a free-kick expert and a 100 per-cent grafter, he settled down quickly at The Alfred McAlpine Stadium and when he retired in June 2003, he was just short of the 600 appearance-mark at club level.

ISLIP, Ernest: Forward: 173 apps. 52 goals Born: Packwood Springs, Sheffield, October 1892. Died: Huddersfield, August 1941.
Islip played for Sheffield Douglas before becoming a professional at Leeds Road in June 1911. In 1919-20 he gained runners-up medals in both the FA Cup and Division Two but collected an FA Cup winner's medal in 1922 when Huddersfield beat PNE. He left Huddersfield for Birmingham in November 1923 for £1,500 but after some useful performances for the Midland club found himself out in the cold at St Andrew's following the emergence of George Briggs. In May 1927 he moved to Bradford City for £400, yet only spent a season at Valley Parade before entering non-League soccer with Kidderminster. He later assisted Ashton National and then came back into the League with Wrexham in November 1928, retiring four months later. During WW1 Islip guested for Rotherham County, Sheffield Wednesday and West Ham. He had the chance to join the Hammers and if he had agreed then he might well have appeared in the first Wembley Cup Final of 1923.

J

JACKSON, Alexander Skinner: Outside-right: 203 apps. 89 goals Born: Renton, Dumbartonshire, May 1905. Died: Egypt, November 1946
Alex Jackson was a pupil at Renton School, he played for Dumbarton Academy before joining Renton Victoria in 1919, transferring to Dumbarton in July 1922 and onto Aberdeen for £100 in March 1923. He spent the whole of the 1923-24 season playing for the USA club Bethlehem Star of Pennsylvania, returning to Pittodrie Park in August 1924. He remained with the Dons until his £5,000 transfer to Huddersfield in May 1925. Five years later in September 1930 he moved to Chelsea for £8,500 and in August 1932 quit League football for Ashton National, later having a brief spell with Margate (February-April 1933) and also with the French club, Nice (during 1933-34).
In his heyday during the 1920s, Jackson's performances on the right-wing impelled the more flowery sports writers to dub him the 'Flying Scotsman', the 'Gay Cavalier' and the 'Wing Wizard.' A superlative footballer, he was certainly one of the greatest outside-rights of his era. A wanderer, liable to pop up and score goals from any position, he was fast, brainy with an immaculate command over the ball.
Capped 17 times by Scotland between 1925-20, he was a League championship winner with Huddersfield in 1925 and also played in losing FA Cup finals (1928 & 1930). He scored eight goals in 40 games for Aberdeen and after leaving Leeds Road netted 29 times in 77 first-class matches for Chelsea. He died in a car crash whilst serving in the army in Egypt.

JACKSON, Peter Alan: Defender: 197 apps. 5 goals Born: Bradford, 6 April 1961
Peter Jackson spent four years as a player with Huddersfield up to September 1994. Prior to that he had made 391 appearances in two spells for Bradford City (June 1977-October 1986 and September 1988-September 1990) and in between times, 72 for Newcastle who signed him for £250,000. He was snapped up by the Terriers on a free transfer and when he left the club it was also on free to Chester.
Jackson was a Third Division championship winner with the Bantams in 1985 and during his career that ended in May 1997, he played on every League ground except Molineux. He made well over 750 senior appearances (651 in the Football League) and scored 42 goals. He is the only man to have served two separate spells as manager of the Terriers. (SEE Managers).

JEE, Joseph William: Outside-left: 224 apps. 46 goals Born: Chorlton-cum-Hardy, Lancashire, 1883 A winger who loved to remain close to the touchline, Joe Jee was fast over the ground, tricky and a battler to the last. He played for Bolton (1906-08) and had a long spell with Brighton in the Southern League before joining Huddersfield for a mere £25 in August 1909. He made 44 appearances in his first season and then, as the Terriers established themselves in the Football League, continued to prove his worth, serving the club until October 1919 when he joined Nelson for £50 while receiving a cheque himself for £150 in lieu of a benefit. One interesting point is that Jee made his first League appearance for Huddersfield in September 1910 - some 32 months after his last for Bolton.

JENKINS, Stephen Robert: Full-back: 295 apps. 4 goals Born: Merthyr Tydfil, 16 July 1972

Welsh international Steve Jenkins served Huddersfield superbly well for eight years, making almost 300 appearances. He joined Swansea as an apprentice and turned professional at The Vetch Field in July 1990. He had to 215 outings for the Swans, helping them win the Autoglass Trophy in 1994 (v. Huddersfield). A positive, totally committed yet composed defender player, he loved to overlap and on many occasions seemed to serve as a direct right-winger. He played for his country at Youth and Under-21 levels before going on to gain 16 full caps. After a loan spell with Birmingham, he left the Terriers for Cardiff City in February 2003 but had rather an uneasy debut for the Bluebirds at Stockport on St David's Day, swallowing his tongue after a clash of heads. Thankfully, the speedy action of physio Clive Goodyear prevented what could have been a rather nasty situation. Jenkins joined Notts County in August 2003, switching to Peterborough United in January 2004.

JEPSON, Ronald Francis: Forward: 124 apps. 42 goals Born: Stoke, 12 May 1963

Ronnie Jepson scored a goal every three games for the Terriers whom he served from December 1993 to July 1996. He played for Nantwich Town, Port Vale, Peterborough, PNE and Exeter before moving to Leeds Road for £80,000. After giving his all for the Terriers he switched to Bury for £40,000 and went on to assist Oldham and Burnley before hanging up his boots in July 2001 having netted 103 goals in 414 competitive matches, 62 of them as a substitute for Burnley. Jepson's (left) only club honour was to win the Second Division championship with Bury in 1997.

JOHNSON, Kevin Peter: Midfield/forward: 87 apps. 23 goals Born: Doncaster, 29 August 1952

After starting his professional career with Sheffield Wednesday in July 1970, Kevin Johnson then had spells with Southend, Gillingham and Workington before doing well with Hartlepool. Recruited by Huddersfield in September 1976, he played wide on the left in the Terrier' midfield and had two excellent seasons at Leeds Road prior to his transfer to Halifax in August 1978. He later returned to Hartlepool, retiring in 1984, having scored 46 goals in a total of 320 League appearances.

JONES, Joseph Patrick Full-back: 76 apps. 4 goals Born: Llandudno, 4 March 1955

Joey Jones had a fine career in both club and international football. Primarily a full-back, he amassed 733 League and Cup appearances and gained 72 full and four Under-23 caps for Wales. He joined Wrexham for the first of three spells as a 15 year-old, turning professional in January 1973. He then made 94 appearances for Liverpool, another 225 for Wrexham and 91 for Chelsea before enjoying his exploits at Huddersfield. Ending his playing days at The Racecourse Ground in 1992 after adding 143 games to his tally, he later became senior coach at the club. With Liverpool he won the European Cup, League championship and Super Cup in 1977 as well as two Charity Shields. He was a Second Division championship winner and Welsh Cup winner with Chelsea in 1984 and Wrexham in 1986 respectively.

JONES, Paul Bernard: Defender: 91 apps. 11 goals Born: Ellesmere Port, 13 May 1953

Paul Jones represented Ellesmere Port Boys & Cheshire Schools before joining Bolton as a junior, turning professional in June 1970. A stylish centre-half, appeared in 506 first-class games for the Whites over the next 13 years before joining Huddersfield in July 1983. He accompanied Dave Sutton and then Sam Allardyce at the heart of the Terriers' defence before his transfer to Oldham in December 1985. He later played for Blackpool, Atherton LR, Stalybridge Celtic, Wigan, Galway United (Ireland), Rochdale and Stockport while also having a spell in South Africa. Jones who retired in 1990 with over 700 senior appearances in his locker, scouted for Blackpool in the 1990s.

huddersfield town
division three play-off winners 2004

the light at the end of the tunnel

the light at the end of the tunnel

the light at the end of the tunnel

K

KELLY, Robert F: Inside-forward: 213 apps. 42 goals Born: Ashton-in-Makerfield near Wigan, 16 November 1893. Died: Fylde, Lancashire, September 1969.

Kelly was one of the most gifted footballers of his generation. A former coalminer, he played for Ashton White Star, Ashton Central, Earlestown (Liverpool) and St Helens before joining Burnley for £275 in November 1913. Over the next 12 years, he scored 97 goals in 299 senior games for the Clarets before moving to Sunderland for a then British record fee of £6,550 in December 1925.

In February 1927, he switched to Huddersfield where he stayed for over five years, producing some outstanding displays while occupying every position in the forward-line. Sold to PNE in July 1932, he was player-manager of Carlisle from March 1935 to October 1936 and bossed Stockport from November 1936 to March 1939. After WW2, Kelly coached Sporting Club de Portugal and held similar positions in Switzerland and the Channel Islands. His last appointment in football was that of manager of Barry Town from December 1960 to May 1961. Capped 14 times by England between 1920 and 1928, Kelly was a League championship winner with Burnley (1921) and played in two losing FA Cup finals with Huddersfield (1928 & 1930). He was neat and tidy in everything he did.

Kelly scored his first League goal for Burnley in 1913 and his last for Carlisle in 1934.

KELLY, Lawrence: Full-back: 239 apps. 2 goals Born: Wolverhampton, 28 April 1925

Kelly played in 70 games for Wolves (including the 1949 FA Cup semi-final) before transferring to Huddersfield for £10,500 in October 1950 - unable to command a regular place in the side owing to the depth of full-back talent at Molineux. He became part of a tremendous defensive formation at Leeds Road that comprised goalkeeper Jack Wheeler, Ron Staniforth and himself at full-back with Billy McGarry, Don McEvoy and Len Quested at half-back. Injuries apart, he was first choice at Leeds Road for six seasons until Tony Conwell came in and Staniforth switched to the left. He left the club to become player-manager of Nuneaton Town in May 1957, spending only a few months in the job. Kelly, who was awarded a benefit cheque for £750 on leaving Molineux.

KENNEDY, Michael Francis Martin: Midfield: 95 apps. 9 goals Born: Salford, 9 April 1961

Mick Kennedy's professional career spanned 15 years: January 1979-May 1994. During that time he appeared in 536 League games, serving in turn, with Halifax, Huddersfield (signed for £50,000, August 1980), Middlesbrough (transferred for £100,000, August 1982), Portsmouth, Bradford City, Leicester, Luton, Stoke, Chesterfield and Wigan. Capped by Republic of Ireland at full (twice in 1986) and Under-21 levels, he anchored the Terriers' midfield with David Cowling and Brian Stanton alongside.

KENNON, Neil Sandilands: Goalkeeper: 80 apps. Born: Regent's Park, Johannesburg, 28 November 1933

'Sandy' Kennon played for Umbilo FC, Berea Park (Durban) and Queen's Park FC (Bulawayo) before joining Huddersfield in August 1956 after an impressive display for a Rhodesia XI against the touring FA XI. He competed for the number one spot with Harry

Fearnley during his first season at Leeds Road before settling in as first choice until February 1959 when Ray Wood arrived from Manchester United. At that point Kennon was transferred to Norwich for whom he appeared in over 200 League games before rounding off his career with Colchester United (1965-67). Kennon, who had his own dance band, 'Sandy Kennon and the Blazers', later ran a bookmaker's business in Norwich.

KINDON, Stephen Michael: Forward: 82 apps. 37 goals Born: Warrington, 17 December 1950

Steve Kindon was a strong, busling forward who preferred to play on the left where his skill at times was most impressive. He joined Burnley on leaving school and turned professional at Turf Moor on his 17th birthday. An England Youth international, he made over 120 appearances for the Clarets before transferring to Wolves for £100,000 in July 1972. In November 1977 - after scoring 31 goals in 177 games for Wolves - he returned to Burnley for £80,000. Three years later, he was snapped up by Huddersfield and gave the club excellent service before retiring in May 1982 with 109 goals to his credit in almost 400 League games. Kindon was employed as Commercial Manager at Leeds Road for five years before becoming a globetrotting sales manager for Rolyat, a firm of basketware importers. He later turned to after dinner speaking. In 1976, Kindon won the professional footballer's 75 metres sprint title.

KRZYWICKI, Ryzard Lech: Winger: 54 apps. 8 goals Born: Penley, North Wales, 2 February 1947.

Dick Krzywicki, whose father was a Polish soldier, moved to Leek with his family when he was just three and after assisting the local Youth club he joined WBA in July 1962, turning professional in February 1965, having made his League debut v. Fulham as a 17 year-old.

Never a first-team regular at the Hawthorns, 'Glass of Whisky' as he was called, transferred to Huddersfield for a record fee of £45,000 in March 1970, having just played in that season's League Cup Final defeat by Manchester City .

He scored four goals at the end of that season as the Terriers sealed the Second Division championship. After spells with Scunthorpe (from February 1973) and Northampton, he then helped Lincoln win the Fourth Division title before quitting League football in 1976 to work in engineering in Batley and later helped run the Moorlands Youth Club at Dewsbury. Krzywicki was capped eight times by Wales and played in three Under-21 internationals. He went on to work in engineering while coaching youngsters in his spare time. Now living in West Yorkshire, his daughter was a Welsh sprinting champion.

L

LAVERICK, Michael George: Outside-right: 88 apps. 12 goals Born: Castle Eden, County Durham, 13 March 1954

Mick Laverick had two spells with Huddersfield. He was signed first of all from Southend in July 1979 and then sold to York in January 1982, only to return to Leeds Road on loan in January/February 1983. Having started his professional career with Mansfield in January 1972, he went on to score 46 goals in 316 League games in a career that ended in May 1983. His brother, Bobby played for Chelsea, Everton, Brighton and Coventry City. Laverick became a prison officer in Nottingham gaol.

LAW, Denis: Inside-forward: 91 apps. 19 goals Born: Aberdeen, 24 February 1940

Law was educated at Hilton Primary, Kitty Brewster Junior and Powis Secondary Modern Schools, and represented Aberdeen Boys before signing for Huddersfield as an amateur in 1955, turning professional two years later. In 1960 Manchester City paid a record fee for his signature of £55,000 (£10,000 more than the previous one) and twelve months later he moved to Torino in Italy for another new transfer record. Returning to England with Manchester United for £115,000 in August 1962, he ended his playing career in the World Cup finals of 1974 having gone back to Maine Road in the summer of 1973. His last League goal of a distinguished career was scored at the age of 34 for City against his former club Manchester United at Old Trafford in April 1974 - a cheeky back-heeler on 82 minutes which decided the contest and sent the Reds into the Second Division! Hugely gifted with balance, vision, alertness, control, a deadly shot and superb heading ability, Law's tally of 325 goals (in 637 appearances in England and for Scotland) included 239 for Manchester United, 33 coming in European matches. He was the world's first £100,000 footballer when he moved to Torino for £115,000 and when he left Italy, Manchester United became the first British club to splash out a six-figure fee on a player, Jimmy Greaves having cost Tottenham £99,999 against Law's fee of £125,000.

Scorer of 30 goals in 55 internationals for Scotland, Law also represented his country in three Under-23 internationals and played for a Football League XI. He netted for Manchester United in their 1963 FA Cup final victory over Leicester, was voted European Footballer of the Year in 1964, gained two First Division championship medals (1965 & 1967) but missed the 1968 European Cup Final with a knee injury. Despite the presence of all-time greats George Best and Bobby Charlton at Old Trafford, Law was regarded as 'The King'...and perhaps only Eric Cantona and to a certain degree David Beckham, have approached this level of hero worship at that club. In his career in Britain Law made 637 appearances. Now living in Bowden, Cheshire, he became an expert radio and TV summariser and after dinner speaker before limiting his activities due to his health.

LAWS, Brian: Full-back: 66 apps. one goal
Born: Wallsend, 14 October 1961
Laws spent 20 years in League football,
serving, in turn, with Burnley (from June 1977,
professional October 1979), Huddersfield
(August 1983 to March 1985), Middlesbrough,
Nottingham Forrest, Grimsby (player-manager),
Darlington and Scunthorpe, finally hanging up
his boots in 1998 after returning to
management with his last club.
Having gained a Third Division championship
winner's medal with Burnley in 1982, Laws won
two League Cups with Forest (1989 & 1990),
the Simod Cup (also 1989), was substitute in
the both 1991 FA Cup and 1992 League Cup
finals and helped the Reds gain promotion to
the Premiership in 1994. Laws (right) made
over 630 appearances, scored 38 goals and
played once for England 'B'. He partnered
David Burke during his time at Leeds Road
before losing his place to Ian Measham.

LAWSON, David: Goalkeeper: 67 apps. Born: Wallsend, 22 December 1947
Lawson joined Newcastle as an apprentice, in April 1964, turning professional two years
later. A trial with Shrewsbury preceded his move to Bradford PA in October 1967 and in
May 1969 he transferred to Huddersfield for £7,000, switching to Everton for £85,000 in
June 1972, onto Luton in October 1978) before winding down with Stockport (March
1979-May 1981). In his 17-year career Lawson amassed over 300 appearances, having
his best spell of 124 outings with Everton. Agile and a fine shot-stopper, he failed to
make the grade at Newcastle, did reasonably well at Bradford and then did much better
at Leeds Road before a record transfer fee for a goalkeeper took him to Goodison Park
where he collected a League Cup runners-up medal in 1977. Lawson is now a postman.

LAWSON, James Joseph: Forward: 273 apps. 46 goals Born: Middlesbrough, 11
December 1947
Jimmy Lawson cost Huddersfield £7,000 when signed from Middlesbrough in May 1968.
He spent eight years at Leeds Road, helping the Terriers win the Second Division
championship in 1970 when he scored six goals in 40 League appearances. However, in
his first season in the top flight he had a disagreement with the club and was transfer-
listed for breach of contract, but thankfully was re-instated and finished the campaign
as leading marksman. Injuries apart, he was a first-team regular for some six seasons at
Leeds Road and accumulated a fine record before his transfer to Halifax in May 1976 in
a £6,000 deal involving Bobby Hoy.
Lawson later became player-manager at The Shay, being replaced as boss in October
1978, but remaining as a player until May 1979. Lawson played in all four Divisions of
the Football League with the Terriers.

LEDGER, Robert Hardy: Forward: 62 apps. 7 goals Born: Chester-le-Street, County Durham, 5 October 1937 Big-hearted Bob Ledger represented Doncaster & Yorkshire Schoolboys before joining Huddersfield as an amateur in 1952, turning professional in October 1954. A fine crosser of the ball, he started out as an orthodox outside-right and spent eight years at Leeds Road during which time he occupied three other front-line positions. In May 1962 he was transferred to Oldham for £6,000. He netted 37 goals in 222 League games for the Latics, helping them win promotion to the Third Division in 1963. In December 1967 he moved to Mansfield and on to Barrow in October 1969, retiring in May 1970.

LEEDS CITY: Huddersfield's record against City is:
Football League

Venue	P	W	D	L	F	A
Home	5	3	1	1	7	5
Away	5	1	0	4	6	13
Totals	10	4	1	5	13	18

Huddersfield's first home win in the Football League (Division two) was against Leeds City on 24 September 1910. They triumphed 3-2 at Leeds Road with goals from Alex McCubbin, Harry Hamilton and Bill Bartlett. The attendance was 7,500. Huddersfield lost the return fixture 5-2. Town's only away win at Leeds followed in December 1912 - 3-0 at Elland Road, Huddersfield lost 5-1 on City soil in March 1914.

LEEDS UNITED: Huddersfield's record against United is:
Football League

Venue	P	W	D	L	F	A
Home	19	11	4	4	45	22
Away	19	11	3	5	32	20
Totals	38	22	7	9	77	42
FA Cup						
Home	1	1	0	0	3	0
Away	2	1	0	1	4	4
Totals	3	2	0	1	7	4
League Cup						
Home	1	0	1	0	1	1
Away	5	1	1	3	7	9
Totals	6	1	2	3	8	10

Huddersfield first met United at League level in September 1924 when they drew 1-1 at Elland Road. The following January the return fixture went in favour of the Terriers by 2-0. The following season Huddersfield won 4-0 at Elland Road and in 1928 Leeds crashed 6-1 at Huddersfield. When they beat Leeds 1-0 in August 1952, it was Huddersfield's first victory in Division Two for 32 years, since they accounted for Lincoln 4-2 in May 1920. Huddersfield played two League games at Elland Road in 1950 following a fire in the main stand at Leeds Road. Huddersfield whipped United 6-1 in a home League game in September 1928, George Brown scoring twice in front of almost 40,000 fans. Alex Jackson scored twice when Leeds were beaten 3-2 in a home 4th round FA Cup-tie in January 1929. Ten years later Billy Price netted a hat-trick when the Terriers won 4-2 at Elland Road, also in the 4th round. It took Leeds three games to knock Huddersfield out of the League Cup in 1974-75.

LEGG, William Campbell Defender: 60 apps. 4 goals Born: Bradford, 17 April 1948
Billy Legg joined Huddersfield as an apprentice in May 1963 and turned professional in May 1965. He wore the number '11' shirt when making his League debut against Wolves in October 1965 and in his next game, in May 1967 v. Cardiff, he lined up at left-back, a position he claimed from Chris Cattlin halfway through the following campaign. After spending nine years at Leeds Road, Legg moved to Bradford Park Avenue in April 1972.

LEICESTER CITY (Fosse): Huddersfield's record against the Foxes is:
Football League

Venue	P	W	D	L	F	A
Home	32	18	8	6	52	28
Away	32	8	8	16	36	53
Totals	64	26	16	22	88	81
Others						
Away	1	0	0	1	0	1

Huddersfield lost their first League game against Leicester 2-1 at Leeds Road in October 1910.That was the same score in the return fixture at Filbert Street before Town won 2-0 at home in October 1911.George Brown scored a hat-trick when Huddersfield beat the Foxes 5-3 at Leeds Road in October 1926. Later that season the Terriers completed the double with a 4-2 win at Filbert Street.

LEIGHTON, Anthony: Centre-forward: 97 apps. 44 goals Born: Leeds, 27 November 1939. Died: April 1978
Although not the tallest of strikers, Leighton was still an aggressive, all-action, tireless player who gave defenders plenty to think about. He joined the groundstaff at Elland Road on leaving school and turned professional in December 1956. He failed to make Leeds' first team and in June 1959 moved to Doncaster for £2,000. He scored 45 goals in 83 Fourth Division games for Rovers before switching to Barnsley in May 1962 and two years later transferred to Huddersfield for £20,000. He continued to find the net and headed the Terriers' scoring charts in 1966-67 with 20 goals in 37 outings. In March 1968 Leighton along with Dennis Atkins left Leeds Road in an exchange deal involving Alex Smith and Paul Aimson, plus a £15,000 cash adjustment.
In July 1970, having moved to the left-half position, he became player-coach at Bradford Park Avenue, retiring as a player in November 1973, quitting as manager early in 1974. During his time with Bradford Leighton also fulfilled the role, of development officer and groundsman and worked part-time for a Dewsbury-based joinery firm.
He later assisted Sligo Rovers and was player-manager of Liversedge, and had a few games at cricket with Leicestershire's second XI. Leighton, sadly at the age of 39, was struck down with a muscular disease which confined him to a wheelchair. His testimonial match drew a crowd of 9,370 at Leeds Road.

LEYTON ORIENT (Clapton Orient): Huddersfield's record against the Orient is:
Football League

Venue	P	W	D	L	F	A
Home	24	14	10	0	35	9
Away	24	6	3	15	25	39
Totals	48	20	13	15	60	48

FA Cup

Home	1	0	1	0	1	1
Away	1	0	0	1	0	2
Totals	2	0	1	1	1	3

Huddersfield encountered Orient for the first time in the League in November 1910, losing 2-0 away, gaining revenge by winning the return fixture by the same score at Leeds Road.

Huddersfield's first post-WW1 League game saw them beat Orient 2-1 at Leeds Road on 30 August 1919.

Huddersfield whipped Orient 6-0 at Leeds Road in September 1982, having been knocked out of the FA Cup by the Londoners in the 4th round seven months earlier.

LILLIS, Mark Anthony Forward/midfield: 242 apps 63 goals Born: Manchester City , 17 January 1960

Mark Lillis represented Manchester City & District Schools, and Lancashire County Youths before joining Manchester City as a junior in 1976, switching to Huddersfield as a professional in July 1978. Seven years later he returned to Maine Road for £150,000 and afterwards served with Derby (signed for £100,000, August 1986), Aston Villa (£130,000, September 1987), Scunthorpe (£40,000, September 1989) and Stockport (September 1991 to May 1992). He then held various coaching positions (including a spell at Huddersfield) before managing Halifax (June 1999 to September 2000).

An attacking player, strong and willing, Lillis was a key member in two Huddersfield sides that climbed out of the Fourth and Third Divisions in 1980 and 1983 respectively and he also helped Aston Villa gain promotion from the Second Division in 1988. He netted well over 100 goals in more than 400 competitive games at club level. Unfortunately he didn't have much success as manager at The Shay.

LIMITED COMPANY: Huddersfield Town FC was registered as a Limited Company on 15 August 1908.

LINCOLN CITY: Huddersfield's record against the Imps is:

Football League

Venue	P	W	D	L	F	A
Home	16	9	2	5	32	17
Away	16	4	7	5	18	23
Totals	32	13	9	10	50	40

FA Cup

	P	W	D	L	F	A
Home	2	1	1	0	5	3
Away	2	0	0	2	0	2
Totals	4	1	1	2	5	5

League Cup

	P	W	D	L	F	A
Away	1	0	0	1	1	2

Others

	P	W	D	L	F	A
Home	2	1	1	0	5	4
Away	1	1	0	0	2	1
Totals	3	2	1	0	7	5

The first League game between the two clubs played at Sincil Bank in December 1910, finished level at 2-2. The return game also ended in a draw, 1-1.

In March 1913 Huddersfield won 5-1 at home, having gone down 3-1 away earlier in the season. Huddersfield started their 1928 FA Cup run with a 3rd round home win over Lincoln by 4-2. The Terriers defeated the Imps over two legs to reach the 2004 Third Division play-off final.

LINLEY, Harry: Half-back: 51 apps. one goal Born: Sheffield circa 1890
Linley joined Huddersfield from Silverwood Colliery in August 1912 and was registered with the club for nine years before transferring to Halifax in July 1921. A strong player, his only goal for the Terriers saved his side a point in a 2-2 draw with Fulham in February 1915.

LIVERPOOL: Huddersfield's record against the Reds is:
Football League

Venue	P	W	D	L	F	A
Home	34	14	7	13	57	48
Away	34	12	10	12	56	65
Totals	68	26	17	25	113	113
FA Cup						
Home	2	1	0	1	2	3
Away	2	2	0	0	3	0
Totals	4	3	0	1	5	3
FA Charity Shield						
Neutral	1	1	0	0	1	0

The first of Huddersfield's 68 League games against Liverpool took place at Anfield in February 1921 and in front of 37,500 fans, the Reds won 4-1, completing the double a week later with a 2-1 victory at Leeds Road.

Liverpool doubled up again the following season and it wasn't until November 1923 that Huddersfield gained their first win over the Reds - 3-1 at Leeds Road.

In November 1934, Huddersfield slammed Liverpool 8-0 in a home League game (their second best win in the competition). Liverpudlian Albert Malam scored a hat-trick, including a penalty.

Two years later (December 1936) Liverpool lost 4-0 at Leeds Road.

In August 1970, back in the top flight for the first time in 14 years, Huddersfield lost their first away game 4-0 at Anfield.

Liverpool lost both League games by 3-2 to Huddersfield in 1949-50, the season they reached the FA Cup final (beaten by Arsenal).

In 1960-61, Liverpool did the double over the Terriers, winning 4-2 at Leeds Road and 3-1 at Anfield.

The Terriers beat Liverpool 2-1 (h) and 1-0 (a) when reaching the 1920 and 1938 FA Cup finals respectively.

A record crowd at The Alfred McAlpine Stadium of 23,678 saw Liverpool beat Huddersfield 2-0 in a 3rd round FA Cup-tie in December 1999.

A crowd of 10,000 saw Tom Wilson's goal give Huddersfield victory over Liverpool in the 1922 FA Charity Shield Game at Old Trafford.

the light at the end of the tunnel

LONG SERVICE: Roy Goodall spent 42 years with Huddersfield Town - 1921-37 as a player and 1937-53 as trainer and reserve team coach.

Terriers' winger Billy Smith was presented with the Football League's long service medal in 1934 to celebrate 21 years as a player at Leeds Road.

LONGEST SEASONS: The 1939-40 season - the first of WW2 - lasted for nine months and eight days, although there was an enforced break of seven weeks during September and October owing to the outbreak of war.

Two domestic seasons have lasted for exactly nine months, those of 1962-63 and 1978-79. The 1946-47 campaign ran for eight months and 27 days while that of 1944-45 covered one day less. The latest finish to a Football League season (not including play-offs) is 26 May 1947 while the earliest start to a Divisional campaign has been 9 August 1969.

LOW, Gordon Alexander: Left-half: 68 apps. 6 goals Born: Aberdeen, 11 July 1940

Gordon Low followed his Powis School chum Denis Law to Leeds Road in October 1955, turning professional two years later. He had one excellent season in the Terriers' line-up, scoring three goals in 37 games in 1958-59. He was transferred to Bristol City March 1961 for £3,000 and appeared in 234 competitive matches for the Robins (15 goals) before moving to Stockport for £3,000 in July 1968, finishing his career with a brief spell at Crewe.

LUCKETTI, Christopher James: Defender: 75 apps. 2 goals Born: Littleborough, 28 September 1971

Chris Lucketti made one League appearance for Rochdale before joining Stockport in August 1990. A year later he moved to Halifax for whom he made 86 appearances, following up with 277 for Bury between October 1993 and June 1999 when he transferred to Huddersfield for £750,000. He spent two seasons with the Terriers before another £750,000 deal took him across country to PNE. Lucketti was a Third Division championship winner with the Shakers in 1997.

LUKE, Charles E: Outside-right or left: 143 apps. 47 goals Born: Esh Winning, Durham, 16 March 1909. Died: Whitstable, October 1983.

A former Durham miner, Luke's playing career spanned 20 years: 1924-44. He served with Ushaw Moor, Portsmouth (trialist), Darlington, Bishop Auckland, Huddersfield (January 1931 to February 1936), Sheffield Wednesday, Blackburn and Chesterfield, retiring during WW2. A prolific marksman with Bishop Auckland for whom he netted 61 goals in 1930-31 when they reached the FA Amateur Cup final, he played his best League football at Leeds Road, his finest season coming in 1933-34 when he scored 18 goals in 45 outings. Short and sprightly, he preferred the right-wing position and his pace caused defenders plenty of problems.

LUTON TOWN: Huddersfield's record against the Hatters is:

Football League

Venue	P	W	D	L	F	A
Home	8	3	1	4	9	8
Away	8	3	1	4	13	17
Totals	16	6	2	8	22	25

FA Cup

Home	1	0	0	1	0	1
Away	1	0	0	1	0	2
Totals	2	0	0	2	0	3

Huddersfield 3 Luton 0 was the result of then first League game between the clubs played in October 1952 at Leeds Road. The Terriers won 2-0 at Kenilworth Road later in the season. After relegation at the end of the 1955-56 season Town were replaced in the top flight by the Hatters.
Huddersfield were defeated by the previous season's beaten finalists Luton 1-0 at Leeds Road in the 4th round of the FA Cup in January 1960.

LYTHGOE, Alfred Peter: Centre-forward: 79 apps. 46 goals Born: Nantwich, 16 March 1907. Died: 1967
Alf Lythgoe scored five goals in a League game for two different clubs in two different Divisions - for Huddersfield against Blackburn (First) in April 1935 and for Stockport against Southport (Third) in August 1934. In a varied career he also played for Crewe Alexandra, Whitchurch, Sandbach Ramblers, Congleton Town, Ashton National and Wolves, , moving to Leeds Road from Molineux in October 1934 and later returning to Edgeley Park (March 1936) before having a second spell with Ashton National. He scored 104 goals in 119 League games for Stockport.

M

MACAULAY, James: Inside-forward: 97 apps. 34 goals Born: Portarlington, Ireland, 1889. Died: October 1945
Macaulay, ex-Preston Rangers, Cliftonville Olympic and Glasgow Rangers, was signed by Huddersfield after assisting Brighton United in October 1910, and made his League debut almost immediately against Wolves at Molineux, starring in a 3-0 win. There had been technicalities surrounding his transfer to Leeds Road but once they had been sorted out, Macaulay gave the Terriers fine service.
An Irish Cup winner with Cliftonville in 1909, he represented the Irish League on five occasions and gained an Amateur cap before becoming Huddersfield's first joint full international when chosen to play against Wales at Belfast in January 1911, his team-mate Charlie Wilson making his debut for the opposition. Macaulay, who gained six caps in total, moved to PNE for £850 in April 1913, and later assisted Leicester Fosse (July 1919), Grimsby (June 1920), Lancaster Town and Morecambe, retiring in 1927, having scored 55 goals in 154 League games.

McEVOY, Donald William: Centre-half: 155 apps. 3 goals Born: Golcar, 3 December 1928
Don McEvoy came to the fore in Huddersfield's side of the early 1950s, forming a splendid half-back line with Billy McGarry and Len Quested. He was signed from Bradley United in November 1945 and established himself in senior side in 1950-51 and two

years later he helped the Terriers gain promotion to the First Division when along with six other players he was an ever-present. Replaced at centre-half by Ken Taylor following an injury, McEvoy moved to Sheffield Wednesday for £15,000 in December 1954. He made over 100 appearances for the Owls and skippered the side when the Hillsborough club won the Second Division title in 1956. After relegation in 1958 he moved to Lincoln and was later player-coach at Barrow, coach at Halifax before succeeding his former colleague Ron Staniforth as manager at Holker Street, guiding Barrow to promotion before enduring a difficult time as manager of Grimsby and Southport. He later ran the Crown Hotel in Brighouse and scouted for Halifax.

McFADYEN, William: Centre-forward: 54 apps. 19 goals Born: Overtown, Lanarkshire, 23 June 1904. Died: 1971.
A remarkably consistent goalscorer, strong, fast and skilful, McFadyen played for Wishaw YMCA and Motherwell before joining Huddersfield in exchange for Duncan Ogilvie in December 1936. He netted on his Terriers' debut against Liverpool (won 4-0) and ended his first season with eight goals to his credit, following up with 11 in 1937-38, eventually transferring to Clapton Orient in May 1939 having failed to appear that season. After WW2 he was manager of Dundee United: 1946-54. In 1931-32, McFadyen set a new Scottish record by scoring 52 goals when helping Motherwell win the First Division title. He was also a Cup finalist in 1931 and 1933 and played in the 1938 FA Cup final for Huddersfield. Capped twice against Wales and Austria in 1934, he also represented the Scottish League.

McGARRY, William Harry: Right-half: 381 apps. 26 goals Born: Stoke, 10 June 1927
Bill McGarry was an inside-right with Northwood Mission before turning professional with Port Vale in June 1945. At both of these clubs he played behind Ronnie Allen whom he succeeded as manager of Wolves. Switching to right-half, he spent six years with the Valiants, up to March 1951 when he transferred to Huddersfield for £10,000. Remaining at Leeds Road until March 1961, he left to become player-manager of Bournemouth (signed for £2,000).
A solid tackler McGarry passed the ball well and helped the Terriers win promotion to the First Division in 1953 when he was part of a terrific ever-present defence. Between 1954-56 he gained four England caps and represented his country's 'B' team.
From Dean Court he took charge of Watford (July 1963-October 1964) and after serving in the same capacity at Ipswich, he switched to Molineux in November 1968 for the first of his two spells as manager. This ended in May 1976 while his second lasted just 61 days, from September to November 1985.
In his first spell, McGarry took Wolves to the 1972 UEFA Cup final, winning the League Cup two years later. After losing his job in 1976, he went abroad to coach in Saudi

Arabia and the UAE, returning in August 1980 as manager of Newcastle. He next scouted for Brighton in 1980 and coached Power Dynamo (Zambia) and the Zambian national team before returning to Wolves. He was out of football for quite awhile before accepting a coaching position in Bophuthatswana in 1993-94.

McGILL, James Morrison: Inside-left: 186 apps. 8 goals Born: Bellshill, Glasgow, 2 November 1946
Jimmy McGill played for Possil Park YMCA (Glasgow) before joining Arsenal in June 1965. He made only 12 appearances for the Gunners who transferred him to Huddersfield for £10,000 in September 1967. Four years later he switched to Hull for £55,000 and later assisted Halifax (February 1976-May 1977) and also San Diego Jaws. He then assisted George Cross FC (Australia) but sustained an injury that virtually ended his career, although he did play a few games for Frickley Colliery before retiring early in 1978 to take up coaching, a job which took him to many different countries as well as clubs. An ever-present in Huddersfield's Second Division championship-winning side of 1969-70, McGill was a probing player who laid on chances a plenty for Frank Worthington and Colin Dobson. A panel beater by trade, he was employed by Huddersfield firm ICI in the 1980s.

McHALE, John Kevin: Forward: 375 apps. 68 goals Born: Darfield, Yorkshire, 1 October 1939
Kevin McHale made his League debut for Huddersfield as a 16 year-old against Leyton Orient in August 1956. Establishing himself in the side he became Denis Law's right-wing partner after turning professional six months after his baptism. He remained first choice for ten years, amassing over 370 senior appearances for the Terriers. He represented Barnsley and England Schools and joined the groundstaff at Leeds Road in May 1955. In January 1968, he moved to Crewe Alexandra (in exchange for John Archer). He helped the Railwaymen gain promotion from Division Four, but then went back down with the same team before joining Chester in October 1970, leaving in May 1972 to take over as player-manager of Hastings United, a position he held for just eight weeks. Later worked for David Brown's, Huddersfield.

McKENNA, John: Outside-right: 139 apps. 9 goals Born: Belfast, 6 June 1926. Died: Blackpool, October 1980.
Fleet-footed and tricky, McKenna took over from Albert Bateman on Huddersfield's right-wing in 1948 and was replaced in 1952 by Alistair Gunn. The son of an Irish boot-maker, and one-time milk tester for the Ministry of Food in his native Belfast, he joined the club for £6,500 from Linfield in August 1948, having played in two Victory internationals for Ireland in 1945-46. A regular for four seasons at Leeds Road, he won seven full caps for his country before leaving for Blackpool in July 1954 with Albert Hobson moving to Huddersfield in exchange. Recruited by Southport in July 1957, he retired two years later.

McLEAN, George: Inside-forward: 131 apps. 46 goals Born: Forfar, 24 August 1897. Died: 1970 McLean played initially for Forfar Athletic before netting 139 goals in 265 League and Cup games in nine seasons for Bradford Park Avenue, helping them win the Third Division (N) title in 1928. He joined Huddersfield in November 1930 and spent almost

five years at Leeds Road before returning to Forfar in September 1935. Having recovered from a broken right leg suffered in a collision with Sam Cowan of Manchester City, in March 1934. He retired in 1939.
* McLean's brother, David, scored 346 League goals during an eight-club playing career between 1907 and 1928. The pair played together at Bradford Park Avenue.

McNAB, Robert: Left-back: 76 apps. Born: Huddersfield, 20 July 1943
In his prime McNab was a fine full-back with good ball control and excellent vision. He played for Rawthorpe CSM and Mold Green Civic Youth Club before joining the Terriers as an amateur in June 1961, turning professional in April 1962. Transferred to Arsenal for £40,000 in October 1966, he became a star performer with the Gunners, helping them win the Fairs Cup in 1970, complete the League and FA Cup double twelve months later and finish runners-up in the FA Cup in 1972. He also collected two League Cup runners-up prizes in 1968 and 1969 while making 365 appearances. Capped four times by England as well as representing the Football League, he left Highbury for Wolves in July 1975 but spent only a season at Molineux before assisting San Antonio in Texas. In September 1977, McNab signed for Barnet but remained at Underhill for only a short time prior to becoming a licensee near the Spurs ground. Later a coach/manager of Vancouver Whitecaps and Tacoma Stars, he now resides in Canada with his wife and family, having opened the Vancouver Racquets Club which, once established, he sold in 1988. Now runs his own recruitment agency watching his daughter develop as a film actress.

MAKEL, Lee: Midfield: 79 apps.5 goals Born: Sunderland, 11 January 1973
Playmaker Makel played in 14 games for Newcastle and 13 for Blackburn before joining Huddersfield for £300,000 in October 1995. He did well with the Terriers prior to his £75,000 departure to Hearts in March 1998. After assisting Bradford City and Livingston, he joined newly promoted Plymouth in 2004.

MANAGERS: Here are details of the men who have managed Huddersfield down the years:

Fred Walker	August 1908-May 1910
Albert Pulan	September 1910-April 1912
Leslie Knighton	April 1912
Arthur Fairclough	April 1912-December 1919
Ambrose Langley	December 1919-March 1921
Herbert Chapman	March 1921-June 1925
Cecil Potter	July 1925-August 1926
John Chaplin	August 1926-May 1929
Clem Stephenson	May 1929-June 1942
Ted Magner	June 1942-September 1943
David Steele	September 1943-June 1947
George Stephenson	August 1947-March 1952
Andy Beattie	April 1952-November 1956
Bill Shankly	November 1956-November 1959
Eddie Boot	January 1960-September 1964
Tom Johnston	October 1964-May 1968

Ian Greaves	June 1968-June 1974
Bobby Collins	July 1974-December 1975
John Haselden	April 1977-September 1977
Tom Johnston	September 1977-August 1978
Mick Buxton	October 1978-December 1986
Steve Smith	January 1987-October 1987
Malcolm Macdonald	October 1987-May 1988
Eoin Hand	June 1988-March 1992
Ian Ross	March 1992-June 1993
Neil Warnock	July 1993-June 1995
Brian Horton	June 1995-October 1997
Peter Jackson	October 1997-June 1999
Steve Bruce	June 1999-October 2000
Lou Macari	October 2000-June 2002
Mick Wadsworth	July 2002-June 2003
Peter Jackson	June 2003 to date

Notes

- Bill Shankly was assistant to manager Andy Beattie at Leeds Road. Both men had played together for PNE against Huddersfield in the 1938 FA Cup final and they were also team-mates in international matches for Scotland against England, Northern Ireland and Wales in the late 1930s.
- Leslie Knighton was 'assistant' from 1914-19 and later managed Arsenal, Birmingham, Bournemouth, Chelsea and Shrewsbury Town.
- George Stephenson was assistant to his brother, Clem from whom he took over in 1952, thus keeping the manager's job in the family!

MANCHESTER CITY: Huddersfield's record against the Blues is:

Football League

Venue	P	W	D	L	F	A
Home	34	12	17	5	39	30
Away	34	10	8	16	42	65
Totals	68	22	25	21	81	95

FA Cup

Home	2	0	1	1	2	5
Away	2	0	1	1	0	4
Totals	4	0	2	2	2	9

League Cup

Home	1	0	1	0	0	0
Away	1	0	0	1	0	4
Totals	2	0	1	1	0	4

Huddersfield lost their first two League games against City - going down 1-0 at home and 3-2 away in early November 1920.

The Terriers' first win came on Boxing Day 1921 when two goals by Clem Stephenson (one a penalty) gave them a 2-0 home victory in front of 33,000 spectators.

George Brown scored a hat-trick when Huddersfield beat City 5-1 (a) in February 1926.

Only 5,482 fans saw Huddersfield beat FA Cup finalists City 1-0 at Leeds Road in May 1933.

By beating City 1-0 on the final day of the 1937-38 Huddersfield saved themselves from relegation but City slipped into the Second Division.

A crowd of 74,799 (the fourth biggest ever to watch Huddersfield play) saw City win a 4th round FA Cup-tie 4-0 at Maine Road in January 1926 - on their way to the final (beaten by Bolton).

Huddersfield suffered their heaviest League (and, indeed, Cup) defeat when crashing 10-1 to City at Maine Road in a Second Division game in November 1987. Three home players (Tony Adcock, Paul Simpson and David White scored hat-tricks).

City beat Huddersfield 4-0 in a 2nd round League Cup replay in 1968-69.

MANCHESTER UNITED: Huddersfield's record against the Reds is:

Football League

Venue	P	W	D	L	F	A
Home	21	8	6	7	39	22
Away	21	1	9	11	21	46
Totals	42	9	15	18	60	68

FA Cup

	P	W	D	L	F	A
Away	3	1	0	2	4	8

Huddersfield first met United in a League game in March 1921 and they celebrated the occasion with a 5-2 win at Leeds Road. A week later they lost the return fixture at Old Trafford by 2-0. In March 1926, Huddersfield beat United 5-0 in a home League game and in September 1930 they went a goal better winning 6-0 at Old Trafford with Gerry Kelly and Alex Jackson both scoring hat-tricks. A crowd of 59,772 saw a cracking 4-4 draw between United and Huddersfield at Old Trafford in November 1947. Huddersfield, in fact, conceded 14 goals in successive League visits to Old Trafford. Besides that drawn game (above) they lost 4-1 in September 1948 and 6-1 in November 1949.

In April 1961, on the last day of the season, the Terriers went down 6-1 to the League runners-up. Ex-Huddersfield starlet Denis Law scored a hat-trick in front of 47,703 spectators when United beat the Terriers 5-0 in a 3rd round FA Cup-tie at Old Trafford in January 1963. The Reds went on to win the final.

MANGNALL, David: Centre-forward: 90 apps. 73 goals Born: Wigan, 21 September 1907. Died: Penzance, April 1962. (right).

In a career spanning some 25 years (first as a player, then as a manager), Mangnall set foot on virtually every ground in the country. He scored 52 goals for Maltby New Church and 35 for Maltby Colliery in successive seasons, before having trials with both Rotherham and Huddersfield. He signed amateur forms for Doncaster in 1926 before turning professional with Leeds United in November 1927. He netted 10 times in a reserve game at Elland Road prior to his £3,000 transfer to Huddersfield in December 1929, signed to replace George Brown. In 1931-32, he rattled in 42 goals for the Terriers but started the next season in the second team! In February 1934, Mangnall moved to struggling Birmingham, moving on to West Ham and then Millwall. As captain he top-scored for the Lions when they won the Third Division (S) title in 1938, having played in the previous season's FA Cup semi-final. He signed for QPR in May 1939, taking over as manager at Loftus Road in 1944. He guided Rangers to the Third Division (S) title in 1948 before leaving in 1952.

MANN, Frank Drury: Centre-forward: 227 apps. 75 goals Born: Newark, 6 March 1891. Died: Nottingham, February 1959.

A champion marksman for the Terriers before, during and after WW1, Frank Mann served the club for 11 years during which time he averaged a goal every three games. He played for Newark Castle United, Newark Castle Rovers, Newark Town, Leeds City, Lincoln and Aston Villa before moving to Leeds Road in July 1912. He top-scored in his first two seasons and despite losing four years due to the conflict in Europe, his goal-touch never waned and he continued to bulge the nets when League football resumed in 1919. He played his part in helping the Terriers reach the 1920 and 1922 FA Cup finals, collecting a winner's medal in the latter and finish runners-up to gain promotion from the Second Division, also in 1920. He joined Manchester United for £1,750 in March 1923 and after the Reds had also gained promotion to the top flight in 1925, he moved on to Mossley (1930) and later Meltham Mills (Huddersfield), retiring in 1932. He scored five goals in almost 200 appearances in seven years at Old Trafford.

MANSFIELD TOWN: Huddersfield's record against the Stags is:

Football League

Venue	P	W	D	L	F	A
Home	6	3	2	1	9	7
Away	6	3	2	1	9	6
Totals	12	6	4	2	18	13
FA Cup						
Home	1	0	1	0	0	0
Away	2	0	0	2	1	6
Totals	3	0	1	2	1	6
League Cup						
Home	2	2	0	0	8	3
Away	2	1	1	0	3	2
Totals	4	3	1	0	11	5
Other						
Neutral	1	0	0*	0	0	0

- Huddersfield lost 1-0 (a) and won 2-0 (h) in their first two League games against Mansfield in 1988-89 (Division Three).
- The Stags knocked Huddersfield out of the FA Cup in 1976-77 and again in 2001-02, winning a 2nd round tie 4-0 at Field Mill in the latter season.
- Mark Lillis netted twice in the Terriers 1st round second leg 5-2 League Cup home win over Mansfield in September 1983 (for a 7-2 aggregate victory). The Stags were beaten in the same competition in 1998-99.

- Huddersfield beat the Stags on penalties (after a 0-0 draw) in the 2004 Third Division play-off final at the Millennium Stadium.

MARGETSON, Martyn Walter: Goalkeeper: 59 apps. Born: Neath, 8 September 1971
Martyn Margetson signed professional forms with Manchester City in 1990 and made only 59 first-team appearances during the next ten years, also having a loan spell with Bristol Rovers before transferring to Southend in August 1998. Twelve months later he moved to Huddersfield (as cover for Nico Vaesen) and spent three seasons with the Terriers before moving to Cardiff in August 2002. A fine shot-stopper he has represented Wales at Schoolboy, Youth, 'B' and Under-21 levels, gaining seven caps in the latter category.

MARSDEN, Christopher: Midfield: 155 apps. 9 goals Born: Sheffield, 3 January 1969
Marsden reached the personal milestone of 500 senior appearances in 2004. Starting his professional career with Sheffield United in January 1988, he then served Huddersfield (July 1988 to January 1994), Coventry City (on loan), Wolves, Notts County, Stockport, Birmingham and Southampton before joining Sheffield Wednesday in May 2004. An FA Cup finalist with Saints in 2003, he prefers to play on the left of the midfield tangent, is totally committed, a real workhorse in the engine-room.

MARTIN, Lee Brendon: Goalkeeper: 63 apps. Born: Huddersfield, 9 September 1968
England Schoolboy international Lee Martin signed professional forms for Huddersfield in July 1987 after two years as an apprentice. He stayed at Leeds Road until July 1992 when he moved to Blackpool (117 appearances), later assisting Rochdale, Halifax and Macclesfield Town where, after retiring in June 2003, he was also engaged as a goalkeeping coach

MASKELL, Craig Dell: Striker: 108 apps. 54 goals Born: Aldershot, 10 April 1968
Scorer of a goal every two games for Huddersfield whom he served from May 1988 until August 1990 when he joined Reading for £250,000, Craig Maskell spent four years with Southampton before his £20,000 switch to Leeds Road. After two seasons with the Royals he moved to Swindon, returning to The Dell in February 1994, again for £250,000 and then serving with Bristol City (loan), Brighton, Dunfermline Athletic (trial), Happy Valley (Hong Kong) and Leyton Orient. A consistent marksmen during the late 1980s/early 90s, he knocked home the 125th goal of his career with Brighton in 1996 when he was the club's top-scorer

MASSIE, Leslie: Inside-forward: 363 apps. 108 goals Born: Aberdeen, 20 July 1935
Massie was a junior with Powis Youth club and Bank o' Dee, before joining Huddersfield in August 1953 but had to wait three years before manager Bill Shankly handed him his League debut against Fulham (September 1956). He established himself in the side towards the end of that season and thereafter was a regular in the Terriers' attack for nine seasons, topping the scoring charts on four occasions. In 1965-66 he notched hat-tricks in home and away games against Middlesbrough and is now one of only four players to have claimed a century of goals for the club. Massie moved to Darlington for £2,500 in October 1966 and later assisted Halifax, Bradford Park Avenue and Workington. He helped the Shaymen gain promotion for the first time in the club's

history and his League career realised 160 goals in 520 games. In the 1990s Massie went into the haulage business and later worked for Haslets, Huddersfield.

MATTIS, Dwayne Antony: Midfield: 80 apps. 3 goals Born: Huddersfield, 31 July 1981
A Republic of Ireland international at Youth and Under-21 levels, Dwayne Mattis joined the Terriers as a junior at the age of 16, turned professional in July 1999 but after 80 first-team outings was released by the club in March 2003.

MAY, Andrew Michael Peter: Midfield: 137 apps. 6 goals Born: Bury, 26 February 1964
An England Under-21 international, Andy May made 150 League appearances for Manchester City and played at Wembley in the Full Member's Cup final v. Chelsea before joining Huddersfield for £36,000 in July 1986. He spent three seasons at Leeds Road, producing some excellent performances. In March 1988 he was loaned out to Bolton and helped the Whites gain promotion from Division Four. He later assisted Bristol City (signed for £90,000 in August 1990) and Millwall

MEAGAN, Michael Kevin: Left-back: 132 apps. one goal Born: Dublin, 29 May 1934
Mick Meagan played for Rathfarnham & Johnville Juniors before joining Everton, turning professional in September 1952. He appeared in over 170 games for the Merseysiders, up to July 1964 when he moved to Huddersfield in a player-exchange deal involving Ray Wilson. In July 1968 he switched to Halifax and afterwards coached at Drogheda, Shamrock Rovers and Bray before working in a Dublin hospital.
An Eire Schoolboy international inside-forward, Meagan developed into a fine wing-half before making his mark as a full-back, gaining a League championship medal in 1963. He did well at Leeds Road and played for the Terriers in the 1968 League Cup semi-final against Arsenal. Capped 17 times by the Republic of Ireland (12 with the Terriers) he also represented his country in one 'B' international and captained Halifax when they gained promotion in 1969.
MEDAL WINNER: Joe Hulme appeared in five FA Cup finals in eleven years...with Arsenal in 1927, 1930, 1932 and 1936 and with Huddersfield in 1938. He was a winner in 1930 and 1936 and a runner-up in the other three finals. He also won three League championship medals and the FA Charity Shield twice with the Gunners – securing 10 club medals in all.

MENDES, Albert Junior Hillyard Andrew: Striker: 15 apps
Born: Balham, 15 September 1976 Career: Chelsea (trainee, April 1993, professional July 1995), St Mirren (free transfer, April 1996), Carlisle United (loan, November-December 1998), Dunfermline Athletic (£20,000, July 2000), St Mirren (free, June 2002), Mansfield Town (free, January 203), Huddersfield Town (free, May 2004) A right-sided forward, keen and aggressive, Junior Mendes had already scored 43 goals in more than 240 senior appearances (including 28 in 154 outings for St Mirren) before joining the Terriers in readiness for the 2004-05 season.

the light at the end of the tunnel

MERCER, William Henry: Goalkeeper: 79 apps. Born: Prescot, June 1892. Died: 5 June 1956

An amateur with Prescot Athletic, Billy Mercer was an exceptionally able goalkeeper who joined Hull in August 1914. He made almost 200 appearances for the Tigers and guested for Stockport in 1918-19 when serving with the Royal Engineers. He moved to Huddersfield in July 1924 and was a League championship winner in 1925 and an FA Cup finalist in 1928 before switching to Blackpool in May 1928, retiring twelve months later. Mercer also played cricket (for Hull CC), billiards and tennis.

METCALFE, Victor: Outside-left: 459 apps. 90 goals Born: Barrow, 3 February 1922. Died: Huddersfield, April 2003

Metcalfe served Huddersfield supremely well for 18 years during which time he scored 103 goals in 516 first-team appearances, 87 coming in 434 Football League games. A skilful, tricky and positive winger and marvellous crosser of the ball (which pleased Jim Glazzard immensely) Educated in the West Riding, he joined Huddersfield from Ravensthorpe Albion in June 1940, turning professional in December 1945, having gained some experience by playing in wartime football. Capped twice by England v. Argentina and Portugal in 1951, he twice represented the Football League and helped the Terriers regain their First Division status in 1953, being one of eight ever-presents in a marvellous side. After his move to Hull in June 1958 he played in six games as the Tigers clinched promotion from Division Three. Retiring in February 1960, Metcalfe opened an electrical shop and returned to Leeds Road as coach in 1961. Four years later he took over as coach/scout at Halifax and was manager at The Shay from June 1966 to November 1967, later scouting for Bradford City.

• Metcalfe's father was a Rugby League full-back with Barrow and Skipton.

MIDDLESBROUGH: Huddersfield's record against the 'Boro is:

Football League

Venue	P	W	D	L	F	A
Home	41	22	9	10	63	38
Away	41	8	8	25	43	86
Totals	82	30	17	35	106	124
FA Cup						
Home	1	1	0	0	4	0
League Cup						
Away	1	0	0	1	1	5

The first two League games between the two clubs both ended in Middlesbrough wins - 2-0 at Ayresome Park and 1-0 at Leeds Road in season 1920-21.

In March 1922, Middlesbrough won 5-1 at home before Huddersfield's gained their first win, 2-1 in the May. In February 1937, Huddersfield lost 5-0 at 'Boro; in September 1950 they succumbed to an 8-0 defeat and crashed 7-2 on the same ground in April 1957. Huddersfield gained revenge with a 5-0 win at Ayresome Park in August 1962 and a double in 1965-66, winning 6-0 at home when Allan Gilliver and Les Massie both hit hat-tricks, and 3-1 away. A crowd of 55,200 saw the Wembley bound Terriers beat Middlesbrough 4-0 in a home 5th round FA Cup-tie in February 1928.

Huddersfield were humbled 5-1 by 'Boro in a 3rd round League Cup-tie at The Riverside Stadium in 1996-97.

MIDLAND LEAGUE: Huddersfield played in the Midland League for one season, 1909-10, finishing 5th with this record:

Venue	P	W	D	L	F	A	Pts
Home	21	15	3	3	53	25	33
Away	21	7	3	11	39	51	24
Totals	42	22	6	14	92	76	57

They won their first game on 2 September 1909, beating Bradford City 3-2 at home with goals from Jack Foster, Jim Roberts (penalty) and Joe Jee.

Leeds City inflicted the first defeat on the Terriers, winning 2-0 at home on 13 September in front of 3,000 spectators.

Huddersfield's biggest win of the 22 recorded was 5-0 away to Worksop Town on New Year's day and their heaviest defeat was 6-2 at Hull on 11 December.

Jee (38), Foster (37), Bill Hooton (37), Bill McCreadie (32), David Ewing (29), goalkeeper Tom Felstead (29), Bill Smith (22), Roberts (21) and A Rowley (20) made the most appearances while Will Smith (15 goals) finished up as leading scorer.

Hooton and Fred Walker were the only players to appear in the North-Eastern League the previous season.

MILLS, Henry: Goalkeeper: 160 apps. Born: Bishop Auckland, 23 July 1922. Died: 1990
Signed from Blyth Spartans to replace the injured Bob Hesford in March 1948, Mills remained at Leeds Road until December 1955 when he moved to Halifax.

Well built and agile and had to battle for his first team place with Jack Wheeler. One game he was brilliant, the next average - like when he conceded eight goals at Middlesbrough in September 1950 and kept a blank sheet a week later.

He did not play during the Terriers' promotion winning season of 1952-53 and after making 49 appearances in three campaigns he left for pastures new. He retired in May 1957 due to his wife's illness.

MILLWALL: Huddersfield's record against the Lions is:

Football League

Venue	P	W	D	L	F	A
Home	12	8	1	3	22	10
Away	12	2	2	8	11	25
Totals	24	10	3	11	33	35

FA Cup

Venue	P	W	D	L	F	A
Home	3	2	0	1	6	4
Away	2	0	1	1	1	3
Totals	5	2	1	2	7	7

Huddersfield completed the double over Millwall when the teams first met in season 1966-67.67, winning 2-0 at home and 3-1 away (Division Two).

Later, the Terriers beat the Lions at home by 5-1 in February 1983 and 4-3 in August 1985 but then lost at The Den by 4-0 in December 1986, 3-0 in May 1987 and 4-1 in March 1988.

On their way to the 1922 FA Cup final, Huddersfield beat Millwall 3-0 at home in the 4th round. Eighty years later the Lions won a 3rd round tie 4-0 at Leeds Road.

MITCHELL, Graham Lee: Defender: 310 apps. 5 goals Born: Shipley, 16 February 1968 Graham Mitchell joined Huddersfield as an associate schoolboy and after his apprenticeship, signing as a non-contract professional in March 1986. He became full-time soon afterwards and developed into an outstanding defender who also produced some sterling displays in midfield as well as up front (in an emergency). After a loan spell with Bournemouth, he moved to Bradford City in December 1994 in a deal that took Lee Sinnott to the Alfred McAlpine Stadium. In October 1996 he joined Raith Rovers, switched to Cardiff in August 1998 and was recruited by Halifax for £45,000 in July 1999, later taking over as player-coach at The Shay. He quit top-class League football in June 2002 with 616 appearances to his credit.

MORRISON, Andrew Charles: Defender: 55 apps. 2 goals Born: Inverness, 30 July 1970 Andy Morrison's professional career spanned 14 years. He served with seven different clubs - Plymouth, Blackburn, Blackpool (two spells), Huddersfield (July 1996 to October 1998), Manchester City , Crystal Palace and Sheffield United before his retirement with a knee injury in March 2002. A six-footer, weighing 14 stone, he was signed by the Terriers for £500,000 and sold for £250,000. He made a total of 310 senior appearances, having his best spell with Plymouth (133 outings).

MOSES, Adrian Paul: Defender: 78 apps. 2 goals Born: Doncaster, 4 May 1975 Ade Moses was capped twice by England at Under-21 level with Barnsley for whom he appeared in 182 first-class matches. He moved from Oakwell to Huddersfield for £225,000 in December 2000 and proved a totally reliable defender able to occupy several positions until his transfer to Crewe Alexandra in July 2003.

MOUNTFORD, Reginald Charles: Full-back: 255 apps. 7 goals Born: Darlington, May 1908. Deceased.
A former miner, Reg Mountford was an amateur with Darlington before joining Huddersfield as a professional in May 1929. He gained a regular place in the side in 1933 and went on to serve the club admirably until the outbreak of WW2, playing in the 1938 FA Cup final. He guested for Brentford, Chelsea, Crystal Palace, Norwich, Rochdale and Southampton during the hostilities when serving as an ARP control officer. In May 1946 he was appointed coach of Combinag (Copenhagen) and later coached the Danish national team that reached the semi-finals of the 1948 Olympic Games in London.

MUTCH, Alexander: Goalkeeper: 252 apps. Born: Inveraray, 9 December 1884. Died: Newcastle, September 1967.

After four years and 82 games for Aberdeen, 'Cody' or 'Sandy' Mutch joined Huddersfield in May 1910. He went straight into the team and with the odd exception, was a permanent fixture at the back of the Terriers' defence for some considerable time. He was one of the most capable 'keepers north of the border and he continued to produce the goods at Leeds Road, helping the Terriers gain promotion to the First Division and reach the FA Cup final in 1920. Two years later he collected a Cup winner's medal in his 249th game for the club. In August 1922, he was sold to Newcastle for £850 and was all set to play in the 1924 FA Cup final but an injury ruled him out at the last minute. After his retirement Mutch became groundsman at St James' Park, retaining that job until 1958.

* Mutch's son, Alex junior, was Newcastle's physiotherapist during the mid-1980s.

N

NAMES: The Huddersfield Town player with the longest name (including Christian names) has been Alexander Hector McMilland MacLeod (30 letters). He was with the club in 1974.

George Edward Holland Richardson (29 letters), Robert Frederick George Perrett (28), Michael Francis Martin Kennedy (27), Christopher Martin Nigel Jones (27), Ronald Frederick John Percival (27, Joseph Harold Anthony Hulme (24), Albert William Thomas Smith (24), James Sydney Dean Rawlings (23), John Graham Anthony Turner (23), Thomas Walter James Wilcox (23), and John Dennis Parkin Tanner (22) are some of the club's other long-named players.

The shortest named players include Denis Law, Henry Raw and Peter Goy (all eight letters)

NEUTRAL GROUNDS: Huddersfield's record of first-class matches, played on a neutral ground:

Season	Competition	Opponents	Result	Venue
1919-20	FAC s/final	Bristol City	2-1	Stamford Bridge
1919-20	FAC Final	Aston Villa	0-1	Stamford Bridge
1921-22	FAC s/final	Notts County	3-1	Turf Moor
1921-22	FAC final	Preston NE	1-0	Stamford Bridge
1921-22	Charity Shield	Liverpool	1-0	Old Trafford
1927-28	FAC s/final	Sheffield Utd	2-2	Old Trafford

1927-28	FAC s/final rep	Sheffield Utd	0-0	Goodison Park
1927-28	FAC s/final 2r	Sheffield Utd	1-0	Maine Road
1927-28	FAC final	Blackburn R	1-3	Wembley
1928-29	FAC s/final	Bolton Wds	1-3	Anfield
1929-30	FAC s/final	Sheffield Wed	2-1	Old Trafford
1929-30	FAC final	Arsenal	0-2	Wembley
1937-38	FAC s/final	Sunderland	3-1	Ewood Park
1937-38	FAC final	Preston NE	0-1	Wembley
1938-39	FAC s/final	Portsmouth	1-2	Highbury
1956-57	FAC 3rd rd	Sheffield Utd	2-1	Maine Road
1963-64	FLC 2nd rd	Plymouth A	2-1	Villa Park
1970-71	FAC 4th rd	Stoke	0-1	Old Trafford
1993-94	AGT final	Swansea	1-1*	Wembley
1994-95	Play-off final	Bristol Rovers	2-1	Wembley
2003-04	Play-off final	Mansfield T	0-0**	Millennium Stadium

* Huddersfield lost 3-1 on penalties
** Terriers won on penalties

Full record

P	W	D	L	F	A
21	11	3	7	25	23

NEWCASTLE UNITED: Huddersfield's record against the Magpies is:

Football League

Venue	P	W	D	L	F	A
Home	28	11	6	11	40	39
Away	28	8	8	12	39	52
Totals	56	19	14	23	79	91

FA Cup

	P	W	D	L	F	A
Home	1	0	1	0	1	1
Away	2	1	0	1	1	2
Totals	3	1	1	1	2	3

Newcastle completed the double over Huddersfield when the teams first met in League combat in 1920-21. The Magpies won 1-0 at home and 3-1 away during February. Huddersfield's first win came in the fourth game - 2-1 before 50,000 fans in the North-East (September 1921).

Huddersfield won both League games v. Newcastle in 1932-33 with a 4-0 scoreline. Newcastle won their home League game by 6-0 in September 1950 and completed the double in 1951-52 with a 4-2 win at Leeds Road and a 6-2 victory at St James' Park. Six months after their 1955 FA Cup final triumph, the Magpies slammed Huddersfield 6-2 at Leeds Road in a First Division encounter.

Some years later, the Terriers also went down 5-2 on Tyneside (December 1983).

Huddersfield won a 4th round FA Cup-tie 1-0 in front of 46,462 spectators at Newcastle in January 1920, to make progress towards the final showdown with Aston Villa.

And on their way winning the trophy in 1955, Newcastle beat the Terriers 2-0 after-extra-time at St James' Park in a 6th round replay. A total of 107,340 spectators attended those two games: 54,960 at Leeds Road and 52,380 at Newcastle.

NEWPORT COUNTY: Huddersfield's record against County is:
Football League

Venue	P	W	D	L	F	A
Home	8	7	0	1	16	4
Away	8	1	2	5	9	14
Totals	16	8	2	6	25	18
FA Cup						
Home	1	0	0	1	1	3
Away	1	0	1	0	3	3
Totals	2	0	1	1	4	6

In October 1975, Huddersfield won the first League game with Newport 2-1 at Leeds Road. Later that season they doubled up with a 2-1 victory at Somerton Park. In January 1981 the Terriers defeated County 4-1 at home.

Newport's only League win on Huddersfield soil was 1-0 in February 1979.

After a thrilling 3-3 draw after extra-time in front of a full-house of 22,500 at Newport in the 4th round of the FA Cup in January 1949, a crowd of 34,183 attended the replay to see the underdogs from South Wales beat First Division Huddersfield 3-1 at Leeds Road.

NICHOLSON, James Joseph: Wing-half/midfield: 310 apps. 28 goals Born: Belfast, 27 February 1943

Jimmy Nicholson attended Methody College (Belfast), and played for Boyland FC before joining the Old Trafford groundstaff in June 1958, turning professional in February 1960. After 68 appearances for the Reds he moved to Huddersfield for £8,000 in December 1964 and spent the next nine years at Leeds Road before going on to assist Bury (late 1973), Mossley and Stalybridge Celtic, retiring in 1979 and later managing a Sports Centre in Sale.

Enjoying rugby and soccer as a youngster, he preferred the round ball game and developed into a fine player who was rewarded with caps at Schoolboy, Youth, Under-23 and senior levels by Northern Ireland by the time he was 18. He went on to play in 41 full internationals as well as adding a 'B' cap to his collection and is the Terriers' most capped player with 31. He was 17 when he made his League debut in 1960 with his senior international debut following a year later. Compared at times with the great Duncan Edwards, he switched to Huddersfield following the arrival of Pat Crerand and amassed over 300 senior appearances for the Terriers, skippering the side in 1969-70 when the Second Division Championship was won. During his career Nicholson made over 500 senior appearances, 422 in the Football League.

NICKNAMES: The Terriers is now Huddersfield's official club nickname. Prior to 1970 the team's nickname was 'Town'.

Over the years several players acquired nicknames, among them Edward 'Ned' Barkas,: George 'Bomber' Brown, Edwin 'Terry' 'TC' Curran, Fred 'Tiny' Fayers, Neil 'Sandy' Kennon, Dick 'Glass of Whiskey' Krzywicki, Alex 'Cody' & 'Sandy' Mutch, Ifem 'Iffy' Onuora, Derek 'Squeak' Parkin, George 'Smiler' Shaw, Frank 'Worthy' Worthington.

NIGHTINGALE, Albert: Inside-forward: 127 apps. 21 goals Born: Thryburgh near Rotherham, 10 November 1923

Nightingale joined Sheffield United from Thurcroft in June 1941. After 225 appearances for the Blades he moved to Huddersfield for £12,000 in March 1948, switched to Blackburn in October 1951) and served with Leeds United from October 1952 until his retirement through injury in May 1957. He later worked as a greengrocer.

A busy, hard-working inside-forward with splendid close control, allied to craft and skill, Nightingale was also subtle and aggressive, being able to wriggle his way past defenders in the tightest of situations before firing in a powerful shot or clipping a short, decisive pass to a colleague. A 'barter deal' took him to Leeds Road and after his year with Blackburn he scored 48 goals in 130 for Leeds where he teamed up with John Charles, having twice slipped through Leeds' grasp earlier in his career.

NORTH-EASTERN LEAGUE: Huddersfield played in this competition for one season, 1908-09, when they finished 16th out of 18 with this record:

Venue	P	W	D	L	F	A	Pts
Home	17	6	3	8	27	33	15
Away	17	4	1	12	20	45	9
Totals	34	10	4	20	47	78	24

Their first game ended in a 2-0 defeat away to South Shields Adelaide on 5 September 1908 and their first win followed a week later, 2-0 at Workington.

Huddersfield's biggest win was 5-0 away to Sunderland RR on 28 December and their heaviest defeat was 6-1 away to Bradford Park Avenue on Christmas Day.

Some 40 players were used during the course of the season, the mainstays being goalkeeper W J Crinson (26 apps), full-backs Tom Jones (21) and Bob Trenham (28), wing-half Bill Hooton (30), inside-forward J Wallace (38 and seemingly the top-scorer with eight goals), outside-left Didymus (29) and player-manager and centre-half Fred Walker (21).

NORTHAMPTON TOWN: Huddersfield's record against the Cobblers is:

Football League

Venue	P	W	D	L	F	A
Home	12	6	2	4	19	9
Away	12	5	2	5	17	16
Totals	24	11	4	9	36	25

FA Cup

Home	1	0	0	1	0	2

League Cup

Away	1	1	0	0	1	0

Huddersfield lost their first home and away League games with the Cobblers by 1-0 in season 1963-64. The Terriers' first win came in January 1965, clinching a 2-0 home victory.

The Cobblers from the Third Division (S) knocked First Division Huddersfield out of the FA Cup in the 4th round in January 1934.

Huddersfield's best win over the Cobblers is 5-0, home, in November 1979.

Bob Newton's goal beat the Cobblers in the 2nd round of the League Cup in 1976-77.

NORWICH CITY: Huddersfield's record against the Canaries is:
Football League

Venue	P	W	D	L	F	A
Home	17	5	10	2	18	13
Away	17	5	5	7	17	29
Totals	34	10	15	9	35	42

FA Cup

	P	W	D	L	F	A
Home	1	0	0	1	2	4
Away	1	0	1	0	1	1
Totals	2	0	1	1	3	5

League Cup

	P	W	D	L	F	A
Away	1	1	0	0	1	0

Huddersfield lost 2-0 at Norwich in the first League meeting between the clubs in October 1960. Huddersfield's first win followed in February 1962 when a brace by Len White gave them a 2-1 scoreline at Carrow Road. After holding the Canaries to a 1-1 draw at Carrow Road, Huddersfield were defeated 4-2 in a 3rd round FA cup replay in January 1987.

NOTTINGHAM FOREST: Huddersfield's record against Forest is:
Football League

Venue	P	W	D	L	F	A
Home	16	7	5	4	23	14
Away	16	8	4	4	21	18
Totals	32	15	9	8	44	32

FA Cup

	P	W	D	L	F	A
Home	1	0	1	0	0	0
Away	1	1	0	0	3	0
Totals	2	1	1	0	3	0

League Cup

	P	W	D	L	F	A
Home	2	0	2	0	3	3
Away	2	0	1	1	1	3
Totals	4	0	3	1	4	6

Forest won the first two League games between the clubs in the 1911-12 season - 2-1 at Leeds Road and 3-1 at The City Ground. Huddersfield beat Forest 3-0 in a 3rd round replay in January 1939. Forest beat Huddersfield on the away goal rule (after a 4-4 aggregate score) in a 2nd round League Cup-tie in 1989-90

NOTTS COUNTY: Huddersfield's record against the Magpies is:
Football League

Venue	P	W	D	L	F	A
Home	12	7	3	2	21	8
Away	12	2	2	8	11	21
Totals	24	9	5	10	32	29

FA Cup

	P	W	D	L	F	A
Home	2	1	0	1	2	2
Neutral	1	1	0	0	3	1
Totals	3	2	0	1	5	3

League Cup

Home	1	1	0	0	2	1
Away	1	0	1	0	2	2
Totals	2	1	1	0	4	3

Huddersfield lost their first League game against County by 3-0 at Meadow Lane in December 1913 but won their first home game 2-1 in April 1914.

Town completed the double over the Magpies at Christmas 1956, winning. 2-1 away and 3-0 at Leeds Road.

Huddersfield beat County 3-1 in the semi-final of the FA Cup at Turf Moor in March 1922 and Jack Beattie scored his only goal for the club in a 4th round win over County in January 1938.

County were knocked out of the League Cup in 1999-2000.

O

O'GRADY, Michael: Forward: 174 apps. 28 goals Born: Leeds, 11 October 1942

O'Grady was a smart utility forward, able to occupy both flanks as well as an inside berth, he joined Huddersfield on leaving school and turned professional in October 1959. He did well at Leeds Road, scoring twice on his England debut against Northern Ireland in October 1962 while gaining three Under-23 caps. In October 1965 he was transferred to Leeds for £30,000 and over the next four years became part of Don Revie's brilliant footballing-machine. He hit 13 goals in 101 appearances, helping United reach successive Fairs Cup finals, gaining a winner's medal in the second in 1968, and clinch the League title in 1969. He also added a second England cap to his collection, and represented the Football League on three occasions. In September 1969, O'Grady joined Wolves for £80,000. He had a loan spell with Birmingham (February 1972), being the Blues' first loan player to make a League appearance before retiring through injury in May 1984 after serving Rotherham. Became licensee of the Royal Oak pub, Aberford, Wetherby and still plays for the Leeds United All Stars (ex-players).

OLDFIELD, John Stephen: Goalkeeper: 171 apps. Born: Lindrick, Notts, 19 August 1943

John Oldfield joined Huddersfield as a 16 year-old and turned professional in August 1961. He made over 170 appearances for the Terriers before transferring to Wolves in December 1969. A competent 'keeper with good reflexes, he had a loan spell with Crewe Alexandra before signing for Bradford City in December 1971. He remained at Valley Parade until May 1973 and later managed amateur side Yeadon Celtic: 1974-76.

OLDHAM ATHLETIC: Huddersfield's record against the Latics is:
Football League

Venue	P	W	D	L	F	A
Home	13	8	4	1	24	13
Away	13	4	4	5	17	25
Totals	26	12	8	6	41	38
FA Cup						
Home	1	1	0	0	6	0
Away	1	0	1	0	1	1
Totals	2	1	1	0	7	1
League Cup						
Home	1	0	0	1	0	2
Away	1	0	0	1	0	1
Totals	2	0	0	2	0	3

Huddersfield's first two League games against the Latics were staged at the end of the 1920-21 season and both resulted in wins for the Terriers - 3-1 at home and 2-1 at Boundary Park. In April 1974, already promoted Oldham whipped the Terriers 6-0 in a Third Division game at Boundary Park.

A nine-goal thriller in September 1986, finished in a 5-4 victory for Town. After a hard fought draw at Boundary Park, Huddersfield went to town and whipped Oldham 6-0 in a 3rd round FA Cup replay in January 1932, Dave Mangnall scoring four times.

ONUORA, Ifem: Striker: 217 apps. 41 goals Born: Glasgow, 28 July 1967
'Iffy' Onuora joined Huddersfield in July 1989 from Bradford University. Over the next five years he caused plenty of problems for defenders with his pace and commitment and scored his fair share of goals. In July 1994 he was transferred to Mansfield for £30,000 and later assisted Gillingham, Swindon, Gillingham (again) and Sheffield United before joining Walsall in May 2004 - having reached the personal milestone of 500 senior appearances while taking his goal haul past the 130 mark. Onuora holds the record for most substitute appearances for the Terriers - 65.

O'REGAN, Kieran Michael: Midfield: 253 apps. 3 goals Born: Cork, 9 November 1963
Kieran O'Regan played for Tramore Athletic, Brighton and Swindon before joining Huddersfield in August 1988. Over the next five years he gave some excellent performances in the engine-room at Leeds Road and made over 250 appearances before transferring to WBA for £25,000, in July 1993. He later assisted Halifax (as player and then player-manager July 1998 to April 1999) and Altrincham, returning to Huddersfield as youth team coach while also working as a soccer summariser on Radio Leeds. Able to also fill in at right-back, O'Regan was honoured by the Republic of Ireland at Youth team level before going on to gain four full caps.

OTHER COMPETITIONS: Over the years Huddersfield have played in several local hospital, charity and Cup and League competitions, as well as various fund games.
- In 1909 they won their first trophy, beating Lindley Temperance 5-0 at Leeds Road to lift the Huddersfield & District League Cup.
- The following year the Bradford & District Hospital Cup was claimed after a 1-0 win over Goole Town at Castleford.

- And the Huddersfield Infirmary & Victoria Nurses' Charity Cup was captured in 1924 when the Terriers beat Heart of Midlothian 2-1 at Leeds Road in front of more than 10,000 spectators.
- Roy Shiner scored both goals when Huddersfield beat Sheffield Wednesday to win the Westmorland Invitation Trophy final in April 1953
- The Shipp Cup was another trophy won by the Terriers who, in July/August 1977 beat both Cambridge United 1-0 and Peterborough 5-1 at Leeds Road and Sheffield Wednesday 2-0 at Hillsborough to gain maximum points and thus take first prize in a mini-League competition.

OVERSEAS PLAYERS: The first overseas (foreign-born) players to be associated with Huddersfield Town football club were two South Africans - Dennis Lindsay (born Benomi, 1916) and George Wienand (born East London, 1912). They joined the club in August 1937.
Two other South Africans, goalkeeper 'Sandy' Kennon (born in Johannesburg in 1933) and John W Carr (born in Durban, 1926) were players at Leeds Road from 1950-52 and 1956-59 respectively. And in 1949, Karl A Hansen, born in Denmark, 1921, became the first 'foreigner' to be signed by the Terriers after WW2. Since then several more foreigners from various countries have served the club as a professionals.

OXFORD UNITED: Huddersfield's record against United is:
Football League

Venue	P	W	D	L	F	A
Home	12	9	2	1	23	9
Away	12	3	2	7	9	19
Totals	24	12	4	8	32	28
League Cup						
Home	1	1	0	0	2	0
Away	1	0	0	1	0	1
Totals	2	1	0	1	2	1

Oxford, elected to the League in 1962, made rapid progress and in 1968-69 met Huddersfield for the first time in the Second Division. Both teams won their respective home game, the Terriers by 2-1 and Oxford by 3-0. The Terriers beat the 'U's' 2-1 on aggregate in the 2nd round of the League Cup in 1982-83.

P

PARKER, Robert William: Full-back: 75 apps. Born: Seaham, 26 November 1935
Bob Parker was signed from Muirton Colliery Juniors in June 1954 and transferred to Barnsley in July 1965, going on to make over 100 appearances for the Tykes. With so many fine full-backs with the club, he had to wait until January 1960 before making his debut and then had his best season the following year when he had 35 outings.

PARKIN, Derek: Full-back: 70 apps. one goal Born: Newcastle-upon-Tyne, 2 January 1948.
After joining Wolves from Huddersfield for £80,000 in February 1968, 'Squeak' Parkin went on to make a record 609 appearances in 14 years with the Molineux club, 501 in the Football League. He also gained two League Cup winner's prizes (1974 & 1980), a Second Division championship medal (1977), won five England Under-23 caps and represented the Football League. Never a reckless tackler, being steady rather than enthusiastic, he had a wonderful left foot and always tried to use the ball rather than hoof it aimlessly downfield. He started his career at Leeds Road as a junior, turning professional in May 1965. After leaving Wolves in 1982 he spent a season with Stoke, retiring to concentrate on a landscape gardening business near Bridgnorth. He is a fine handicap golfer.

PARSLEY, Neil Robert: Full-back: 75 apps. one goal Born: Liverpool, 25 April 1966
Neil Parsley played for Witton Albion, Leeds United and Chester (on loan) before joining Huddersfield in July 1990. After a loan spell with Chester, he signed for WBA for £25,000 in December 1993. He later assisted Exeter and Leeds (on trial), had two further spells with Witton Albion and two with Guiseley, the second as manager: 2001-04. An efficient full-back, he produced some excellent displays for Huddersfield before moving to The Hawthorns, and was one of three ex-Terriers' players in the Baggies' side when masking his debut against Middlesbrough in September 1993 (the others were Kevin Donovan and Kieran O'Regan).

PAYTON, Andrew Paul: Striker: 52 apps. 20 goals Born: Clitheroe, 23 October 1967,
In a wonderful career spanning 20 years, Andy Payton(right) scored 226 goals in 588 competitive games, 80 coming in 176 outings for Burnley and 57 in 165 for Hull. He joined the apprentice ranks at Boothferry Park in 1983 and turned professional two years later. Signed by the Terriers from Barnsley for £350,000 in July 1996 he remained at Leeds Road until January 1998 when he moved to Turf Moor. He also played for Middlesbrough, Celtic and Blackpool.

the light at the end of the tunnel

PENALTY KICK:

- Tom Jones had the pleasure of scoring Huddersfield's first penalty - in a 3-0 home win over Carlisle in a North-Eastern League game on Boxing Day 1908.
- In the 2-2 home draw with Workington on 31 March 1909, P Hartley scored both Huddersfield's goals from the penalty spot.
- The first player to score from the penalty spot in a League game for Huddersfield was Bill Bartlett in a 3-0 win over Wolves at Molineux on 29 October 1910.
- The first penalty converted by Huddersfield in the FA Cup was by Jim Roberts in the 6-0 home win over South Kirby Colliery on 6 November 1909.
- The first Huddersfield player to score from the spot in a League Cup-tie was John Coddington in the 1-1 home draw with Burnley on 1 February 1961.
- Billy Smith scored the only goal from the penalty spot in the 1922 FA Cup final against PNE at Stamford Bridge. This was, in fact, the first time a penalty had decided such a final.
- Preston gained revenge 16 years later when George Mutch scored with a last minute penalty at the end of extra-time after Huddersfield's Alf Young was said to have brought down Mutch inside the area - when TV footage later confirmed that the incident had taken place outside the 18-yard area.
- In home League games against Wolves in October 1937 and February 1939, visiting defender Stan Cullis conceded a late penalty for hands in both encounters. Bill Hayes successfully scored from the spot to earn Huddersfield two 1-0 victories.
- Fred Fayers scored three penalties in four League games during February and March 1913.
- Outside-left Vic Metcalfe scored 33 penalties for Huddersfield - 31 in competitive games, 29 League, 2 FA Cup, and two in other matches).
- Roy Goodall netted 21 spot-kicks: 19 in the League, two in the FA Cup. Six were scored in 1927-28, a club record at the time, later equalled by Vic Metcalfe: 1951-52 & 1955-56.
- After missing a penalty in the last minute of their final League game of the 1923-24 season against Birmingham at St Andrew's, Cardiff's 0-0 draw saw them finish as runners-up to Huddersfield in the First Division championship. Victory for the Welsh side would have given them the title. The Terriers won the title by just 0.024 of a goal, their goal-average of 1.8181 beating Cardiff's 1.7941.

Penalty Shoot-outs

- It was heartbreak for Huddersfield at Wembley in May 1994 when they lost to Swansea on penalties (3-1) in the final of the Autoglass Trophy. Earlier, in round two, the Terriers knocked out PNE 5-4 in a penalty shoot-out.
- In an early round of the Autoglass Trophy in 1991-92 Huddersfield were held to a 1-1 home draw by Blackpool before going through 3-1 on penalties.
- Huddersfield defeated Brentford 4-3 on penalties to reach the 1994-95 Second Division play-off final.
- In 2001-02 after drawing 0-0 with neighbours Halifax in the first round of the LDV Vans Trophy, the Terriers made progress with a 4-3 victory in the penalty shoot-out.
- Huddersfield beat Mansfield 4-1 on penalties in the Third Division play-off at Cardiff's Millennium Stadium in May 2004. Neither side scored in outfield play.
- Huddersfield's intermediate team defeated Hull (a) 8-7 on penalties (after a 2-2 draw) in the FA Youth Cup in 2002-03

PETERBOROUGH UNITED: Huddersfield's record against the Posh is:

Football League

Venue	P	W	D	L	F	A
Home	6	1	2	3	5	6
Away	6	3	1	2	9	8
Totals	12	4	3	5	14	14

FA Cup

Home	2	2	0	0	5	1

Others

Home	1	0	0	1	1	2
Away	1	0	1	0	2	2
Totals	2	0	1	1	3	4

Huddersfield met Posh for the first time in a League game on the opening day of the 1974-75 season at Leeds Road and in front of 7,334 spectators succumbed to a 2-1 defeat. Posh also won their home game by the same score.

Huddersfield beat Posh (then of the Midland League) 3-1 in a 4th round FA Cup-tie in November 1956. A crowd of 48,735 saw the contest.

Peterborough beat Huddersfield over two legs in the 1991-92 play-off semi-final.

PLAY-OFFS: Huddersfield's record in the play-offs is:

Venue	P	W	D	L	F	A
Home	3	0	2	1	4	5
Away	3	1	2	0	5	4
Neutral	2	1	1*	0	2	1
Totals	8	2	5	1	11	10

Huddersfield's first taste of the end-of-season play-offs came in 1991-92 after they had finished third in Division Three. Unfortunately they failed to overcome Peterborough in the semi-final, losing 4-3 on aggregate.

After a 2-2 at London Road (attendance 11,751), Eoin Hand's side became favourites to go through to Wembley, but it all went wrong and in front of more than 16,000 fans they lost the return leg 2-1 at Leeds Road after taking an early lead through Phil Starbuck.

In 1994-95, Huddersfield gained promotion from the Second Division after beating Bristol Rovers 2-1 in the Wembley final before a crowd of 59,175.

In the two-legged semi-final the Terriers overcame Brentford 4-3 on penalties after both legs had ended in 1-1 draws.

Chris Billy scored the winning goal at Wembley on 81 minutes after Andy Booth had equalised Martin Grainger's 18th minute penalty on the stroke of half-time.

Then, in 2003-04, the Terriers again reached the play-offs, this time after finishing fourth in Division Three behind Doncaster, Hull and Torquay. They overcame Lincoln in the two-legged semi-final, fighting back from two down to draw the return game 2-2 having won 2-1 at Sincil Bank. It was a nervous occasion at Cardiff's Millennium Stadium as Huddersfield battled it out with Mansfield for that final promotion spot. The game ended level after extra-time and so it was all down to penalties - Huddersfield winning the shoot-out 4-1 to make a welcome return to the First Division.

PLYMOUTH ARGYLE: Huddersfield's record against the Pilgrims is:

Football League

Venue	P	W	D	L	F	A
Home	21	14	2	5	39	23
Away	21	5	9	7	25	29
Totals	42	19	11	12	64	52

FA Cup

Home	2	2	0	0	9	3
Away	3	2	1	0	4	1
Totals	5	4	1	0	13	4

League Cup

Home	1	0	1	0	3	3
Away	1	0	1	0	2	2
Neutral	1	1	0	0	2	1
Totals	3	1	2	0	7	6

In season 1952-53, Huddersfield won their first two League games against the Pilgrims - 4-0 at Leeds Road (thanks mainly to a Roy Shiner hat-trick) and 2-0 at Home Park. Another double followed in 1959-60, Town winning 3-1 at Home Park and 2-0 at Leeds Road. All these games were in the Second Division.

Argyle won both League games in 1960-61 - winning 5-1 at Huddersfield and 2-1 at Plymouth. The following season Town won 5-1 at home but lost 4-2 away and in April 1963, Argyle were defeated 4-2 on Terriers' soil, Derek Stokes and Les Massie both scoring twice. Huddersfield played Plymouth six times during the 1963-64 season. The two Second Division League games ended 0-0 at Home Park and 4-3 to the Terriers at Leeds Road. A third round FA Cup-tie at Plymouth saw Town win 1-0, while in the first round of the League Cup, after 2-2 and 3-3 draws at Home Park and Leeds Road respectively, Huddersfield won 2-1 in the second replay at Villa Park.

In August 1987 Plymouth slammed the Terriers 6-1 in South Devon.

On their way to the 1920 FA Cup final, Huddersfield defeated Southern League Argyle 3-1 in a 5th round tie at Leeds Road. After drawing 1-1 at Home Park in the 3rd round in January 1934, Huddersfield brushed aside the Pilgrims to win the replay 6-2, Dave Mangnall scoring a hat-trick in front of almost 19,000 spectators.

POINTS: (Three points awarded for a win since 1981-82).

- The most League points gained by Huddersfield in a season (2 for win) is 66 in season 1979-80 and (3 for a win) it is 82 in the 1982-83 campaign.
- Huddersfield gained 65 points in 1989-90 (3 for a win) and 64 in 1919-20 (the first season when 42 League games were played).
- A total of 53 home points were won in 1982-83 and 37 in 1979-80.
- 30 points (out of 42) were obtained from away League games in season 1924-25 and 29 were secured on the road in 1982-83
- Huddersfield collected only 15 points in home League games in 1971-72 and mustered only seven from their away games in 1946-47 and 1951-52.
- In 1987-88, only 28 points were obtained all season (home and away) while 25 were claimed in 1971-72.
- When Huddersfield won the First Division championship in 1924-25, they picked up more points away from home (30) than they did at Leeds Road (28).

POOLE, Terence: Goalkeeper: 231 apps. Born: Chesterfield, 16 December 1949.
An ever-present when Huddersfield won the Second Division championship in 1969-70, Poole had joined the Terriers in August 1968 from Manchester United where he had acted a reserve to Alex Stepney and Jimmy Rimmer. Tall and agile with a safe pair of hands, he remained at Leeds Road until January 1977 when he moved to Bolton, ending his career in 1981 after a loan spell with Sheffield United. Poole now lives in Wingerworth near Chesterfield and is manager of a cash 'n' carry video wholesalers.
* His younger brother, Andy, played for Northampton, Wolves, Port Vale and Gillingham.

PORTSMOUTH: Huddersfield's record against Pompey is:
Football League

Venue	P	W	D	L	F	A
Home	47	21	12	14	79	54
Away	47	7	8	32	46	100
Total	94	28	20	46	125	154

FA Cup

	P	W	D	L	F	A
Home	1	0	0	1	2	3
Away	1	0	1	0	1	1
Neutral	1	0	0	1	1	2
Totals	3	0	1	2	4	6

A total of 279 goals have so far been scored in the 94 League fixtures played between the two clubs - a Huddersfield record in terms of goals in games.
The first encounter took place on Christmas Eve 1927 when Pompey won 2-1 at Fratton Park. Huddersfield gained revenge by winning the return game on the last day of the season by 4-1, Alex Jackson scoring twice for the FA Cup finalists.
A poor display in November 1934 saw the Terriers slammed 5-0 by Pompey at Fratton Park.
In 1953-54 a total of 13 goals were scored in the two League games between the clubs. Town won 5-1 at home but lost 5-2 away.
Huddersfield doubled up over Pompey in 1959-60 - winning 6-3 at home and 2-0 away - and did it again in 1969-70 with 4-0 home victory and a 3-1 triumph at Portsmouth.
The Terriers lost 4-1 at Fratton Park in February 1986
Having knocked Huddersfield out of the competition in 1935, Pompey again put the Terriers out of the FA Cup by winning the 1939 semi-final showdown at Highbury 2-1 in front of more than 60,000 fans.

PORT VALE: Huddersfield's record against the Valiants is:
Football League

Venue	P	W	D	L	F	A
Home	16	8	4	4	33	22
Away	16	2	4	10	10	29
Totals	32	10	8	14	43	51

FA Cup

	P	W	D	L	F	A
Home	1	1	0	0	2	1
Away	1	0	0	1	0	1
Totals	2	1	0	1	2	2

the light at the end of the tunnel

League Cup

Venue	P	W	D	L	F	A
Home	1	0	0	1	1	2
Away	1	1	0	0	3	1
Totals	2	1	0	1	4	3

Having replaced Leeds City in the Football League, Port Vale first encountered Huddersfield in the competition on 2 January 1920 but suffered a 4-1 defeat at Leeds Road, Jack Swann scoring a hat-trick. Huddersfield's best win over the Potteries club is 7-1, achieved at home in September 1979. Both FA Cup-ties were close contests. Rod Belfitt and Steve Baines scored for the Terriers in their 2-1 home win in December 1975. Huddersfield beat Vale 4-3 on aggregate in a 1st round League Cup-tie in 1995-96.

PRESTON NORTH END: Huddersfield's record against the Lillywhites is:
Football League

Venue	P	W	D	L	F	A
Home	38	20	10	8	64	39
Away	38	9	11	18	40	62
Totals	76	29	21	26	104	101

FA Cup

Home	1	1	0	0	4	0
Away	1	1	0	0	2	0
Neutral	2	1	0	1	1	1
Totals	4	3	0	1	7	1

League Cup

Home	2	0	1	1	2	3
Away	1	0	0	1	0	1
Totals	3	0	1	2	2	4

Other

Home	1	0	1*	0	0	0

* Huddersfield won this Autoglass Trophy game 5-4 on penalties.

The first League game between Huddersfield and PNE ended level at 1-1 at Leeds Road in October 1912. PNE won the return fixture 2-1 while Town's first win followed in January 1915, away at Deepdale by 3-2. A double over PNE in 1920-21 was followed by a 6-0 home win for the Terriers in April 1922, Ernie Islip and Billy Smith both scoring hat-tricks in the FA Cup final rehearsal. Two more big results for Town were a 4-0 home win in September 1923 and a 4-1 victory at Deepdale in April 1925, George Brown netting a treble on this occasion. PNE goalkeeper Fred Mitchell wore spectacles against Huddersfield in the 1922 FA Cup final, won by the Terriers 1-0, courtesy of Billy Smith's penalty. Sixteen years later another penalty decided the 1938 final, George Mutch firing home from the spot in the last minute of extra-time time to give Preston a revenge 1-0 victory. Over 44,000 saw Huddersfield beat PNE 4-0 in a home 5th round FA Cup tie in February 1932.

PRICE, Albert John William: Forward: 60 apps. 31 goals Born: Hadley near Wellington, 10 April 1917. Died: 1995
Billy Price was signed from Wrockwardine Wood Juniors in October 1937. A wonderfully consistent marksman he netted well over 260 goals in more than 350 appearances at club level during a 15-year career. Besides his peacetime efforts for Huddersfield, scored 191 goals in 215 WW2 games and if he hadn't lost those 'seven' years to conflict, one

wonders what sort of record he would have achieved. He claimed 16 hat-tricks for the Terriers (one FA Cup, 15 in WW2), scored in eight consecutive games between April and September 1943 and in seven up to February 1943, while bagging a seven-timer in an 11-0 home Regional victory over Rochdale in March 1941. He could shoot with both feet, was also a fine header of the ball, was deceptively fast and elusive and a tremendous snapper up of the half-chance - and he created openings for his colleagues as well with his off-the-ball running. It was a pity the war came when it did for hot shot Price who was transferred to Reading for £5,000 in October 1947, later assisting Bradford City before retiring in May 1952.

PROGRAMMES: Matchday programmes (right is a 2004/05 cover) have been produced by Huddersfield Town FC since 1910. Initially the official publication comprised eight pages and over the years it increased in size and content. There were periods, especially during the two World Wars, when issues were reduced accordingly owing to a restriction on paper, but from the late 1940s/early '50s Town's programme has proved to be a good read. It won several awards during the 1980s/90s and is now rated as one of the best lower Division publications in the country.

PROMOTION: Huddersfield have gained promotion as follows:
1910 - elected into the Football League (Division Two).
1920 - promoted to the First Division
1953 - promoted to the First Division
1970 - promoted to the First Division
1980 - promoted to the Third Division
1983 - promoted to the Second Division
1992 - promoted to the Second Division
1995 - promoted to the First Division
2004 - promoted to the First Division

PUGH, Daral James: Midfield: 94 apps. 8 goals Born: Crynant, Neath Wales, 5 June 1961 Daral Pugh played for Doncaster before spending three years at Leeds Road, from September 1982 until July 1985. He then assisted Rotherham, Cambridge United and Torquay before joining Bridlington Town in 1990. Capped twice by his country at Under-21 level, he appeared in over 425 competitive games (389 in the Football League) and scored almost 40 goals. He helped the Terriers to third place in Division Three in 1983

PUGH, John Graham: Midfield: 87 apps. 2 goals
Born: Hoole near Chester, 12 February 1948
Graham Pugh started his professional career with Sheffield Wednesday in February 1965. He made 156 appearances for the Owls, gaining an FA Cup runners-up medal in 1966 and represented England at Under-23 level, before transferring to Huddersfield in May 1972. He did well at Leeds Road, partnering Steve Smith and Les Chapman in the engine-room. He moved to Chester in February 1975 and assisted Barnsley and Scunthorpe. He later ran a pub near Hillsborough.

HUDDERSFIELD TOWN.
★★★

Prime Time
Main Club Sponsor

Coca-Cola
FOOTBALL LEAGUE

the official matchday magazine of huddersfield town afc

up!

HUDDERSFIELD TOWN v TRANMERE ROVERS
kick-off tuesday 19th october 2004: 7.45pm

coca cola football league one

issue no: 08   £2.50

Admiral.
Official Kit
Supplier

BBC RADIO LEEDS
92.4, 95.3 FM & 774 AM
Main Radio Partner

TAYLOR &
WHITELEY
Match Sponsor

Corporate
Match Ball Sponsor

Q

QUEEN'S PARK RANGERS: Huddersfield's record against QPR is:

Football League

Venue	P	W	D	L	F	A
Home	10	6	2	2	13	9
Away	10	0	2	8	9	25
Totals	20	6	4	10	22	34

FA Cup

Home	4	3	1	0	13	2
Away	3	1	1	1	2	2
Totals	7	4	2	1	15	4

Huddersfield and QPR first met in the League in 1967-68 (Division Two) and both teams won their respective home games, the Terriers by 1-0 and Rangers by 3-0.

Over 31,000 fans saw Huddersfield beat Rangers 4-0 in a home 4th round FA Cup-tie in January 1932 as they made their way through to the quarter-finals. And there were a similar number of spectators present when Rangers were whipped 5-0 in a 3rd round replay in January 1949.

QUESTED, Wilfred Leonard: Left-half: 236 apps.9 goals Born: Folkestone, 9 January 1925
A tireless, totally committed wing-half, Len Quested represented Folkestone & Kent Schools and played in the Southern League with Folkestone before going on to make 188 appearances for Fulham who secured his signature on amateur forms in 1941, giving him professional status in August 1946 on demob from the navy. He helped the Cottagers win the Second Division championship in 1949 and gained an England 'B' cap v. Holland the following year. In October 1951 he moved to Huddersfield in exchange for Jeff Taylor. He became a star performer at Leeds Road, helping the Terriers reach the First Division in 1953 as part of a wonderful ever-present back division. Quested emigrated to Australia in July 1957. He later became an Australian League club director where his son was a star player.

QUIGLEY, John: Inside-right: 71 apps.6 goals Born: Glasgow, 28 June 1935
Quigley played for Glasgow Ashfield before going on to score 58 goals in 270 appearances for Nottingham Forest who he joined in July 1957. He left the City Ground for Huddersfield in February 1965 and spent eighteen months at Leeds Road, producing some fine displays before transferring to Mansfield for £3,000 in July 1968, later acting as player-manager and also trainer-coach at Field Mill. In 1972, he went to coach in the Middle East. He gained an FA Cup winner's medal with Forest in 1960 and was captain of Mansfield when they had a fine Cup run in 1969.

R

RANKIN, Andrew George: Goalkeeper: 81 apps. Born: Bootle, 11 May 1944

Andy Rankin joined Everton as an amateur in June 1959 and turned professional in October 1961. He spent ten years at Goodison Park before transferring to Watford for £20,000 in November 1971, moving to Huddersfield in December 1979 and retiring in May 1981.

The first goalkeeping substitute used by Everton (v. Nuremburg, Fairs Cup in October 1965) he understudied Gordon West for most of his stay at Goodison Park. Technically sound with fine reflexes and a safe pair of hands, Rankin had set his mind on quitting the game to join the police force but was persuaded to continue in soccer and in the end the decision was right. He played in 299 League games for Watford before giving good service to Huddersfield for 18 months. He gained one Under-23 cap for England. Rankin later worked as a warehouseman in Huddersfield.

RAW, Henry: Wing-half/Inside-forward: 70 apps. 11 goals Born: Tow Law, County Durham, 6 July 1903

Raw represented Tow Law & Crook Schools, Tow Law Town (as an amateur) and Durham County before joining Huddersfield in May 1925. A schemer with go-ahead ideas, a player of commendable steadiness, he played in the Terriers' championship winning side of 1925-26 and gained an FA Cup runners-up medal in 1930. He moved to WBA for £1,500 in February 1931 as a reserve to England internationals Tommy Magee and Joe Carter and spent most of his time in Albion's second XI, gaining three Central League championship medals to go with the one he won with Huddersfield. Joining Lincoln for £250 in July 1936, he retired in May 1939 and died in Durham West in November 1965.

READING: Huddersfield's record against the Royals is:

Football League

Venue	P	W	D	L	F	A
Home	18	8	3	7	27	20
Away	18	3	4	11	17	28
Totals	36	11	7	18	44	48

FA Cup

Home	1	0	1	0	0	0
Away	1	0	0	1	1	2
Totals	2	0	1	1	1	2

League Cup

Away	1	0	0	1	0	1

Huddersfield and Reading first met in League football in the Fourth Division season of 1975-76. The Royals won 2-0 at Elm Park and Town 3-0 at Leeds Road. In September 1980 Reading lost 4-1 at Leeds Road and in February 1982 they crashed 6-1 on the same ground.

Reading knocked Huddersfield out in the 3rd round of both the FA Cup (January 1986) and the League Cup (October 2003).

RECORDS: In 1919-20, Huddersfield set up several club records: most wins (16), most away wins (12), total number of wins (28), most 'doubles' over opponents (9) and least 'doubles' against (none). They finished runners-up in the First Division.

REDFERN, Levi: Inside-forward: 63 apps. one goal Born: Burton-on-Trent, 18 February 1905. Died: 1976 Redfern was a creator rather than taker of goal chances in a fine career that began with York. He served with Huddersfield from May 1927 to December 1932 and later assisted Bradford City, Rochdale and Sheffield United, retiring in 1936. * Redfern's brother, Les, played for Wolves, Southend and Crewe Alexandra

REFEREE:
- Former Huddersfield manager Arthur Fairclough was once a first-class referee.
- Ex-Huddersfield footballer Steve Baines became a fully qualified Football League referee after retiring as a player.
- Referee Dennis Howell (later a M.P) was pelted with orange peel and paper/plastic cups during the League game between Plymouth and Huddersfield in February 1961. After an inquiry, Home Park was closed for two weeks.
- In the 1950s, goalkeeper Les Wood was with Huddersfield in the 1950s and his father was a senior referee. As a result the Football League had to ensure that Wood senior did not officiate in a game which involved his son.
- A League match between Liverpool and Huddersfield at Anfield in March 1948 remains unique because the second-half restarted without the referee. Play had been in progress for about 40 seconds before the ball went into touch. At this point one of the players noticed that the referee was not on the pitch - presumably a spectator had blown the whistle to start proceedings after the interval.

REID, Paul Robert: Midfield: 93 apps.7 goals Born: Oldbury, 19 January 1968
Left-sided midfielder Paul Reid joined Leicester as an apprentice and turned 'pro' at Filbert Street in January 1986. He scored 25 goals in 189 appearances for the Foxes before transferring to Bradford City for £25,000 in July 1992 (after a loan spell at Valley Parade), moving to Huddersfield for £70,000 in May 1994. He served the Terriers up to March 1997 when he moved to Oldham for £100,000, switching to Bury on a 'free' in July 1999, switching to Swansea in July 2002 and ending up with Carmarthen Town in March 2004. He amassed in excess of 620 club appearances, including 100 for Bradford, 106 for the Latics and 126 for Swansea.

RELEGATION:
- Huddersfield were relegated from the First Division with Sheffield United at the end of the 1955-56 season. They were replaced in the top flight by Leeds United and Sheffield Wednesday - the only time four clubs from the same county have been involved in promotion and relegation issues from two Divisions in Football League history.
- Paul Garner was with Huddersfield when they were relegated from the Second Division in 1973 and from the Third in 1975. He then joined Sheffield United who were relegated from the First in 1976, from the Second in 1979 and from the Third in 1981. Eventually after five relegation campaigns, Garner's luck changed and in 1982 he helped the Blades gain promotion from the Fourth Division and followed up two years later with promotion from the Third.

RESERVES: When Huddersfield's first XI won the Football League championship three seasons running, the reserves also did extremely well in the Central League, winning the title in 1924-25 and 1925-26, and finishing second in 1923-24 (beaten on goal-average by WBA). The Huddersfield skipper in the mid-1920s was Marshall Spence. Three players, E Barkas, W Mercer and C Wilson, added Central League winner's medals to those they won with Huddersfield in the Football League.

Former player Jack Foster was 'manager' and Jack Eastwood trainer of the second XI during the mid-1920s

RICHARDSON, George Edward Holland: Outside-right: 132 apps.9 goals Born: Seaham Harbour, County Durham, 4 December 1891. Died: April 1969.

A fast-raiding winger, George Richardson played for Huddersfield before, during and after WW1, appearing in a further 30 games between 1915-19. He joined Huddersfield from Seaham Harbour in May 1914 and remained at Leeds Road until December 1923 when he moved to Bradford City, later serving with Hull (signed for £1,000), Bradford City (on trial), Hartlepool United and Lancaster Town. He rejoined Huddersfield as third team trainer in 1946, later promoted to assistant-trainer.

He helped the Terriers gain promotion to the First Division in 1920, played in the 1922 FA Cup winning side and was rewarded with a benefit that same year.

* Christened George Edward Holland Richardson, those 29 letters give him the honour of being the Huddersfield player with the longest name!

RICHARDSON, James Robert: Inside-right: 125 apps. 32 goals Born: Ashington, County Durham, 8 February 1911. Died: 1964

Jimmy Richardson, a motor engineer, played for Blyth Spartans before joining Newcastle for £200 in April 1928. He scored 53 goals in 164 appearances for the Magpies, scored the first of two goals that beat Arsenal in the famous 'over the line goal' 1932 FA Cup final, was capped twice by England and represented the Football League prior to his £4,000 transfer to Huddersfield in October 1934. He proved a good servant to the Terriers, scored some important goals and the club even made a small profit when they sold him back to Newcastle for £4,500 in October 1937. A Second Division championship winner in 1938, he switched to Millwall that same year and during WW2, guested for Aldershot, Charlton, Fulham and Leyton Orient. Taking as player-trainer at Brisbane Road in 1948, he retired as a player three years later and was then assistant-trainer at Millwall in 1956-57.

ROBERTS, Iwan Wyn: Striker: 182 apps. 68 goals Born: Bangor, 26 June 1968

When he quit Premiership-bound Norwich to become player-coach at Gillingham at the end of the 2003-04 season, 6'3" and 14st 2lb striker Iwan Roberts had scored over 230 goals in more than 700 League, Cup and international appearances in a professional career that started in July 1986 with Watford. He moved from Vicarage Road to Huddersfield for £275,000 in August 1990, transferred to Leicester for £100,000 in November 1993, joined Wolves for £1.3 million in July 1996 and switched to Norwich for £900,000 in July 1997. Strong in the air and a real gutsy performer, a great target man, Roberts has won Schoolboy, Youth, one 'B' and 15 full caps for Wales. He was a huge favourite with the Terriers' supporters and had his best season with the club in 1991-92 when he netted 30 goals.

ROBINS, Ian: Forward: 186 apps. 67 goals Born: Bury, 22 February 1952
Robins was a prolific marksman, he joined Oldham as a junior and was an England
Youth international trialist before turning professional in February 1970. Scorer of 40
goals in 220 League games for the Latics, whom he helped win the Third Division
championship, he joined Bury for £25,000 in July 1977. In September 1978 he switched
to Huddersfield where he remained for four years during which time he scored more
than a goal every three games, gaining a Fourth Division championship medal in 1980.
To the amazement of the Terriers' fans Robins retired in May 1982. In later years he
worked for Port Petroleum and was also landlord of Clown's Bar in Wigan.

ROBINSON, Frederick James: Left-back: 84 apps. 2 goals Born: Rotherham, 29 December
1954.
Fred Robinson played for Rotherham from 1971 to 1975 and then made over 120
appearances for Doncaster before joining Huddersfield in August 1979. He retired in May
1982.

ROBINSON, Philip John: Midfield/defender: 95 apps. 6 goals Born: Stafford, 6 January
1967. Red-haired Phil Robinson was registered with Aston Villa from 1981 to 1987 when
he joined Wolves for £5,000. He then served with Notts County and Birmingham (loan)
before Huddersfield secured his £50,000 transfer in September 1992. He later assisted
Northampton (loan), Chesterfield (signed for £15,000, December 1994), Notts County,
Stoke and Hereford (as player-coach) before becoming manager of Stafford Rangers in
May 2002. Equally adept in defence or midfield, Robinson always gave a good account of
himself. He helped Wolves win the Fourth and Third Division titles and SVT, was a key
member of Notts County's Third Division promotion winning side (1990) and helped Blues
lift the Leyland DAF Cup a year later. Robinson, who ventured into physiotherapy while
playing for Hednesford, appeared in 534 games at competitive level (51 goals).

ROCHDALE: Huddersfield's record against the 'Dale is:
Football League

Venue	P	W	D	L	F	A
Home	7	5	2	0	17	4
Away	7	2	5	0	8	4
Totals	14	7	7	0	25	8
FA Cup						
Home	1	0	1	0	1	1
Away	2	2	0	0	6	4
Totals	3	2	1	0	7	5
League Cup						
Home	2	1	0	1	3	2
Away	1	1	0	0	4	2
Totals	3	2	0	1	7	4

Huddersfield drew 1-1 with Rochdale at Spotland in the first League game between the
clubs in October 1973 (Division Three). The Terriers easily won the return game 5-0 at
Leeds Road - Ian Lawson and Alan Gowling both scoring twice. In December 1979 Town
won 5-1 at Leeds Road - their best victory over the 'Dale. Huddersfield were held at
home 1-1 by the 'Dale in a 1st round FA Cup-tie in November 1988 but they won the

replay at Spotland 4-3, former England international Peter Withe opening the scoring with his first goal for the club. Huddersfield beat the 'Dale 7-3 on aggregate in a 1st round League Cup-tie in 1981-82 but were then beaten at home at the same stage of the competition in 2001-02.

ROTHERHAM UNITED (County, Town): Huddersfield's record against the Millermen is:

Football League

Venue	P	W	D	L	F	A
Home	20	15	1	4	37	15
Away	20	6	10	4	29	26
Totals	40	21	11	8	66	41

FA Cup

Home	2	1	1	0	6	5
Away	1	0	0	1	1	2
Totals	3	1	1	1	7	7

League Cup

Home	1	0	0	1	1	3
Away	1	0	1	0	4	4
Totals	2	0	1	1	4	7

Others

Away	2	0	1	1	1	4

The first League encounter between the two Yorkshire clubs took place on 25 December 1919 when the Terriers claimed their best win so far over Rotherham, beating them 7-1 at Leeds Road. Jack Swann and Frank Mann both scored hat-tricks. The following day, Town completed the double with a 3-1 victory at Millmoor. Huddersfield lost 2-1 at Rotherham in an FA Cup 4th qualifying round replay in November 1909 - their first defeat in the competition. In January 1962, the Millermen were defeated 4-3 in an exciting 3rd round FA Cup clash at Leeds Road. After fighting back to draw 4-4 in the first leg of their 2nd round League Cup-tie v. Rotherham in 1987-88, Huddersfield slipped up badly by losing the return leg 3-1 at Leeds Road.

ROUGHTON, George: Full-back: 171 apps. Born: Manchester City , 11 December 1909. Died: Southampton, June 1989.
The son of a prize-wining athlete, Roughton played for Droylesden before joining Huddersfield in October 1928, turning professional a month later. He spent eight years at Leeds Road, helping the Terriers, forming a fine full-back partnership with Roy Goodall while also representing the Football League and touring Canada with the FA in 1931. Signed by Manchester United in September 1936, he guested for the Terriers during WW2, was appointed player-manager of Exeter in November 1945 and was in charge of Southampton from May 1952 to September 1955. A heart by-pass operation ended his association with the game

RUSSELL, Colin: Forward: 81 apps. 25 goals Born: Liverpool, 21 January 1961.
A £15,000 buy from Liverpool in September 1982, on the strength of his second XI performances at Anfield, Russell did well during his two years at Leeds Road before losing his place. A loan spell with Stoke preceded his transfer to Bournemouth in August 1984 and afterwards he served with Doncaster and Scarborough.

S

SANDERCOCK, Philip John: Left-back: 89 apps. one goal Born: Plymouth, 21 June 1953
Phil Sandercock played for Torquay (with his brother Ken) before joining Huddersfield in June 1977. After two very useful seasons at Leeds Road he moved to Northampton and quit League football in 1981 with over 350 League appearances to his credit.

SAUNDERS, John: Defender: 133 apps. 3 goals Died: Worksop, 1 December 1950. Died: 4 January 1998
Registered with Mansfield from 1968, Saunders became a rock-solid performer at the heart of the Huddersfield defence following his transfer from Field Mill in October 1972. In December 1975 he moved to Barnsley whom he skippered to promotion from Division Four, and later assisted Lincoln, Doncaster (signed for £5,000), Matlock Town (briefly) and Worksop Town who he later managed (1983-84) before becoming chairman and owner of Tigers Club.

SAWARD, Patrick: Left-half: 63 apps. one goal Born: Cobh, County Cork, 17 August 1928. Died: Newmarket, September 2002.
Saward played for Cork & Cobh County Schools, Beckenham, Crystal Palace (trialist), Millwall and Aston Villa before joining Huddersfield in March 1961. Moving to Coventry City in October 1963 as player-coach, later assistant-manager (July 1967), he was in charge of Brighton (1970-73) and NASR Al/ Saudi Arabia (1973-75) before running a bar in Menorca. A tough competitor, Saward who occasionally occupied an inside-forward berth, was a valuable member of Villa's 1957 FA Cup and 1960 Second Division championship-winning sides, gained 18 caps for the Republic of Ireland and as a manager, guided Brighton to promotion from Division Three in 1972. He died from Alzheimer's disease in a Newmarket nursing home.

SCHOFIELD, Daniel James: Midfield: 136 apps. 23 goals Born: Doncaster, 10 April 1980
Danny Schofield quickly established himself in the Huddersfield side as a wide midfielder with smart control, good passing skills and fine temperament. He was signed from Brodsworth for £2,000 in February 1999 and helped the Terriers win promotion from Division Three in 2004, netting eight goals in 40 League games.

SCULLY, Patrick Joseph: Defender: 89 apps. 3 goals Born: Dublin, 23June 1970
Pat Scully started his career with Arsenal. He had loan spells with PNE and Northampton before joining Southend for £100,000 in January 1991, transferring to Huddersfield in March 1994. A strong defender, he remained with the Terriers until the summer of 1994 when he was released after turning down a move to York. A Republic of Ireland international at schoolboy, Youth (3), 'B' (2), Under-21 (9), Under-23 (1) and senior (1) levels, he helped the Terriers win the 1995 Second Division play-off final v. Bristol Rovers.

SCUNTHORPE UNITED: Huddersfield League record against the Iron is:

Football League

Venue	P	W	D	L	F	A
Home	12	8	1	3	23	14
Away	12	6	3	3	21	15
Totals	24	14	4	6	44	29

FA Cup

Venue	P	W	D	L	F	A
Home	1	1	0	0	2	1
Away	1	0	1	0	0	0
Totals	2	1	1	0	2	1

League Cup

Venue	P	W	D	L	F	A
Home	3	1	2	0	5	2
Away	3	1	0	2	5	5
Totals	6	2	2	2	10	7

Other

Venue	P	W	D	L	F	A
Home	1	1	0	0	4	1

Almost 14,000 fans saw the first League game between Huddersfield and the Iron at Leeds Road in December 1958 (Division Two). Scunthorpe won 1-0 but the Terriers gained revenge with a 3-0 victory at The Old Show Ground in their penultimate game of the season.

In April and December 1977 Huddersfield beat the Iron 4-0 (a) and 4-1 (home) in League game games.

The Iron lost to the Terriers in a 1st round FA Cup replay in 1992-93, while the Terriers went out 5-4 on aggregate (after extra-time) in the 1st round of the League Cup in 1988-89. Huddersfield then won 4-2 and 2-0 (both on aggregate) at the same stage in 1994-95 and 1999-2000 respectively.

The Iron were defeated 4-1 in the LDV Vans Trophy in 2001-02.

SEASONS: The 2004-05 campaign is Huddersfield's 84th season of Football League action.

SECRETARIES: The first honorary secretary of Huddersfield was Mr J H R Appleyard who was appointed in 1908 with Mr T H Kaye acting as the club's official auditor.

Albert 'Dick' Pudan took over as secretary-manager in September 1910 and in April 1912 Arthur Fairclough assumed the same role.

Immediately after WW1, Ambrose Langley was appointed secretary-manager (December 1919) and then Herbert Chapman took office in March 1921, followed by Cecil Potter in July 1925. Over the last 78 years - from August 1926 - only seven other people have held the position of secretary of the club. They are: Harry Brewer (August 1926-February 1958), Anthony 'Tony' Galvin (February 1958-March 1970), William Brook (March 1970-February 1974), George S Binn (February 1974-summer 1991), Mr C D Patzelt (July 1991-May 1993), Alan Sykes (May 1993-May 1999) and Ann Hough who is still in office at The Alfred McAlpine Stadium.

SENDINGS-OFF:
- Ernie Islip was one of the first Huddersfield players to get sent-off in a League game after WW1. He was dismissed for a foul on the Notts County goalkeeper Albert

Iremonger during a game at Leeds Road in November 1924. Later in a rather heated encounter, the visiting defender Willie Flint was also sent-off in the 0-0 draw. Both players were suspended for a month following an FA inquiry.

- Huddersfield goalkeeper Lee Martin was sent-off for a professional foul in the 57th minute of the Third Division game with Bury in December 1990. With Bury leading 1-0 Kieran O'Regan took over in goal but was called on to take a penalty in the 77th minute which he converted to bring the scores level. The Terriers went on to win the game after Bury's Ronnie Mauge was also sent-off.
- Goalkeeper Nico Vaesen was sent-off at Blackburn in a League game in April 2001, allowing Martyn Margetson to come off the subs' bench for his debut in a 2-0 defeat.
- John Pugh was sent-off in the final of the West Riding Cup v. Bradford City in August 1973.
- Huddersfield players collected over 100 disciplinary points during 1975-76.

SHARP, Kevin Philip: Defender: 43 apps. Born: Ontario, Canada, 19 September 1974
Competent defender Kevin Sharp played for Auxerre (France) before joining Leeds United for £60,000 in October 1992. Recruited by Wigan for £100,000 in November 1995, he made 216 appearances for the Latics and then assisted Wrexham before joining Huddersfield on a free transfer in August 2002. An England Schoolboy and Youth international, he won the FA Youth Cup with Leeds in 1993, the Third Division and AWS with Wigan in 1997 and 1999. He moved to Scunthorpe United in July 2003.

SHEARER, Duncan Nicol: Striker: 96 apps.48 goals Born: Fort William, 28 August 1962
Scorer of a goal every two games for the Terriers, Duncan Shearer (right) - who played initially for Inverness Clachnacuddin - paid back his £10,000 transfer fee with interest. Signed from Chelsea in March 1986, he served Huddersfield for just over two seasons, moving to Swindon in June 1988 and later assisting Blackburn. He ended his League career with 118 goals to his name in 250 games. He was capped seven times by Scotland

SHEFFIELD UNITED: Huddersfield's record against the Blades is:
Football League

Venue	P	W	D	L	F	A
Home	42	18	14	10	62	46
Away	42	15	15	12	62	56
Totals	84	33	29	22	124	102

FA Cup

	P	W	D	L	F	A
Home	5	2	2	1	6	4
Away	2	0	1	1	1	3
Neutral	4	2	2	0	5	3
Totals	11	4	5	2	12	10

The first League game between the Terriers and the Blades, played at Bramall Lane in December 1920, ended 1-1. Later in the season Huddersfield won 1-0 at Leeds Road.
The following season (March 1921) the Huddersfield-Blades League derby at Leeds Road realised ground record gate receipts (at that time) of £1,802
The Terriers did the double over United in 1925-26, winning 4-1 at home and 3-2 away and when they did likewise in 1933-34, they scored 10 goals with wins of 6-1 at home and 4-1 at Bramall Lane. In November 1927, United were crushed 7-1 at home by a rampant Town side. This was, in fact, Huddersfield's biggest winning margin in an away League game at that time. The following season Alex Jackson scored a hat-trick when Town beat United 6-1 at Leeds Road.
Jim Glazzard was another hat-trick hero when he helped the Terriers beat the Blades 6-3 in a First Division home game in September 1953.
The Terriers lost 5-1 at Sheffield in March 1989. Huddersfield beat the Blades 1-0 in a 2nd replay of the 1928 FA Cup semi-final at Maine Road (following 2-2 and 0-0 draws at Old Trafford and Goodison Park). In the only season of FA Cup football when the scores of both the home and away games were added together (1945-46) the Terriers lost to United 3-1 on aggregate in the 3rd round. In January 1957, a 3rd round tie between the clubs also went to a second replay before the Terriers won 2-1 at Maine Road.
Huddersfield have met United more times in the FA Cup than they have any other club.

SHEFFIELD WEDNESDAY: Huddersfield's record against the Owls is:

Football League

Venue	P	W	D	L	F	A
Home	18	12	3	3	39	15
Away	18	5	5	8	31	35
Totals	36	17	8	11	70	50

FA Cup

	P	W	D	L	F	A
Home	1	0	0	1	1	2
Neutral	1	1	0	0	2	1
Totals	2	1	0	1	3	3

League Cup

	P	W	D	L	F	A
Home	1	1	0	0	2	1
Away	1	0	0	1	0	3
Totals	2	1	0	1	2	4

The first Huddersfield-Wednesday Yorkshire League derby took place at Hillsborough in September 1926 in front of 32,493 spectators. It ended level at 1-1. Later in the season a seven-goal thriller at Leeds Road went in favour of the Terriers by 4-3, Bob Kelly scoring a hat-trick before a crowd of 22,329.
A year later (December 1927) George Brown netted three times when Huddersfield won 5-0 to Huddersfield at Hillsborough and Dave Mangnall followed up with a treble to beat Wednesday 6-1 at home in January 1932.
A crowd of 69,292 saw Huddersfield beat Wednesday 2-1 at Old Trafford in the semi-

final of the FA Cup in March 1930. Alex Jackson scored both goals. The Terriers also won a 5th round tie 2-1 as they slowly edged towards the 1966 Wembley final.

Huddersfield lost 4-2 on aggregate in a 3rd round League Cup-tie in 1984-85

SHREWSBURY TOWN: Huddersfield's record against the Shrews is:

Football League

Venue	P	W	D	L	F	A
Home	10	7	2	1	13	10
Away	10	1	3	6	9	22
Totals	20	8	5	7	22	32

FA Cup

Home	1	0	0	1	0	3

League Cup

Home	1	0	0	1	0	2
Away	1	1	0	0	3	2
Totals	2	1	0	1	3	4

Huddersfield won their first League game against the Shrews 1-0 at Leeds Road in November 1973 but lost the return 3-0 at Gay Meadow when the turn out was only 1,675.

Huddersfield's only League win on Shrews' soil has so far been 2-1 in February 1987, while Shrewsbury won both home and away games by 5-1 in 1984-85.

When Shrewsbury beat Huddersfield 3-0 in a 3rd round FA Cup-tie in January 1981, all three goals were scored against different goalkeepers. Chris Topping conceded an own-goal before Terrier's ' keeper Andy Rankin went off injured. His replacement, Steve Kindon was then beaten by Stephen Cross and late in the game after Mark Lillis had taken over between the posts, Chic Bates added Shrewsbury's final goal.

Huddersfield lost 4-3 on aggregate to the Shrews in a 1st round League Cup in 1985-86.

SIDEBOTTOM, Arnold: Defender: 66 apps.6 goals Born: Barnsley, 1 April 1954

Sidebottom played in 16 League games for Manchester United before joining Huddersfield in January 1976. He gave some sterling displays at the heart of the Terriers' defence before transferring to Halifax in October 1978, retiring in May 1979 to concentrate on playing cricket with Yorkshire for whom he took 285 wickets in 122 games. He also appeared in one Test Match for England v. Australia in 1985. His son later played for England in Test Matches.

SIMPSON, Ronald: Forward: 118 apps. 26 goals Born: Carlisle, 25 February 1934

Simpson (right) played in every position in the forward-line for Huddersfield but during his first five seasons with the club managed only 15 senior appearances. However, once he had established himself in the side (in 1955) he produced some fine displays before going on to play in over 200 games for Sheffield United, helping the Blades reach the FA Cup semi-final and gain promotion to the First Division in 1961. He joined the Terriers in February 1951 from Holme Head Works team and left Leeds Road for Bramall Lane in May 1958, switching to Carlisle in December 1964 and on to Queen of the South in July 1966.

SINNOTT, Lee: Defender: 100 apps. Born: Pelsall, West Midlands, 12 July 1965
Sinnott's League career spanned 17 years. In that time he made over 600 appearances while serving with Walsall (signed as a professional in November 1982), Watford, Bradford City (three separate spells), Crystal Palace, Huddersfield (signed for £105,000, December 1994 to July 1997) and Oldham, moving to Scarborough in September 1999. An England Youth and Under-21 international, he read the game superbly and was always in the thick of the action.

SLADE, Howard Charles: Right-half/inside-forward: 130 apps. 7 goals Born: Bath, 29 January 1891. Died: Doncaster, April 1971.
Charlie Slade helped Huddersfield gain promotion from Division Two in the first season after WW1 and played in two FA Cup finals, 1920 & 1922, earning a winner's medal in the second. An honest campaigner in whatever position he occupied, he served with Bath City, Stourbridge and Aston Villa before moving to Leeds Road in March 1914. He made his debut immediately, guested for Reading and played during and after the hostilities for the Terriers before transferring to Middlesbrough in October 1922 (having recovered from a fractured leg). He later assisted Darlington (1925-27) and Folkestone (briefly); coached in Turkey, Venezuela, Mexico and Scandinavia and at Rotherham (1929) and Aldershot (1930). He worked for the Middlesex Schools Authority as a soccer instructor (1934-39), was scout, then joint-manager and chief scout of Crystal Palace between 1946 and 1955) and also played cricket for Yorkshire clubs Bradley Mills and Lockwood.

SMITH, Mark Cyril: Forward: 111 apps. 13 goals Born: Sheffield, 19 December 1961
Mark Smith played for Sheffield United, Worksop Town, Gainsborough Trinity and Kettering Town before joining Rochdale in July 1988. He made his League debut later that year and after 33 games for the 'Dale transferred to Huddersfield in February 1989. He remained at Leeds Road until March 1991 when a £55,000 deal took him to Grimsby, later assisting Scunthorpe (1993-95).

SMITH, Martin Geoffrey: Forward: 85 apps. 29 goals Born: Sunderland, 13 November 1974
Martin Smith was a trainee at The Stadium of Light before signing professional forms for his home-town club in September 1992. He scored 28 goals in 145 appearances for the Wearsiders before transferring to Sheffield United in August 1999, moving to Huddersfield in February 2000 for £300,000. He switched to Northampton Town on a 'free' in March 2003. Capped by England at Schoolboy, Youth and Under-21 levels, he has terrific pace, good close control and has the ability to take on and beat defenders. He was a First Division championship winner in 1996 with Sunderland.

SMITH, Stephen: Forward: 388 apps. 34 goals Born: Huddersfield, 28 April 1946.
The club's only local-born manager, Smith gave the Terriers tremendous service for

almost 25 years, first as a player (October 1961 to August 1977) and then as chief scout, youth team coach, reserve team manager, caretaker-manager and non-contract player (September 1979 to July 1988). Said to have been the 'perfect professional', Smith had two years as an apprentice before signing professional forms at Leeds Road in October 1963, making his League debut against Newcastle in September 1964. A year later he was the first substitute used by Huddersfield (v. Preston) and went on to make over 380 appearances before moving to Halifax in 1977, having had a loan spell with Bolton. A Second Division championship winner in 1969-70 when he and Frank Worthington netted 23 League goals between them, Smith had to work hard in a struggling side at The Shay. On his return to Leeds Road he quickly settled back into the club.

His spell as caretaker-manager was from January to October 1987 when he stepped in following the departure of Mick Buxton and the arrival of Malcolm Macdonald. In April 1990 Smith took over as Youth Development Officer at Bradford City, also acting as coach at Valley Parade.

SMITH, William Henry: Outside-right or left: 575 apps.126 goals Born: Tantobie, County Durham, 23 May 1895. Died: April 1951

A Huddersfield legend, Billy Smith spent virtually all of professional playing career at Leeds Road, he started out with Hobson Wanderers before joining the Terriers in 1913. He scored his first League goal in October 1913 (v. Hull) and his last more than 20 years later v. Sheffield United in February 1934. Blessed with a long, raking stride, he was quick, elusive and clever and formed a celebrated left-wing partnership with Clem Stephenson. He created scoring opportunities aplenty for his colleagues while tucking away his fair share of goals himself. He was the first player to find the net direct form a corner (v. Arsenal in October 1924).

A promotion winner with the Terriers in 1920 but missed that season's FA Cup final defeat by Aston Villa through suspension after being sent-off in a League game at Stoke on Easter Monday. He soon made amends, however, by scoring the winning penalty against Preston in the 1922 final. He helped the Terriers win the League championship three years running in the mid-1920s, won both Charity Shield and West Riding Cup medals, gained three caps for England and represented the Football League on three occasions. He finally left Leeds Road in July 1934 to become player-coach of Rochdale, later trainer and then manager until November 1935.

Smith was presented with the Football League's Long Service medal soon after his final game for the Terriers. Billy Smith - Mr Huddersfield' - is the oldest player ever to appear for the club.

* His son, Conway Smith, was a Huddersfield reserve.

SODJE, Efetobore: Defender: 43 apps. Born: Greenwich, 5 October 1972.Career: Macclesfield (signed from Stevenage, £30,000, August 1997), Luton (free transfer, August 1999), Colchester (loan, March 2000), Crewe Alexandria (free transfer, July 2000), Huddersfield Town (free, August 2003).An extremely versatile player Nigerian World Cup player Efe is a firm favourite with the fans. Brother Akpo, a striker, joined the Terriers in September 2004 on a short term deal.

SOUTHAMPTON: Huddersfield's record against the Saints is:
Football League

Venue	P	W	D	L	F	A
Home	9	6	0	3	20	10
Away	9	3	2	4	13	16
Totals	18	9	2	7	33	26

League Cup

Home	1	0	0	1	0	1
Away	1	0	0	1	0	4
Totals	2	0	0	2	0	5

The first two League games between the clubs were played in 1952-53 and Huddersfield won them both, 5-0 at home and 2-0 at The Dell.
In 1960-61 Huddersfield won 3-1 at Leeds Road and the Saints 4-2 at The Dell. Huddersfield's 5-0 aggregate drubbing in the League Cup came in 1994-95.

SOUTHEND UNITED: Huddersfield's record against the Shrimpers is:
Football League

Venue	P	W	D	L	F	A
Home	11	7	2	2	20	11
Away	11	6	2	3	16	16
Totals	22	13	4	5	36	27

FA Cup

Home	1	0	0	1	1	2

Huddersfield lost their first League game with Southend by 5-2 at Roots Hall in November 1973 (Division Three). They also lost their first home game 1-0 and another 1-0. The Shrimpers knocked Huddersfield out of the FA Cup in the 3rd round in 1992-93.

SOUTHPORT: Huddersfield's record against Southport is:
Football League

Venue	P	W	D	L	F	A
Home	4	3	0	1	8	4
Away	4	1	3	0	5	4
Totals	8	4	3	1	13	8

On 27 December 1975 Huddersfield played and beat Southport for the first time in a League game, winning 2-1 at Haig Avenue in front of 2,546 spectators. However, the seaside club gained revenge with a 2-1 victory at Leeds Road late in the season.

SPENCE, Marshall Bonwell: Defender: 82 apps. Born: Ferryhill, 21 February 1899. Died: 1982
Signed from Ferryhill Athletic in May 1923, Marshall Spence gave the Terriers tremendous service for a decade before retiring at the end of the 1932-33 season. A solid, uncompromising defender, he played local junior football before becoming a professional with Huddersfield at the age of 24. Reserve to Tom Wilson and Billy Watson, he had to wait until October 1924 before making his senior debut v. Arsenal. Unfortunately, he didn't make enough appearances to qualify for a medal in any of the three championship-winning campaigns but skippered the reserves to a Central League triumph.

STANIFORTH, Ronald: Right-back: 118 apps. Born: Newton Heath, Manchester City , 13 April 1924. Died: 1988 Staniforth was educated at Hague Street School and represented Manchester City Boys before joining Newton Albion in 1938, signing as a professional for Stockport in October 1946. Transferred to Huddersfield in May 1952 (after 223 League outings for the Hatters) he became an England international, winning one 'B' and eight full caps. A right-back in the classical tradition, stylish and polished, he remained unruffled throughout his career. Rarely ever spoken to by the referee, he was a fine footballer who formed part of that wonderful Huddersfield defence of the early 1950s when promotion was gained to the First Division (1953). In July 1955, after three splendid seasons at Leeds Road, Staniforth moved to Sheffield Wednesday with striker Roy Shiner in exchange for Tony Conwell and Jackie Marriott. He made over 100 appearances for the Owls, twice helping them win the Second Division title (1956 & 1959). Appointed player-manager/coach of Barrow in October 1959, he retired as a player in 1961 but continued as a manager until July 1964. He later had two spells as coach back at Hillsborough.

STANTON, Brian: Midfield: 241 apps. 54 goals Born: Liverpool, 7 February 1956.
A bargain at £15,000 from Bury in September 1979, attacking midfielder Stanton gained a Fourth Division championship medal at the end of his first season at Leeds Road, making 41 League appearances. He remained a regular in the side for the next four years and gave some superb displays - certainly a shrewd buy by manager Mick Buxton. It is likely that Stanton holds the record for scoring the fastest hat-trick for the Terriers as a non-forward - netting three times in the space of six minutes against Bradford City on New Year's Day 1983. He actually scored four times that day in a 6-3 home win. Starting off as an amateur with New Brighton, he turned professional with Bury in October 1975 and after six-and-a-half years with Huddersfield moved to Wrexham on trial in March 1986. Three months later he was engaged by Morecambe but Rochdale then resurrected his Football League career in December 1986. After switching to full-back he eventually quit the game in 1988

STARBUCK, Philip Michael: Striker: 177 apps. 47 goals Born: Nottingham, 24 November 1968
Between April 1985 when he joined Nottingham Forest as an apprentice, turning professional in August 1986, and May 1998 (when released by Plymouth), Phil Starbuck scored 54 goals in 306 first-class matches. He had by far his best years with Huddersfield who signed him for £100,000 in August 1991 and sold him to Sheffield United for £150,000 in October 1994. Before joining the Terriers he had loan spells with Birmingham, Hereford and Blackburn and besides his time at Bramall Lane (where he was converted into a midfield player) he also played for Bristol City and Oldham. On leaving the Pilgrims he signed for Cambridge City, later assisting Hucknall Town.

STARLING, Alan William: Goalkeeper: 126 apps. Born: Dagenham, Essex, 2 April 1951 Alan Starling was an apprentice with Luton before signing professional forms at Kenilworth Road in April 1969. He made only seven League appearances for the Hatters and after a loan spell with Torquay and a brief spell at Leicester (where he was taught a lot by Peter Shilton) he moved to Northampton in June 1971. He did superbly well for the Cobblers, playing in more than 250 first-class matches, scoring one goal, a penalty v. Hartlepool in April 1976. Signed for £8,000 by Huddersfield as a replacement for the injured Terry Poole and Dick Taylor in March 1977, he adapted well to conditions at Leeds Road, being a regular until December 1979 when he damaged his ribs against Torquay. Replaced by Andy Rankin, he qualified for a Fourth Division championship medal that season (22 games) but was forced to retire in October 1980. Three years later he returned to the game with Bradley Rangers (July 1983) and was surprisingly signed by former Terriers' star Trevor Cherry as cover goalkeeper at Bradford City five months later.

STEAD, Jonathan Graeme: Striker: 77 apps. 24 goals Born: Huddersfield, 7 April 1983
There is no doubt that the six goals scored by 6' 3" striker Jonathan Stead during the second half of the 2003-04 season kept Blackburn in the Premiership. After two years as a trainee with Huddersfield, Stead became a full-time professional in November 2000. With a goal virtually every three games for the Terriers, he developed quickly in League football - so much so that in February 2004 Graeme Souness, the manager at Ewood Park, paid £1.2m for his services and what a signing he's turned out to be! He has already gained a handful of England Under-21 caps - with more representative honours to come!

STEELE, David Morton: Wing-half: 203 apps. 3 goals Born: Carluke, Lanarkshire, 29 July 1894. Died: Stanningley, 25 May 1964. A former miner, David Steele played for Armadale, Paisley St Mirren and Douglas Water Thistle in Scotland and Bristol Rovers of the Southern League (from November 1919) before joining Huddersfield with colleague Joe Walter for £2,500 in May 1922. After recovering from pneumonia, Steele became the Terriers first Scottish international when capped against Ireland in March 1923, later adding two more to his collection. Forming a brilliant half-back partnersip with Tom Wilson and Billy Watson, Steele helped Huddersfield win the League championship three seasons running and appeared in the 1928 FA Cup final defeat by Blackburn. In July 1929 he joined PNE on a free transfer and later assisted both Bury and Ashton National as player-coach and the Danish side Bold Klubben FC and Sheffield United as a coach. Steele then managed Bradford Park Avenue from May 1936 until February 1952 and during WW2 tuned out for the club aged 48 and celebrated the occasion with a goal against Sheffield Wednesday in October 1942.

He returned to Leeds Road in September 1943 as Huddersfield manager, holding the position until June 1947. Having worked on the family's fruit farm, he was tempted back into management by Bradford City in August 1948 later scouted for the club and was a licensee in Stanningley when he died (see under Managers).

STEPHENSON, Clement: Inside-forward: 276 apps. 50 goals Born: New Delaval, County Durham, 6 February 1890. Died: Huddersfield, 24 October 1961.
A junior with Bedlington, New Delaval Villa, West Stanley and Blyth Spartans (for three months), Stephenson signed as a full-time professional with Durham City in 1909.
After some impressive displays he was transferred to Aston Villa for just £175 in March 1910 - and what a career he had after that! Following a loan spell with Stourbridge (August 1910-February 1911), he went on to score almost 100 goals in 216 appearances for Villa. Indeed, he made tremendous progress after arriving in the Midlands. He netted on his League debut in a 4-0 win over Spurs, represented Birmingham against London in 1913 and collected his only England cap versus Wales in 1924 (there should have been more). He claimed two FA Cup winner's medals - in 1913 v. Sunderland and 1920 v. Huddersfield and, in fact, prior to the 1913 final he had dreamt that Villa would win 1-0 and that the goal, a header, would be scored by Tommy Barber. That's precisely what happened.
A wonderful schemer, Stephenson passed the ball with fine judgement, was no mean goalscorer, could shoot with both feet, possessed good pace and was never afraid to 'rough it' with the burly defenders. He spent two years in Royal Naval Air Service as a PT instructor at the Crystal Palace; guested for Leeds City (February 1919) and assisted South Shields & District before embarking on a 21-year association with Huddersfield in March 1921, signed for £3,000. A year later he was an FA Cup winner as the Terriers beat PNE and as team captain, quickly gained three League championship medals in a row before receiving another Cup runners-up medal in 1928.
On retiring as a player in May 1929; he became manager at Leeds Road, holding office until May 1942, steering the Terriers two more FA Cup finals, losing them both in 1930 and 1938. Stephenson, who later became a caterer in Huddersfield, had two footballing brothers, George Ternent and James who both played for Aston Villa like himself.

STEWART, William Paul Marcus: Striker: 160 apps. 68 goals Born: Bristol, 7 November 1972
An England Schoolboy international, Marcus Stewart joined Bristol Rovers as an apprentice in April 1990 and turned professional in July 1991. Developing into a top-class marksman, he netted 80 goals in 207 games for Rovers before joining Huddersfield for a record fee of £1.2 million in July 1995. After three-and-a-half excellent years with the Terriers he was transferred to Ipswich for £2.5 million in

February 2000 and went on to claim 37 goals in 93 outings for the Tractormen prior to his £3.25 million move to Sunderland in August 2002.

He continued to do the business, scoring 28 goals in 85 appearances up to May 2004, having helped the Wearsiders reach the First Division play-off final.

STOCKPORT COUNTY: Huddersfield's record against the Hatters is:
Football League

Venue	P	W	D	L	F	A
Home	20	11	6	3	36	16
Away	20	6	5	8	18	32
Totals	40	17	11	11	54	48
Other						
Away	1	1	0	0	1	0

Huddersfield's third away game in the Football League on 3 October 1910 saw them lose 1-0 at Stockport. The Terriers gained sweet revenge, however, with a 4-1 home victory in the January when Jim Richardson scored twice.

In February 1980, Huddersfield ran up their best win over County - 5-0 at Leeds Road.

STOKE CITY: Huddersfield's record against the Potters is:
Football League

Venue	P	W	D	L	F	A
Home	33	15	9	9	51	39
Away	33	6	12	15	29	56
Totals	66	21	21	24	80	95
FA Cup						
Home	1	0	1	0	0	0
Away	1	0	1	0	3	3
Neutral	1	0	0	1	0	1
Totals	3	0	2	1	3	4
League Cup						
Home	1	0	0	1	0	2
Away	1	0	1	0	0	0
Totals	2	0	1	1	0	2

Founder members of the Football League, Stoke, first met Huddersfield in the competition in April 1920 - having regained their Second Division status after a spell in the Southern League. Huddersfield won both fixtures - 1-0 at The Victoria ground and 3-0 at Leeds Road.

Stanley Matthews, aged 46, made his 'return' to Stoke for the Second Division game with Huddersfield in October 1961. The Potters won 3-0 in front of 35,974 fans - 27,500 more than had attended the game at The Victoria Ground. Stoke knocked Huddersfield out of the FA Cup in 1970-71, winning a 4th round, 2nd replay at Old Trafford by a goal to nil and they eliminated the Terriers from the League Cup in 1983-84

STOKES, Derek: Centre-forward: 170 apps. 69 goals Born: Normanton, 13 September 1939

Stokes impressed in junior football with Snydale and then after almost two years of intermediate competition with Bradford City he was upgraded to the professional ranks at Valley Parade in April 1958. After scoring 55 goals in 106 outings for the Bantams, he was transferred to Huddersfield for £22,500 plus Stan Howard in June 1960. During his National Service he played against The Army for the RAF and FA XI (1961-62) and also won four England Under-23 caps (1962-63). He was the Terriers' leading scorer four seasons in a row before returning to Valley Parade in January 1966. Adding a further 11 goals in 35 games to his tally, he then moved to Dundalk for £1,500 in 1966, retiring the following year.

SUBSTITUTES: Substitutes today play a big part in the game and it is sometimes hard to appreciate that their use in the Football League has only been allowed since 1965 (passed at the AGM on 29 May of that year). Initially there was only one 'sub' allowed and that for an injured player, and in the 1965-66 season, a total of 746 substitutes were used in League matches all over the country, Huddersfield's contribution being just eight.
The two substitute rule was introduced for the 1987-88 season and three were allowed to be utilised for the first time in 1996-97

Subs' Bench
- Ian Lawson and John Thorrington made 15 substitute League appearances for the Terriers in 1996-97 and 2002-03 respectively but the club record for most 'sub' appearances in any one season (in the Football League) is held by Iain Dunn who, in 1994-95 was called off the bench on 26 occasions. He was also used as a 'sub' in seven other games for an overall total of 33.
- Iffy Onuora made 21 'sub' appearances in his first 26 senior appearances for the Terriers and 18 of veteran striker Peter Withe's 44 outings for the club came as a 'sub'.
- Simon Baldry has made most senior 'sub' appearances for the terriers: 69.
- The first 'sub' used in a League game by Huddersfield was Steve Smith who replaced John Coddington during the Second Division home game with PNE on 18 September 1965.
- The club's first League Cup substitute was Jimmy McGill, in the semi-final, second leg clash with Arsenal at Highbury on 6 February 1968.
- Colin Dobson was Huddersfield's first FA Cup substitute, taking the field in the second-half of the 4th round replay with Stoke on 26 January 1971.
- Huddersfield used two substitutes (Ian Bray and Peter Ward) for the first time in a League game on 22 August 1987 in a 6-1 defeat at Plymouth.
- All three 'subs' came off the bench for the first time against Barnsley at Oakwell on 25 August 1996. They were Simon Collins, Paul Dalton and Paul Reid.
- Geoff Vowden was the first substitute to score a hat-trick in a League game - for Birmingham against Huddersfield in September 1968 (Division Two).

SUNDERLAND: Huddersfield's record against the Wearsiders is:
Football League

Venue	P	W	D	L	F	A
Home	40	15	14	11	60	49
Away	40	4	12	24	40	83
Totals	80	19	26	35	100	132

the light at the end of the tunnel

FA Cup

Away	1	0	0	1	0	6
Neutral	1	1	0	0	3	1

League Cup

Home	2	1	0	1	4	1
Away	3	3	0	0	9	5
Totals	5	4	0	1	13	6

Huddersfield drew 0-0 (h) and lost 2-1 (a) in their first two League games with Sunderland in September/October 1920.

The Terriers' first win in the competition followed at the eighth attempt in December 1923 when they triumphed 3-2 at Leeds Road.

Twelve months later Sunderland were defeated 4-0 at Leeds Road - and on Christmas Eve 1955 that scoreline was repeated in favour of the Terriers.

Huddersfield's last game before WW2 ended in a 0-0 draw at Sunderland on 24 April 1939. The attendance was only 7,729

Two heavy Huddersfield away defeats suffered at the hands of Sunderland have been 7-1 in April 1952 and 4-1 in August 1955. In the first minute of a League game at Sunderland on 21 February 1948, Huddersfield goalkeeper Bob Hesford broke his ankle in a collision with Frank Bee. The game, due to kick--off at 3.15pm, actually commenced at 3.10 and by the time the original start time arrived, Hesford was on his way to hospital. Sunderland won 2-0.

Huddersfield beat Sunderland 3-1 in the FA Cup semi-final at Ewood Park, Blackburn in March 1938 in front of almost 48,000 spectators.

A crowd of 55,097 saw the Terriers suffer their heaviest defeat in the FA Cup when losing a 3rd round tie at Roker Park by 6-0 in January 1950.

After winning 6-1 on aggregate in the 2nd round of the League Cup in 1991-92, the following season Huddersfield won a 1st round tie on the away goal rule after a 3-3 aggregate draw. The Terriers then won 4-2 at The Stadium of Light in a 2nd round League Cup-tie in September 2003.

SUTTON, David William: Defender: 284 apps. 15 goals Born: Tarleton near Preston, 21 January 1957

Despite being born 300 miles away, Dave Sutton started his career in Devon, signing as an apprentice for Plymouth in May 1972, turning professional in July 1974. He had five seasons at Home Park, his most sustained spell in the first team being during the Pilgrims' stay in the Second Division from 1975-77. Having lost his place in the side following relegation, he was taken on loan by Huddersfield for a month before signing permanently for £15,000 in April 1978. An ideal successor to Steve Baines at the heart of the defence, Sutton went on to give the Terriers supreme service for seven years, gaining a Fourth Division championship medal in 1980 when he was an ever-present. In June 1985 he joined Third Division Bolton for £12,000, appearing in both relegation and promotion sides in successive seasons. Moving in July 1988 to nearby Rochdale, he retired at the end of that season through injury. He remained at Spotland as a coach, taking over as caretaker-manager for a month in March 1989 prior to the appointment of another former Huddersfield star Terry Dolan. Appointed manager himself in 1991, he remained at Spotland until November 1994 and four months later became manager of Chorley.

SWANN, Jack: Inside-forward: 74 apps. 36 goals. Born: Easington, County Durham, 10 July 1892. Died: circa 1975

An aggressive, all-action forward, Swann played for Seaham Colliery FC before joining Huddersfield in October 1919. He remained at the club for just over two years, transferring to Leeds United in November 1921 and later assisting Watford, QPR, Thames and Lovells Athletic, retiring in 1930 with over 150 goals under his belt (109 in the Football League). He did very well alongside Sid Taylor in his first season at Leeds Road, his scoring 22 goals in total helping the Terriers gain promotion to the top flight and reach the FA Cup final.

* Some reference books spell this player's surname thus, Swan.

SWANSEA CITY (Town): Huddersfield's record against the Swans is:
Football League

Venue	P	W	D	L	F	A
Home	22	14	6	2	45	20
Away	22	5	7	10	24	34
Totals	44	19	13	12	69	54
FA Cup						
Away	1	0	0	1	0	1
Other						
Neutral	1	0	1*	0	1	1

* Huddersfield lost this 1994 Autoglass Trophy final, 3-1 on penalties.

Huddersfield met Swansea for the first time in the League over the festive period in 1952 (Division Two). Over 28,500 saw the Terriers win 3-0 at Leeds Road on Christmas Day and almost 25,000 were present at The Vetch Field 48 hours later to witness a thrilling 3-3 draw.

The Swans dumped Huddersfield out of the FA Cup in 4th round in January 1965. A crowd of 47,773 witnessed the AGT final in April 1994. Richard Logan scored in normal play for the Terriers - their first goal at Wembley since 1928.

SWEENEY, Alan: Right-back: 71 apps. Born: Paisley, Glasgow, 31 October 1956

After serving his apprenticeship at Leeds Road, Sweeney turned professional at the age of 18 and remained at the club until July 1978 when he dropped down the ladder with Emley, returning to League football with Hartlepool in September 1979 and staying until May 1981. He had his best season with the Terriers in 1975-76, making 40 appearances.

SWINDON TOWN: Huddersfield's record against the Robins is:
Football League

Venue	P	W	D	L	F	A
Home	14	5	5	4	20	15
Away	14	4	2	8	15	30
Totals	28	9	7	12	35	45
FA Cup						
Home	1	0	0	1	1	2
Away	1	0	0	1	0	1
Totals	2	0	0	2	1	3

League Cup
Away   1   0   0   1   1   4
Huddersfield completed the double over Swindon when the teams first met in a League season - 1963-64. The Terriers won 2-0 at home and 2-1 away.
Huddersfield's best League win over the Robins is 5-1 at The County Ground in April 1982.
Swindon eliminated the Terriers from the FA Cup in 1912-13 and 2002-03 and beat them in the League Cup in 1991-92.

T

TAYLOR, Edward Hallows: Goalkeeper: 129 apps. Born: Liverpool, 17 March 1887. Died: Manchester City , 5 July 1956
Ted Taylor played for Marlborough Old Boys (Liverpool), Liverpool Balmoral and Oldham before joining Huddersfield for £1,950 in June 1922. He spent almost five years at Leeds Road, up to February 1927 when he transferred to Everton. He later assisted Ashton National (September 1928) and Wrexham (from November 1928, retired May 1929).
Capped eight times by England between 1923-26, Taylor also played for the Football League (1923-24), for the Professionals against The Amateurs in the Charity Shield games of 1923 and 1924 along with his Leeds Road colleague Sam Wadsworth and appeared in an amateur international trial match. He understudied Howard Matthews at Oldham before WW1 and after receiving a benefit match (v. Manchester United in 1922), subsequently replaced Alex Mutch at Huddersfield. He won two League championship medals with the Terriers (1923-24 and 1925-26), sadly missing a third after breaking his leg v. Manchester City in October 1924.
Not the tallest of 'keepers, he was nevertheless a fine one, quick thinking, competent on and off his line, being without any noticeable weakness. He won a third League championship medal with Everton in 1928 and all told Taylor amassed almost 300 appearances at various levels. He worked in the cotton trade in Manchester City for many years prior to his death.

TAYLOR, Jeffrey Neilson: Forward: 71 apps. 29 goals Born: Huddersfield, 20 September 1930
Jeff Taylor signed amateur forms for Huddersfield in 1945 while singing as a boy soprano at the local town hall. He was also studying geology and later gained honours at London University as well as a diploma in teaching. A member of the YMCA, he signed professional forms at Leeds Road in September 1947 (after serving in the RAF) and remained at the club until November 1951 when he moved to Fulham. He later assisted Brentford before attending the Royal Academy of Music. His first senior engagement was with the Halle Orchestra and he also appeared regularly at Covent Garden and Glyndebourne. He used his middle name on stage, appearing as Neilson Taylor. His brother Kenneth Taylor (q.v) also played for the Terriers.

TAYLOR, Kenneth: Defender: 269 apps. 14 goals: Born: Huddersfield, 21 August 1935
Besides his footballing exploits, cricketer-footballer Taylor also opened the batting for
England and Yorkshire. He also studied at the Huddersfield School of Art and at the
Slade School of Fine Art, London. He signed amateur forms for the Terriers in May 1950
(after a spell with Yorkshire Amateurs), turned professional in September 1952 and
made his League debut v. Liverpool in March 1954 when taking over at centre-half from
Don McEvoy. After almost 13 years' service at Leeds Road (he missed the 1964-65
season because he was coaching in New Zealand) he joined Bradford Park Avenue
(February 1965), retiring from soccer May 1967.
After working as a part-time games and arts teacher, he travelled to Cape Town (South
Africa) where he combined his teaching with cricket and football coaching. On his return
to the U.K. he took employment as a cricket coach in Norfolk.
On the cricket field, he was awarded his county cap in 1957 and helped Yorkshire win
seven titles between 1959 and 1968 and also the Gillette Cup. He scored over 13,000
first-class runs and took 129 wickets. Brother of Jeff Taylor (q.v) Ken's son, Nicholas,
played cricket for Yorkshire and Surrey.

TAYLOR, Richard Herbert: Goalkeeper: 119 apps. Born: Huddersfield, 24 January 1957
An England Youth and Under-21 international, Dick Taylor joined Huddersfield as an
apprentice in May 1973 and turned professional in January 1974. He remained at Leeds
Road until his enforced retirement in 1982, having his best season in the first XI in
1975-76 when he missed only four games (out of 53). Unfortunately injury ruined his
career and in fact, some people believe he was the unluckiest goalkeeper ever to play
for the club. He had a spell on loan with York in March 1980.

TAYLOR, Samuel James T: Forward: 67 apps. 45 goals Born: Sheffield, 17 September
1893. Died: Sheffield, February 1973
Sam Taylor was a wonderfully consistent marksman whose career realised a fine set of
statistics - 346 senior appearances and 127 goals. A junior player with the Atlas &
Norfolk Ironworks team, he then starred for Silverwood Colliery FC and guested for
Rotherham County and Bradford Park Avenue during WW1 before joining Huddersfield in
May 1919. A member of the promotion and FA Cup final sides of 1920, he rattled in no
fewer than 41 goals that season (35 in the League).
But Taylor wanted a bigger stage and in January 1921 moved to Sheffield Wednesday.
He did very well at Hillsborough and later served with Mansfield, Southampton, Halifax,
Chesterfield, Grantham and Llanelli. On retiring from football Taylor and his wife became
well-known variety entertainers on the South Yorkshire circuit. He loved classical jazz
and was no mean billiards player either.

TEMPEST, Dale Michael: Forward: 72 apps. 29 goals Born: Leeds 30 December 1963
Dale Tempest was an apprentice and then professional with Fulham before joining
Huddersfield for £15,000 in August 1984. He spent two seasons at Leeds Road during
which time he averaged a goal every three games while also having a loan spell with
Gillingham (March-April 1986). He played for Lokeren (Belgium) before returning with
Colchester United (August 1987-May 1989).

TERRIER FLEDGLINGS: Huddersfield Town's 2004-05 squad comprises of several youngsters who hopefully will become 'stars of the future.'

- Pawel Abbott (right), a forward, born in York in 1982 and formerly with the Polish club LKS Loda, Preston North End and Bury (on loan). He joined the Terriers in February 2004.
- Chris Brandon, born in Bradford in 1976, was signed on a free transfer from Chesterfield in June 2004. Initially a forward, now a defender, he started his career with Bradford Park Avenue and then assisted Torquay United.
- Nathan Clarke, aged 21 from Halifax, is a central defender who joined the club as a trainee and turned 'pro' in 2001.
- Lee Fowler, a 21 year-old from Cardiff, joined the Terriers from Coventry City in August 2003. A midfielder, he has been capped by Wales at youth and Under-21 levels.
- Andy Holdsworth, a right wing-back, born in Pontefract in 1984, came through the club's Academy to sign professional forms in December 2003.
- Anthony Lloyd who was born in Taunton in 1984, plays as a ;left wing-back and spent two years as a trainee at the club before signing professional forms in August 2003.
- David Mirfin comes from Sheffield. Born in 1985, 6ft 2in tall, he plays in midfield and signed professional forms for the club in December 2003 after two years as a trainee.

THORNLEY, Benjamin Lindsay: Midfield: 126 apps. 8 goals Born: Bury, 21 April 1975
Ben Thornley made 14 appearances for Manchester United and gained an FA Youth Cup winner's medal (1992) before joining Huddersfield for £175,000 in July 1998, having previously been on loan with the Terriers (February 1996) as well as with Stockport. An England Schoolboy international who later gained three Under-21 caps, he was initially a skilful left-sided player who later switched to the centre of midfield. He moved from Huddersfield to Aberdeen in August 2001 and in December 2002 signed for Blackpool, switching to Bury in September 2003.

THORRINGTON, John: Winger: 75 apps. 8 goals Born: Johannesburg, South Africa, 17 October 1979 Thorrington played for Mission Viejas Pateadores (California) before joining Manchester United in October 1997. He failed to break into the first team at Old Trafford and in May 1999 moved to Bayer Leverkusen in Germany, returning to England with Huddersfield in March 2001. Capped once by the USA, Thorrington played a small part in helping the Terriers reach the play-offs before transferring to Grimsby Town in March 2004.

TORQUAY UNITED: Huddersfield's record against the Gulls is:
Football League

Venue	P	W	D	L	F	A
Home	7	4	2	1	15	8
Away	7	3	0	4	8	9
Totals	10	7	2	5	23	17

FA Cup

Away	1	1	0	0	1	0

Huddersfield lost 3-2 at home to Torquay in the first League game between the clubs in

October 1975. The return game at Plainmoor ended in a 3-1 win for the Terriers. Huddersfield's best win over the Gulls is 4-2 (h) in April 1980.

A record crowd of 21,908 attended the Torquay-Huddersfield 4th round FA Cup-tie at Plainmoor in January 1955. Jim Glazzard scored the game's only goal to give the Terriers a narrow victory.

TOTTENHAM HOTSPUR: Huddersfield's record against Spurs is:

Football League

Venue	P	W	D	L	F	A
Home	18	10	6	2	28	18
Away	18	4	7	7	22	26
Totals	36	14	13	9	50	44

FA Cup

Venue	P	W	D	L	F	A
Home	2	2	0	0	8	1
Away	1	0	0	1	0	1
Totals	3	2	0	1	8	2

League Cup

Venue	P	W	D	L	F	A
Away	1	0	0	1	1	2

Huddersfield's first two League games against Spurs took place over a period of three weeks halfway through the 1919-20 season. A crowd of 27,000 saw the 1-1 draw at Leeds Road and 35,000 saw Spurs win 2-0 at White Hart Lane.

Huddersfield's first win followed in April 1921 when they defeated the FA Cup winners of that season 2-0 at home, Jack Swann scoring both goals. Huddersfield drew 5-5 with Spurs in a League game at White Hart Lane in September 1925. A crowd of almost 21,000 saw Alex Jackson net a hat-trick for the Terriers (in the 4th, 13th and 70th minutes). Spurs led 5-3 halfway through the second-half but the visitors stormed back and George Brown headed an equaliser with four minutes remaining. With a Wembley final in sight, George Brown scored four times when Huddersfield beat Spurs 6-1 in a 6th round FA Cup-tie at Leeds Road in March 1928. The attendance was 52,390.

TOURS

The first official overseas tour made by Huddersfield was in 1921 when they played in France.

The first lengthy one came in 1955 when they toured North America, playing nine games and losing only one, 3-2 to Sunderland in a challenge match in New York.

TRANMERE ROVERS: Huddersfield's record against Rovers is:

Football League

Venue	P	W	D	L	F	A
Home	14	8	4	2	16	6
Away	14	2	3	9	9	24
Totals	28	10	7	11	25	30

FA Cup

Venue	P	W	D	L	F	A
Home	1	0	0	1	1	2
Away	2	1	0	1	4	2
Totals	3	1	0	2	5	4

Both League games in 1973-74 between Huddersfield and Rovers (the first time they had played each other) ended in draws - 1-1 at Prenton Park and 0-0 at Leeds Road. Huddersfield lost 4-0 at Prenton Park in September 1989. Huddersfield's Cup win over Rovers was achieved in the 2nd round in December 1980 when Ian Robins scored twice.

TRANSFERS:
Major transfers involving the Terriers:
Players Signed

£1.2 million	Marcus Stewart from Bristol Rovers, July 1996
£500,000	Andy Morrison from Blackpool, July 1996
£350,000	Andy Payton from Barnsley, July 1996
£250,000	Lee Duxbury from Bradford City, December 1994
£245,000*	Iwan Roberts from Watford, July 1990
£110,000	Terry Austin from Mansfield, December 1980
£65,000	Alan Gowling from Manchester United, June 1972
£45,000	Dick Krzywicki from WBA, March 1970
£22,500	Willie Davie from Luton Town, December 1951
£15,500	Ronnie Burke from Manchester United, June 1949
£10,000	Albert Nightingale from Sheffield United, March 1948
£10,000	Peter Doherty from Derby County, December 1946
£6,000	Bob Kelly from Sunderland, February 1927
£5,000	Alex Jackson from Aberdeen, May 1925
£3,000	Clem Stephenson from Aston Villa, March 1921

* Some reference books have this fee down as £275,000

Players Sold

£2.7m	Andy Booth to Sheffield Wednesday, July 1996
£2.5m	Marcus Stewart to Ipswich Town, February 2000
£1.2m	Jonathan Stead to Blackburn Rovers, February 2004
£375,000	Simon Charlton to Southampton, June 1993
£300,000	Iwan Roberts to Leicester, October 1993
£250,000	Craig Maskell to Reading, July 1990
£250,000	Duncan Shearer to Swindon, June 1988
£132,500	Mark Lillis to Manchester City, August 1985
£100,000	Trevor Cherry to Leeds United, December 1980
£80,000	David Lawson to Everton, June 1972
£80,000	Derek Parkin to Wolves, February 1968
£55,000	Denis Law to Manchester City, March 1960
£27,000	Harold Hassall to Bolton Wanderers, January 1952
£8,500	Alex Jackson to Chelsea, September 1930
£5,000	George Brown to Aston Villa, August 1929
£4,100	George Shaw to WBA, December 1926
£2,500	Jack Cock to Chelsea, October 1919

Transfer Talk
- In 1935 John Ball was transferred from Manchester United in the Second Division to Huddersfield in the First and then to Luton in the Third South in the space of seven weeks.

- In July 1955, Sheffield Wednesday and Huddersfield were involved in a major transfer deal in which two players from each side joined the other club with money changing hands. Tony Conwell and Jackie Marriott moved from Hillsborough to Leeds Road while Ron Staniforth and Roy Shiner went in the opposite direction.
- Denis Law was the first British footballer to be transferred for a six-figure fee when he moved from Turin (Italy) to Manchester United for £115,000 in 1962.
- When future Terriers' star Bob Kelly joined Sunderland from Burnley in December 1925 it was for a then British record fee of £6,550.
- On 29 January 1975 Huddersfield sold Paul Smith to Cambridge United for just £1.

TREVITT, SIMON: Full-back: 285 apps. 4 goals Born: Dewsbury, 20 December 1967
An apprentice with Huddersfield before turning professional in June 1986, Trevitt spent more than eleven years with the Terriers. A fine, over-lapping right-back who could cross on the run, he had his best spell in the first team during the early 1990s and it was a surprise when he left to join Hull in November 1995. He assisted Swansea (on loan, December 1997) and signed for Guiseley in June 1998.

TURNER, HUGH: Goalkeeper: 394 apps. Born: Wigan, 6 August 1904. Died: 1997
Rather small for a goalkeeper, Turner was capped twice by England, replacing Birmingham's Harry Hibbs against France and Belgium in 1931. He also represented the Football League v. the Irish League that same year. Starting his career with Felling Colliery (Darlington), he then assisted High Fell (Northern Alliance) before joining Huddersfield in April 1926. Taking over from Ted Taylor, he gave the Terriers splendid service for over a decade, playing in the 1930 FA Cup final against Arsenal. Possessing fine agility and anticipation, he had inspired days when he could not be rivalled. He moved to Fulham in May 1937 and was an ever-present for the Cottagers in the last full season before WW2. He retired in 1940.

U

UNDEFEATED:
- Over a period of 16 months, between May 1982 and September 1983, the Terriers were unbeaten in 28 consecutive home League games.
- The team had a record unbeaten away League run of 18 games between 29 November 1924 and 31 October 1925.
- The club record of unbeaten League games (home and away) is 27 - set between 24 January and 17 October 1925 (16 of those games were won).
- Huddersfield remained undefeated in 25 home FA Cup games (24 won, one drawn) over a period of 19 years, starting with a 3-1 win over Swindon on 15 January 1913 and ending on 27 February 1932 when Arsenal, the subsequent Cup winners, triumphed 1-0 in front of 67,037 spectators.

V

VAESEN, Nico Jos-Theodore: Goalkeeper: 153 apps. Born: Ghent, Belgium, 28 September 1969
Nico Vaesen, 6' 3" tall, played for three Belgian clubs - Tongeren, CS Brugge and SC Eendracht Aalst - before moving to Huddersfield for £80,000 in July 1997. He missed only four League games in three seasons with the Terriers before his £800,000 transfer to Birmingham in June 2001, helped Blues gain promotion to the Premiership in his first season at St Andrew's before losing his place to Maik Taylor. During the second half of 2003-04 he had loan spells with Gillingham, Bradford City and Crystal Palace, performing splendidly for the Eagles as they climbed into the Premiership.

VINCENT, Jamie Roy: Defender: 66 apps. 2 goals Born: Wimbledon, 18 June 1975
Jamie Vincent was an apprentice with Crystal Palace for two years before turning professional in July 1993. A loan spell with Bournemouth preceded his £25,000 transfer to Dean Court in August 1996. After almost 140 outings for the Cherries he moved to Huddersfield for £440,000 in March 1999 and performed consistently during his time with the Terriers which ended in February 2001 when he moved to Portsmouth for £800,000.

W

WADSWORTH, Samuel John: Full-back: 313 apps. 4 goals Born: Darwen, 13 September 1896. Died: Eindhoven, Holland, 6 September 1961
Sam Wadsworth played for Darwen, Blackburn (as an outside-left, 1914-19) and Nelson before joining Huddersfield in April 1921. Converted into a left-back, he became an England international, winning nine caps (four v. Scotland) between 1922 and 1926. He skippered both club and country, was a League championship winner with the Terriers three seasons running (1923-26) and also gained an FA Cup winner's medal in 1922 and a loser's prize in 1928.
A prominent figure in the Huddersfield defence, he was fast, constructive and always tried to use the ball, very rarely choosing to blast it aimlessly downfield. He left Leeds Road for Burnley in September 1929 and later assisted Lytham. (1931-32). After retiring he became manager-coach of PSV Eindhoven in Holland, where he spent the rest of his life (apart for the war years). Wadsworth once worked in a brewery with Jimmy Ruffell (West Ham) and John Townrow (Clapton Orient and Chelsea).
* In September 1927, Wadsworth was suspended for a week by Huddersfield after he had criticised the Central League.

WALSALL: Huddersfield's record against the Saddlers is:
Football League

Venue	P	W	D	L	F	A
Home	10	5	5	0	21	12
Away	10	1	5	4	10	18
Totals	20	6	10	4	31	30

FA Cup

Home	1	1	0	0	3	0
Away	1	1	0	0	1	0
Totals	2	2	0	0	4	0

Huddersfield beat Walsall 4-2 in the first League game between the clubs played at Leeds Road in September 1961. The return fixture at Fellows Park ended goalless. Huddersfield's second home game saw them win 4-0 and their only success on Walsall soil so far followed in August 1989 (3-2).

Huddersfield's last pre-WW2 FA Cup win was against Walsall (h) in the 5th round in February 1939. Billy Price scored twice in the 3-0 victory in front of 33,543 spectators.

WALTER, Joseph Dorville: Outside-right: 57 apps. 5 goals Born: Eastville, Bristol, 16 August 1895. Died: 1995

Joe Walter played for Horfield United and Bristol Rovers before joining Huddersfield in May 1922. A strong and efficient winger, he gained a League championship medal in 1923-24 and left Leeds Road for Taunton United in May 1925. Later associated with Blackburn, Bristol Rovers (for a second spell) and Bath City, he retired in 1933.

WARTIME FOOTBALL: Huddersfield's record in wartime football

Years	P	W	D	L	F	A
1915-19	42	64	29	49	223	192
1939-46	273	127	47	89	634	463
Totals	415	191	76	138	857	655

(1939 void League games & 1946 FA Cup games not included)

War Cry

- Huddersfield competed in the Midland Section Principal and Supplementary Competitions throughout the First World War.
- They finished third in both competitions in 1915-16; took 4th and 6th places respectively in 1916-17, claimed 8th and 7th spots in 1917-18 and finished sixth and runners-up in the two competitions in 1918-19.
- During WW2 Huddersfield participated in the Regional League North-East Division and the Football League War Cup North in 1939-40, winning the championship of the former. The following season they played in the North Region League (claiming 11th place) and Football League War Cup North (beaten in the first round)
- In seasons 1941-42, 1942-43, 1943-44 and 1944-45 they were members of the Football League North Regional Section First & Second Championships, finishing moderately in the first three campaigns before winning the title of the First Championship in 1943-44. They also competed in the Football League War Cup North Regional Section in 1943-44 and 1944-45.
- In the transitional 1945-46 season, Huddersfield played in the Football League (N)

and their final position was a disappointing 15th. Huddersfield recorded nine successive wins between 23 December 1939 and 16 April 1940.The team went 15 games undefeated between 2 December 1939 and 3 June 1940. Of 38 games played during the 1942-43 season, Huddersfield scored in 37 of them.
- Billy Price scored in eight successive games between 22 April and 23 September 1943. Earlier Price had netted in seven consecutive games up to February 1943.
- Only 356 spectators paid to watch Huddersfield beat Rochdale 11-0 in a North Regional League game at Leeds Road on 22 March 1941

WATFORD: Huddersfield's record against the Hornets is:
Football League

Venue	P	W	D	L	F	A
Home	9	6	1	2	15	8
Away	9	3	3	3	8	9
Totals	18	9	4	5	23	17
League Cup						
Home	1	1	0	0	2	1
Away	1	0	1	0	2	2
Totals	2	1	1	0	4	3

Huddersfield and Watford first opposed each in a League game in September 1969 when a crowd of 17,548 witnessed the 1-1 draw at Vicarage Road (Division Two). On the last day of that season the Terriers won 3-1 at Leeds Road, Dick Krzywicki scoring twice for the champions in front of almost 28,000 spectators. Huddersfield won a 2nd round League Cup-tie 4-3 on aggregate in 1983-84 - the season the Hornets reached the FA Cup final.

WATSON, James: Inside-right: 148 apps. 32 goals Born: Cowie, Stirlingshire, 16 January 1924. Deceased.
A Scottish international, capped twice, once with Motherwell, 1948 and once with Huddersfield, 1954, Watson also represented the Scottish League. A thoroughly skilful player, he had a wonderful right-foot which he put to good use during his years at Leeds Road.
He started his career with Armadale, moving to Motherwell in 1944. He was a League Cup and Scottish Cup winner in 1951 and 1952 respectively before transferring to Huddersfield in May 1952. Transferred to Dunfermline Athletic August 1957. On retiring in the summer of 1959 he became a licensee in Dunfermline and later went into business in that town

WATSON, William, senior: Defender: 323 apps. one goal Born: Bolton-on-Deane, 1893. Died: Huddersfield, April 1962.
Signed from Bolton-on-Deane FC in November 1912, Billy Watson made his League debut for Huddersfield against Preston (a) in February 1913. His second outing followed in March 1915 and, in fact, up to the start of the 1919-20 season he managed only six first team games. After that, however, he became a class player, and was part of a great half-back line which also featured Tom Wilson and David Steele. A promotion winner and FA Cup finalist in 1920, he helped the Terriers win the Cup in 1922 and also collected three League championship medals in succession. Retiring as a player in May 1928, he immediately joined the Leeds Road coaching staff, occasionally skippering the

second XI. He left the club in May 1929 but the family tradition continued when his sons Albert and William junior, made 18 and 11 appearances respectively either side of WW2. William junior also played cricket for Yorkshire and England and died in South Africa in April 2004.

WEBSTER, Simon Paul: Defender: 134 apps. 4 goals Born: Hinckley, 20 January 1964
Simon Webster spent five years with Spurs (from 1980) and had a loan spell with Exeter (1983-84) before joining Huddersfield for £15,000 in February 1985. He gave the Terriers three seasons of total commitment as a solid defender prior to his £35,000 move to Sheffield United in March 1988. He later served with Charlton, West Ham and while also having loans spells with Oldham and Derby. On retiring in November 1995 (after failing to regain full fitness following a broken leg suffered in 1992) Webster studied physiotherapy at the University of East London.

WEST BROMWICH ALBION: Huddersfield's record against the Baggies is:
Football League

Venue	P	W	D	L	F	A
Home	33	17	8	8	56	36
Away	33	9	8	16	43	57
Totals	66	26	16	24	99	93
FA Cup						
Home	1	1	0	0	2	1
Away	1	0	1	0	1	1
Totals	2	1	1	0	3	2

On the last day of the 1910-11 season, Huddersfield played the Albion at The Hawthorns in front of a 30,000 crowd. The Baggies won 1-0 and the all-important goal was scored by Fred Buck from the penalty spot after 15 minutes. The two points gained clinched the Second Division championship for Albion.
The first game at Leeds Road - played on 24 December 1910 - resulted in a 2-0 win for the Baggies. In October 1920, the Terriers thrashed Albion, the reigning League champions, 5-1 at Leeds Road but lost the return game 3-0 a week later. In 1923 the Terriers beat Albion 4-1 (h) and 4-2 (a) in April and October respectively.
Albion finished runners-up to Huddersfield in the League championship in 1924-25 and then the Terriers were third in the table behind Wolves (champions) and Albion in 1953-54.
The Terriers lost 5-1 at The Hawthorns a week before the 1938 FA Cup final. Full-back George 'Teapot' Shaw was transferred from Huddersfield to Albion for a then record fee of £4,100 in November 1926. Huddersfield knocked Albion out of the FA Cup in the 6th round in 1928-29.

WEST HAM UNITED: Huddersfield's record against the Hammers is:
Football League

Venue	P	W	D	L	F	A
Home	15	11	2	2	36	13
Away	15	6	4	5	23	26
Totals	30	17	6	7	59	39

the light at the end of the tunnel

FA Cup

Home	4	2	1	1	7	6
Away	2	1	0	1	5	5
Totals	6	3	1	2	12	11

League Cup

Home	2	2	0	0	3	0
Away	1	0	0	1	0	3
Totals	3	2	0	1	3	3

Huddersfield's first League game with the Hammers took place at Leeds Road in February 1924 and ended in a 1-1 draw. Soon afterwards the Terriers travelled to London and won the return game 3-2 at Upton Park, Charlie Wilson scoring twice. George Brown hit a hat-trick in a 5-2 home win over West Ham in January 1928 and later that year Alex Jackson weighed in with a treble as Town earned an early Christmas present by beating the Hammers 4-0 at home. Ken Taylor scored four times when the Terriers whipped the Hammers 6-2 at Leeds Road in February 1957 (Division Two). The Hammers trounced Huddersfield 4-0 in a 3rd round FA Cup-tie at Upton Park in January 1954 but six years later, in January 1960, the Terriers pulled off a splendid 3rd round replay win by 5-1, Les Massie (2), John Connor (2) and Bill McGarry the goalscorers. Huddersfield's best of their two home Cup wins over the London club is 4-2, achieved in the 5th round in February 1972.

WHEELER, William John: Goalkeeper: 182 apps. Born: North Littleton near Evesham, 13 July 1919.

After plying his trade as a goalkeeper with Littleton Juniors and Evesham Early Closers FC, Jack Wheeler developed his game with Cheltenham before joining Birmingham in March 1938. WW2 disrupted his progress at St Andrew's and after failing to gain a regular first team place he switched his allegiance to Huddersfield in August 1948. He became part and parcel of a terrific back division for the Terriers, comprising himself, full-backs Ron Staniforth and Lawrie Kelly and half-backs Billy McGarry, Don McEvoy and Len Quested. All six were ever-present when the Second Division championship was won in 1952-53. Wheeler finally left Leeds road in July 1956, signing for Kettering Town, later assisting Evesham Town. Then employed as trainer by Notts County from 1957 to 1982, he had a spell as caretaker-manager at Meadow Lane in 1968-69.

WHITE, Leonard Roy: Centre-forward: 110 apps. 39 goals Born: Skellow near Doncaster, 23 March 1930. Died: Huddersfield, 17 June 1994

Learning his football with Upton Colliery, Len White then helped Rotherham win the Third Division (N) championship in 1951 before signing for Newcastle for £12,500 in February 1953. He spent nine years at St James' Park during which time he scored 153 goals in 270 appearances, gaining an FA Cup winner's medal in 1955 and twice representing the Football League for whom he scored a hat-trick in eight minutes against the Irish League in 1958. In February 1962, White - strong and mobile - was recruited by Huddersfield in an exchange deal involving Jimmy Kerray plus £10,000. He continued to find the net for the Terriers before enjoying a fruitful swansong to his career with Stockport (signed for £4,000 in January 1965 to May 1966). He then played in non-League circles with Altrincham, Ossett Town, Brown Tractors FC, Elland Road FC, Huddersfield YMCA and a handful of other Huddersfield intermediate sides as well as assisting the Irish club Sligo Rovers. In later years he was assistant-coach at Bradford City. He died after losing a long battle against cancer.

WHITTINGHAM, Alfred: Forward: 68 apps. 17 goals Born: Altofts, 19 June 1914. Died: Yorkshire, 1993 Able to occupy a number of front-line positions but preferring the number '9' shirt. Whittingham was almost 33 years of age when he joined Huddersfield from Bradford City in February 1947, having scored 25 goals in 94 first-class games for the Bantams. Starting his career with local club Altofts WRC, he joined Bradford in 1936 and on leaving Leeds Road in March 1949 signed for Halifax, retiring in April 1950. He had his best period with the Terriers in 1947-48, scoring nine goals in 42 games.

WIGAN ATHLETIC: Huddersfield's record against the Latics is:
Football League

Venue	P	W	D	L	F	A
Home	10	5	5	0	15	5
Away	10	4	1	5	11	11
Totals	20	9	6	5	26	16
FA Cup						
Home	1	1	0	0	2	0
Others						
Away	2	1	0	1	3	5

The first League game between the Terriers and the Latics, played on 7 October 1978 at Leeds Road, resulted in a 1-1 draw. The return fixture that season saw Wigan 2-1 at Springfield Park.
Huddersfield's FA Cup win over the Latics was achieved in the 1st round in November 1973. Bob Newton scored both goals in front of 9,557 spectators at Leeds Road.

WIJNHARD, Clyde: Striker: 72 apps. 18 goals Born: Surinam, 9 November 1973
Wijnhard played (and scored) for four Dutch clubs, Ajax Amsterdam, Groningen, RKC Waelwijk and Willem II, before joining Leeds United for £1.5m in July 1998. Struggling to hold down a place at Elland Road, he was transferred to Huddersfield for £750,000 in July 1999 and quickly got into his stride, top scoring in his first season with 16 goals. After five months with PNE (from March 2002) he moved to Oldham but was released by the Latics in May 2004 and a month later joined Vitoria Guimaeres of Portugal.

WILLIAMS, John James: Outside-right: 50 apps. 14 goals Born: Aberdare, Glamorgan, 29 March 1911. Died: Wrexham, 12 October 1987
Diminutive right-winger, 5ft 5ins tall, dark haired and quick, Jimmy Williams played for Aberaman and Llanelli before joining Huddersfield in November 1932.
He spent three years at Leeds Road before transferring to Aston Villa for £2,000 in November 1935, later going on to play for Ipswich, Wrexham, Colwyn Bay (guest in 1945-46) and Runcorn. Capped by Wales against France in 1939 when with Wrexham, he also helped Ipswich win the Southern League title in 1937 and appeared in the Portman Road club's first-ever League game v. Southend in August 1938 (Division Three South). After leaving football Williams worked as a storekeeper for Hunt's Capacitors (Wrexham).

WILLIAMS, John Joseph: Winger: 60 apps. 6 goals Born: Rotherham, 4 June 1902. Died: circa 1980.

A smart winger, Joe Williams joined the Terriers from Rotherham in May 1924 and left Leeds Road for Stoke in March 1926, switching to Arsenal in September 1929, then onto Middlesbrough in March 1932 before ending his career with Carlisle United. He played for the Professionals v the Amateurs in the 1929 Charity Shield and toured South Africa with the FA party but missed the 1930 FA Cup final (against the Terriers) through injury. With Rotherham when they were relegated from Division Two in 1923, he then helped Huddersfield win the League title in 1925. After his transfer to Stoke, he suffered relegation from Division Two in 1926 and gained a Third Division (N) championship medal in 1927 before helping the Gunners take the First Division crown in 1931.

WILLINGHAM, Charles Kenneth: Wing-half: 270 apps. 5 goals Born: Sheffield, 1 December 1912. Died: 1975

A Football League representative, Ken Willingham won 12 England caps between 1937 and 1939. An enthusiastic right-half, the noteworthy facet of his play was his speed both in going forward to assist his forwards and in his recovery to get back to help his defence. - a legacy of his schoolboy days when he was a champion runner. Willingham started his career with Ecclesfield FC (Sheffield) and after a spell with Worksop Town, joined Huddersfield's groundstaff in July 1930, turning professional in November 1931. An FA Cup finalist in 1938, besides his first-class appearances for the Terriers, he also starred in 194 WW2 matches, taking his overall appearance record with the club to 464. On leaving Leeds Road in December 1945 he joined Sunderland for £5,000 and later played for Leeds United (March 1947-May 1948). He remained on the coaching staff at Elland Road for another two years and thereafter was a licensee in Leeds.

* Willingham holds the record for scoring the fastest first-class goal for Huddersfield - netting after just 10 seconds of a First Division game v. Sunderland on 14 December 1935. It won the game.

WILSON, Charles: Centre-forward: 107 apps. 62 goals Born: Atherstone, 30 March 1895. Died: 1971

Wilson joined Spurs from Coventry City's junior side during WW1 and when competitive football resumed he struck home a hat-trick on his League debut against South Shields in September 1919. Surprisingly he never quite established himself at White Hart Lane and in November 1922 joined Huddersfield. He was top-scorer in each of his first three seasons at Leeds Road, gaining championship medals in 1923-24 and 1924-25. Following the emergence of George Brown, Wilson moved to Stoke in March 1926, helping them win the Third Division (N) title a year later. He netted 112 goals for the Potteries club before quitting top-class football in 1931. He went on to assist Stafford Rangers, Wrexham (briefly) and Shrewsbury

WILSON, Philip: Midfield: 272 apps. 17 goals
Born: Hemsworth, 16 October 1960
Wilson was an apprentice with Bolton before
accepting professional status at Burnden Park
in October 1978. Three years later, in August
1981, he moved to Huddersfield on a free
transfer. He stayed at Leeds Road for six
seasons during which time he aided and
abetted Steve Boyle in the engine-room,
producing some impressive displays while
helping the Terriers gain promotion from the
Third Division in 1983. Signed by York for
£5,000 in August 1987 he went on to play for
the Minstermen in Divisions Three and Four and
so joined the elite band of footballers to have
appeared in all four Divisions of the Football
League. In July 1989 Wilson moved to
Macclesfield Town and later played for
Scarborough after a trial with the Dutch club,
Nijmegan.

WILSON, Ramon: Left-Back: 283 apps. 6 goals Born: Shirebrook, 17 December 1934
Signed by Huddersfield as a wing-half from the Langwith Boys' Club (Mansfield) in May
1952, Wilson developed rapidly and in the mid-1960s was rated as the greatest left-
back in world soccer. He gained a regular place in the Terriers' line-up in 1957 and won
the first of his 63 full England caps as a Huddersfield player in 1960. In June 1964, he
was transferred to Everton for £25,000 (plus Mick Meagan, valued at £15,000) and two
years later twice jigged round Wembley Stadium first as an FA Cup winner and then as
a World Cup victor after England had beaten West Germany. He played in Everton's
losing FA Cup final of 1968 before he left Goodison Park for Oldham in July 1969,
having made over 150 appearances for Everton. Twelve months later he took over as
youth team coach at Bradford City and later worked as assistant-manager and
caretaker-boss at Valley Parade. In December 1971, a month after competing in his final
match, Wilson retired to join his brother-in-law in the family joinery and undertaking
business at Outlane near Huddersfield.
* Wilson was named after the film star Ramon Navarro.

WILSON, Thomas: Centre-half: 501 apps. 5 goals. Born: Seaham, County Durham, 16
April 1896. Died: Barnsley, 2 February 1948
Having started his career with Seaham Colliery, Wilson then had a spell with Sunderland
before returning to his former club only to move on quickly to Huddersfield in June
1919. A 'stopper' centre-half, hard and robust, Wilson gave nothing away, going in for
every ball with gusto, a real competitor who never shirked a challenge. He was strong
with both feet and head and after winning the ball with one of his ferocious tackles he
always tried to place it to the feet of a colleague rather than bang in hopefully
downfield (that's unless danger threatened near his own goal). He helped the Terriers
win three League championships (1924-25-26) and the FA Cup (1922) while collecting

runners-up medals in three losing FA Cup finals (1920, 1928 and 1930). He gained one full England cap, playing on that disastrous day in 1928 when Scotland's 'Wembley Wizards' won 5-1 in London. Second only to Billy Smith in Huddersfield's all-time appearance list, Wilson's tally includes a run of 52 consecutive Cup games. He was transferred to Blackpool in November 1931 but returned to Leeds Road as assistant-trainer in June 1932, holding that position September 1939. During WW2 he worked for British Dyes and assisted in the training sessions at Leeds Road when duty allowed. From 1945 until his death he was trainer of Barnsley.

WIMBLEDON: Huddersfield's record against the Dons is:
Football League

Venue	P	W	D	L	F	A
Home	6	3	1	2	9	5
Away	6	1	2	3	5	9
Totals	12	4	3	5	14	14
FA Cup						
Home	2	0	1	1	2	3
Away	1	0	0	1	1	3
Totals	3	0	1	2	3	6
League Cup						
Home	1	0	0	1	1	2

Huddersfield met the Dons for the first time at League level in December 1977 (Division Four) and in front of 3,544 hardy supporters at Leeds Road, took the points with a 3-0 victory. Later in the campaign the Dons won 2-0 at Plough Lane.

The Dons knocked Huddersfield out of the FA Cup in the 3rd round in 1996 and in the 2nd round two seasons later and did likewise in the League Cup in 1999-2000. For the 2004-05 season Wimbledon changed their name (and ground) to Milton Keynes Dons.

WINTER, Julian: Midfield: 108 apps. 5 goals Born: Huddersfield, 6 September 1965
An apprentice for two years, Winter signed as a professional for Huddersfield in July 1982 and remained at Leeds Road for a further seven years before transferring to Sheffield United for £50,000 in July 1989. A sprightly player, confident and zestful, he had two good seasons with the Terriers, the first in 1986-87, the second in 1988-89 after recovering from a broken leg suffered against Derby in April 1987 and a loan spell with Scunthorpe. Winter failed to make headway at Bramall Lane and left after twelve months.

WINS:
- The Terriers' biggest League win is 10-1 v. Blackpool (h), Division 1 on 13 December 1930.
- The Terriers' biggest win in the FA Cup is 11-0 over Heckmondwike (a) in a 4th preliminary round tie on 18 September 1909. They later ran up three 7-0 victories, against Rothwell White Rose (h) in the 2nd qualifying round on 16 October 1909, against. Lincoln United (h), 1st round, 16 November 1991 and against Chesterfield (h) 3rd round, 12 January 1929.
- In the League Cup (under the competition's various guises) the biggest win has been 5-1 v. Mansfield (h), 1st round 2nd leg, 13 September 1983.

- The most home League wins recorded in a season by the Terriers is 16 - in 1919-20, 1933-34 and 1979-80.
- The most away wins in one campaign is 12 - also in 1919-20.
- The most wins, home ad away, is 28, achieved in 1919-20.
- The fewest home League wins in a season is 4 - in 1971-72 and 1987-88.
- In 1936-37 the Terriers failed to win a single away League game.
- The fewest number of wins (home and away) is 6 - in 1971-72 and 1987-88.
- The Terriers had a run of 11 consecutive home League wins between 28 December 1925 and 30 August 1926.
- Between 24 January and 10 April 1925 the Terriers claimed five consecutive away wins in the League.
- The Terriers won eleven League games in succession (home and away) between 5 April and 4 September 1920.
- The Terriers failed to win any of 22 League games played between 4 December 1971 and 29 April 1972. They went 17 without a win during the 2000-01 season and 15 in 1997.
- In 1971-72, the Terriers had a run of 11 home League games without a win and during the period 22 February 1936 to 18 September 1937, they played 31 away League games without registering a single victory.
- Huddersfield recorded five successive 2-0 wins in League games during March/April 1923.
- On 26 April 1994, a ding-dong League game away at Cambridge United ended in a win for the Terriers by 5-4. At half-time the visitors led 3-1, were pegged back to 3-3 then led 5-3 before United scored again in the last minute.
- Huddersfield won 6-0 away at Bury in April 1989 to achieve their biggest goal-margin of victory since beating Everton 8-2 in home League game in April 1953. It was also their best away win in the League since whipping Sheffield United 7-1 at Bramall Lane in November 1927.

WOLVERHAMPTON WANDERERS: Huddersfield's record against the Wolves is:
Football League

Venue	P	W	D	L	F	A
Home	34	20	4	10	56	34
Away	34	7	8	19	47	89
Totals	68	27	12	29	103	123
FA Cup						
Home	2	2	0	0	5	2
Away	3	0	2	1	2	4
Totals	5	2	2	1	7	6
League Cup						
Home	1	1	0	0	1	0

The first League clash between Huddersfield and Wolves took place in October 1910 before a 12,000 Molineux crowd, the Terriers won 3-0, Bill Bartlett scoring one of the goals from the penalty spot - the Terriers' first in the competition. Terriers completed the double with a 3-1 win at Leeds Road.

Fifteen goals were scored in the two League games between the clubs in 1932-33. Town won 3-2 at Leeds Road but lost 6-4 at Molineux, Charlie Luke's hat-trick being in vain.

In League games against Wolves at Molineux, Huddersfield lost 6-1 in October 1946, 7-1 in October 1948, 7-1 again in September 1949 and 3-1 in December 1950. They also crashed to a 7-1 home defeat at the hands of the Wanderers in September 1951. In May 1949, the Terriers beat the FA cup winners from that season 4-0 at Leeds Road.
In February 1955 Wolves again beat the Terriers 6-4 at Molineux and this time it was Jim Glazzard who netted a hat-trick for the loser's.
In November 1988 Huddersfield recorded their last 'big' result over Wolves, winning 4-1 in the Black Country. After drawing at Molineux in 3rd round FA Cup-ties in January 1961 and January 1985, Huddersfield won the replay each time by 2-1 and 3-2 respectively. Wolves' only Cup win over the Terriers has been 2-0 (h) in the 5th round in February 1951 in front of 52,708 spectators. Huddersfield beat First Division Wolves 1-0 in a 2nd round League Cup-tie at Leeds Road in 1967-68.

WOOD, James William: Right-back: 145 apps. Born: Sunderland, 8 March 1893. Died: circa 1970
James Wood played for Hylton Colliery, Sunderland and South Shields (twice winners of the North-Eastern League title) before joining Huddersfield in February 1915. He remained with the club throughout WW1 and went on to appear in well over 220 first team matches (including 78 in wartime).
A promotion winner and FA Cup finalist with the Terriers in 1920, Wood received a Cup winner's medal in 1922 before his transfer to Blackpool in October of that year. He made 59 appearances for the Seasiders prior to his retirement in May 1926.

WOOD, Raymond Ernest: Goalkeeper: 223 apps. Born: Hebburn, County Durham, 11 June 1931. Died: Bexhill, East Sussex, 7 July 2002.
An amateur with Newcastle in 1948, Ray Wood turned professional with Darlington in September 1949 and three months later joined Manchester United for £5,000. He spent nine years at Old Trafford, transferring to Huddersfield in December 1958. After a brief spell with Toronto FC (Canada) he moved to Bradford City (October 1965) and ended his career with Barnsley (August 1966-May 1968). Having gained his FA coaching badge in 1962, he later coached in Cyprus, Greece, Kuwait, Kenya, Northern Ireland, UAE, USA and Zambia.
Signed by Manchester United as cover for Jack Crompton, he made his First Division debut against Newcastle in December 1949 - the first of more than 200 appearances for the Reds. He had to wait until 1953-54 before establishing himself in the side but then he produced some superb displays with lightning reflexes. He helped United win the League title in 1956 and 1957 and also played in the 1957 FA Cup final when he was injured in a collision with Aston Villa's Peter McParland and had to leave the field. He bravely returned late on but had to withdraw again as Villa took the trophy 2-1.
A survivor of the Munich air crash Wood gained three full England caps, plus others at 'B' and Under-23 levels and had three games for the Football League. After being replaced by Harry Gregg, he moved to Huddersfield whom he served wonderfully well for almost seven years.

WORKINGTON: Huddersfield's record against the Cumbrian side is:

Football League

Venue	P	W	D	L	F	A
Home	2	2	0	0	4	1
Away	2	1	0	1	4	3
Totals	4	3	0	1	8	4

FA Cup

	P	W	D	L	F	A
Home	1	1	0	0	5	0
Away	1	0	1	0	1	1
Totals	2	1	1	0	6	1

League Cup

	P	W	D	L	F	A
Away	1	0	0	1	0	1

Huddersfield won their first-ever League game against Workington by 2-0 at Borough Park in October 1975 and later repeated that scoreline at Leeds Road to complete the double.

Workington were blitzed out of the FA Cup in a 1st round replay in November 1981, Mike Laverick scoring two of Huddersfield's five goals.

WORTHINGTON, Frank: Forward: 200 apps. 50 goals Born: Halifax, 23 November 1948 Worthington appeared in 757 League matches in his career, firmly establishing himself in the top 12 of all-time appearance-makers in English football. A flamboyant character, an original happy-go-lucky centre-forward, he brought a sparkle to the game with his cavalier approach and swash-buckling displays, a personality in his own right. His charismatic humour, his style, his arrogant ball control, his popularity all made him one of the country's likeable footballers. He joined Huddersfield as an apprentice, taking professional status in November 1966. In June 1972, a proposed £150,000 move from Huddersfield to Liverpool was called off because of Worthington's high blood pressure but a little over two months later,

he was transferred to Leicester for £70,000. During his five years at Filbert Street he scored 78 goals in 239 senior outings - his best spell with any of his major clubs. On leaving the Foxes in September 1977 he moved to Bolton for £87,000 and was both the Wanderers' and the First Division's top-scorer in 1978-79 with 24 goals despite his team finishing 17th in the table. Following a loan period with Philadelphia Fury Worthington moved to Birmingham in November 1979 for £150,000. He certainly contributed greatly in helping Blues gain promotion and also consolidate their position in the First Division. After netting 33 goals in 88 appearances for the Midland club and following a loan spell with Tampa Bay Rowdies (NASL), Worthington switched to Leeds United in March

1982 in a part-exchange deal involving Byrom Stevenson. Nine months later he teamed up with Sunderland, diverting to Southampton in June 1983. A year later, one of soccer's nomadic journeymen was on the move again, this time to Brighton from where he switched to Tranmere in July 1985 as player-manager. In February 1987, Worthington was off again, this time to PNE (as a player). Nine months on he signed for Stockport and in April 1988 was recruited by Cape Town Spurs (South Africa). On his return to England he joined Chorley and later served with Stalybridge Celtic, Galway United (Ireland), Weymouth, Radcliffe Borough, Guiseley, Hinckley Town (as player-manager) and Halifax (part-time coach, 1991-92). Worthington also turned out in charity matches before hanging up his boots in 1998 to concentrate on his 'after dinner' speeches.

Capped by England on eight occasions, he also represented his country in two Under-23 internationals, played once for the Football League and helped both Huddersfield (1970) and Bolton (1978) win the Second Division title. He scored at least one League goal in each of 21 consecutive seasons: 1966-67 to 1987-88, amassing 234 goals in total. In all competitions (world wide) he netted almost 300 goals in 905 appearances - a fine record! He was granted a benefit by the PFA in 1991.

Two of Worthington's brothers - Dave and Bob - both started their careers as full-backs with Halifax, while his nephew Gary was on Manchester United's books in 1984-85.

WORTHINGTON, Jonathan Alan: Midfield: 69 apps. 3 goals Born: Dewsbury, 16 April 1983

An energetic midfielder, Jon Worthington grabbed the opportunity of first-team football with both hands when given his chance by manager Peter Jackson. Signed as a trainee in June 1999, he turned professional in September 2001 and won the 'Player of the Year' award in 2004.

WREXHAM: Huddersfield's record against the Red Dragons is:
Football League

Venue	P	W	D	L	F	A
Home	6	5	1	0	16	4
Away	6	1	3	2	5	9
Totals	12	6	4	2	21	13

FA Cup

Home	1	1	0	0	2	1
Away	1	0	1	0	1	1
Totals	2	1	1	0	3	2

League Cup

Home	1	1	0	0	3	0
Away	1	1	0	0	2	1
Totals	2	2	0	0	5	1

Others

Away	2	1	0	1	2	2

The result of the first League game between the two clubs, played at Wrexham in September 1973, was a goalless draw. Later in the season the Terriers won 2-1 at Leeds Road

In March 1983 Huddersfield ran up their best League win over City - 4-1 at Leeds Road. Huddersfield beat Wrexham in a 4th round FA Cup replay in January 1999, having eased to a 5-1 aggregate win in a 1st round League Cup-tie in 1996-97. The two 'other' matches were both in the LDV Vans Trophy in 2001-02 and 2002-03.

WYCOMBE WANDERERS: Huddersfield's record against the Chairboys is:
Football League

Venue	P	W	D	L	F	A
Home	3	1	1	1	2	2
Away	3	1	1	1	5	4
Totals	6	2	2	2	7	6

Huddersfield's first League game against Wycombe was also the first to be staged at The Alfred McAlpine Stadium - the visitors winning 1-0 on 13 August 1994. The Wanderers went on to complete the double over the Terriers that season.

Y

YATES, Stephen: Defender: 41 apps. one goal Born: Bristol, 29 January 1970
Signed from Sheffield United on a 'free' in August 2003, Yates played his part in helping the Terriers win promotion to the Second Division with some sterling displays. Earlier, he made 238 appearances for Bristol Rovers (1988-93), 149 for QPR (1993-99), 137 for Tranmere (1999-2002) and 13 for the Blades, gaining a Third Division championship medal in 1990.

YORATH, Terry: Assistant Manager: Born Cardiff 27 March 1950, the Welshman made his name as a midfielder with Leeds United playing in 120 games including two European Cup Finals in 1973 and 1975. He played for Coventry, Tottenham Hotspur, Bradford City and Vancouver Whitecaps.
Terry has managed and coached Wales, Swansea, Bradford, Cardiff and Sheffield Wednesday.
A popular assistant to Peter Jackson he joined the Terriers in June 2003.
His daughter Gabby is a well known football presenter on TV.

YORK CITY: Huddersfield's record against the Minstermen is:

Football League

Venue	P	W	D	L	F	A
Home	7	3	1	3	10	8
Away	7	4	1	2	13	7
Totals	14	7	2	5	23	15

FA Cup

Home	1	1	0	0	2	1
Away	1	0	1	0	0	0
Totals	2	1	1	0	2	1

League Cup

Away	2	1	0	1	2	1

Other

Home	1	1	0	0	3	0

The first Yorkshire League derby between Huddersfield and City was at Bootham Crescent in April 1974. A crowd of 10,189 saw the Minstermen win 2-1 and they completed the double over the Terriers four days later with a 1-0 victory at Leeds Road. Huddersfield recorded their first victory at the fifth attempt, winning 1-0 at home in November 1978. In March 1980, the Terriers won 4-0 at Bootham Crescent.

After beating WBA and Middlesbrough from the First Division, York were defeated 2-1 by Huddersfield in the 6th round of the FA Cup after a replay in March 1938.

YOUNG, Alfred: Defender: 309 apps. 6 goals Born: Sunderland, 4 November 1905. Died: 1977

Signed from Durham City in January 1927, Young gave the Terriers ten years dedicated service as a solid, confident and resolute defender. He understudied Tom Wilson initially at Leeds Road before securing a regular place in the side in 1930-31. He only missed games through injury and quite often played through the pain barrier.

The player and captain who was wrongly adjudged to have tripped Preston's George Mutch in the 1938 FA Cup final which resulted in a last-gasp extra-time spot-kick winner, Young was transferred to York in November 1945 (having guested for the Minstermen during WW2). He coached the Danish side Koge Boldklub before spending almost four years on the coaching staff at Leeds Road (August 1948 to May 1952).

He later managed Bradford and coached again in Denmark before returning for a third spell with Huddersfield as coach in December 1960. He then served for a year (1964-65) as the club's chief scout before taking over as groundsman of a local police sports ground.

the light at the end of the tunnel